W9-CII-713

DATE DUE

WHEN WILL JESUS COME?

Dave Hunt

HARVEST HOUSE™ PUBLISHERS

EUGENE, OREGON

Scripture quotations in this book are taken from the King James Version of the Bible.

Cover by Koechel Peterson & Associates, Inc., Minneapolis, Minnesota

WHEN WILL JESUS COME?
Copyright © 1993 by Dave Hunt
Published by Harvest House Publishers
Eugene, Oregon 97402

ISBN 0-7394-3730-5

Printed in the United States of America.

*Dedicated to all those citizens of heaven for
whom this world has lost its appeal.
And who, loving Christ with their whole heart,
long to be at home with Him in His Father's house.*

Contents

"I Will Come Again"

Let not your heart be troubled: ye believe in God, believe also in me. In my Father's house are many mansions: if it were not so, I would have told you. I go to prepare a place for you. And if I go and prepare a place for you, I will come again, and receive you unto myself; that where I am, there ye may be also (John 14:1-3).

I will come again." What a promise from our Lord! Yet there has been a consistent blindness from the very beginning to the true meaning of these words—a blindness even going back all the way to those who first heard this comforting pledge from His own lips. The indisputable fact is that when Christ made this startling declaration on the eve of His betrayal, not one of His astonished disciples understood what He meant. Even John the Baptist, though chosen by God to introduce the Messiah to Israel, was as ignorant as were Christ's sworn enemies, the rabbis, of the momentous truth that two Messianic comings had been prophesied.

That blindness to the Old Testament prophecies created great confusion concerning Christ's identity and the purpose of His first advent. If we are to gain accurate insights into the Second Coming, we must go back to discover the reasons for the misunderstandings when Christ first came. And we must make certain that we do not fall prey to similar confusion.

The problem was not skepticism concerning the prophesied coming of the Messiah. Almost everyone in Israel in Christ's day was looking for that promised One—and so are the Jews today. But that He should come *twice* was and still is unthinkable heresy to a Jew. Surprisingly, a similar prejudice against the thought of two comings of Christ being yet future is growing even in the evangelical Church.

The Mystery of Two Comings Remains

Christians have no problem with two comings of Christ, if one is in the past and one in the future. He came once, and will come again as He promised. That there are yet two comings still in the future, however—the Rapture and the Second Coming—separated by seven years, is not generally accepted in the Church. Yet we will see that the Bible clearly indicates that Christ's promise, "I will come again," refers not to one event but two, seven years apart. The rejection of this fact in our day is creating a serious misunderstanding among many Christians, a misunderstanding similar to that which caused such confusion at Christ's first advent.

For the Jews in Jesus' day, the thought of two comings had serious implications. It could only mean that the Messiah would be rejected the first time, perhaps even killed. Otherwise, why would He have to come again? At the very least it would mean that His mission would be aborted and the Kingdom not established. Yet the Kingdom was the very reason for the Messiah's coming. It had to be established. That He would come *twice* was therefore unthinkable.

The same view prevails among Jews today. Visit Israel and ask any Israeli if he or she is expecting the Messiah. Almost without exception the answer will be in the affirmative, some even declaring with conviction that He is somewhere on the earth already, waiting to be recognized. And what about *two* comings? No, it couldn't be possible that He has already come once—certainly not that Jesus was the rejected, crucified Messiah! Never!

The ultimate purpose of the Messiah's coming is clearly stated in Scripture: to establish a Kingdom of everlasting peace. Jesus didn't do that. It is therefore reasoned that He couldn't have been the Messiah. Whoever establishes peace in the Middle East and throughout the world—and it will be established temporarily—will be hailed as the long-awaited Messiah, both by Israel and the world. That man, for whom the entire world waits, will, in fact, be the Antichrist. "Him ye will receive," said Christ (John 5:43), and all for a lack of understanding what the prophets have said!

Truth by Implication

There is absolutely no excuse for such ignorance today. Nor was there any excuse when Jesus came the first time. The Hebrew prophets, whose utterances concerning Messiah's advent comprise a major part of Scripture, had clearly indicated that He would come *twice*. After coming to Israel through a lowly virgin birth, He would leave this earth and then, after a period of great persecution for Jews worldwide and their return to their homeland, He would come again in glory and power to rescue His chosen people at Armageddon and rule the world from Jerusalem. It was all there in the writings of the prophets for anyone who had eyes to see. Oddly, however, the meaning was hidden even from rabbis who read the Hebrew prophets religiously each day.

Of course, the specific words, "two comings of the Messiah" or "Messiah will come twice," were not to be found in the pronouncements of the prophets. The truth was there by implication only. All that the prophets had revealed concerning the Messiah obviously could not occur in one time frame and one event. There were seeming contradictions that could be reconciled in no other way than by two comings. For example, He would be "cut off out of the land of the living" (Isaiah 53:8) yet He would "prolong his days [forever]" (53:10); He would be rejected and killed (53:3,9) yet would reign forever (Isaiah 9:7). The deduction was inescapable. The Messiah *had* to come twice. It was as simple as that.

Despite their diligent study of the Scriptures, there was not one rabbi in Israel at the time of Christ's first advent who comprehended the two comings of the Messiah. Rabbi Nicodemus, in contrast to the other religious leaders, believed that Jesus was the Messiah sent by God. Yet even he did not understand that the Messiah had to be rejected and slain. Surely had he understood, he would have attempted to point out the relevant prophecies to his colleagues, but he did not.

How was such blindness possible? Even more important, could it happen again? Astonishingly, a prophetic ignorance of equal magnitude characterizes our own day. This is true among both Jews and Christians, making a book such as this not only necessary but urgent.

A Prevailing Prophetic Illiteracy

A lack of interest in the Rapture and the Second Coming (the distinction between the two will be examined later), and the ignorance that inevitably accompanies indifference, have settled like an obscuring fog over the Church. Few, indeed, are the Christians today who could point out and explain the meaning of the key Old Testament prophecies of which Christ's contemporaries were so tragically ignorant. This is true even among those who pride themselves on their general knowledge of God's Word.

"I will come again!" After nearly two millennia, that wonderful but as yet unfulfilled promise remains shrouded in misunderstanding. What should be one's attitude today concerning this solemn promise made by Christ to His disciples and to each of us? If the promise is to be taken literally, then why such a long delay?

Yes, a very long time has passed since Christ gave His pledge to return. No matter how many centuries have come and gone, however, the One who conquered death must be taken seriously—both as to His promise and the warnings He uttered—lest His return take us by surprise and find us uninterested and unprepared.

Unfortunately, the same prophetic illiteracy which contributed largely to the rejection of Christ the first time He came is still with us and could have equally serious consequences upon His return. Our purpose is to clarify the misunderstandings and to bring Christ's promise into clear focus once again. It is, of course, axiomatic that without a proper understanding of Christ's first coming one could hardly expect to have any real insight as to His Second Coming.

Jewish Lineage of the Messiah

Genesis 3:15 gives us the first promise of the Messiah's coming and explains the purpose: to destroy Satan and to rescue mankind from God's judgment. Nine chapters later we learn that the virgin-born "seed of the woman" will be a descendant of Abraham (12:3). How else could a blessing come to "all the families of the earth" except through the Messiah? Next we learn that through Isaac's lineage all the world will be blessed (Genesis 26:4); then we are told it will be through the seed of Jacob (28:14). The Messiah's ancestral line is further narrowed down to the tribe of Judah (Genesis 49:10), then the family of Jesse (Isaiah 11:1), and finally to the house of David (2 Samuel 7:12-16; Psalm 89:3,4,28-36; Jeremiah 23:5).

No wonder the New Testament begins with the genealogy of Jesus. It is traced through Joseph in Matthew 1:1-16 (though not his father, he was head of the house), and through Mary, his mother, in Luke 3:23-38, beginning there with Joseph's father-in-law, Heli. That Jesus was descended from David was absolutely essential, for the Messiah had to fulfill every relevant prophecy and His lineage was foundational. As Christ emphasized to His disciples:

> All things must be fulfilled, which were written in the law of Moses, and in the prophets, and in the psalms concerning me (Luke 24:44b).

Numerous and very specific are the Old Testament references to the coming Messiah: That He would be born in Bethlehem (the city of David), that He would be called out of Egypt, that He would live in Nazareth, that His own people would hate and turn Him over to the Gentiles, who would crucify Him. Many more details were prophesied, as we shall see. Why? A major reason, of course, would be so that the Messiah, when He came, could be identified beyond any shadow of doubt.

That the life, death, and resurrection of Jesus of Nazareth fulfilled to the letter all of the requisite prophecies cannot be denied by any honest investigator. The evidence establishes beyond question that Jesus of Nazareth was and is the Messiah. His first coming to earth is an indisputable fact of history. As Peter declared in his second sermon in Jerusalem to thousands of Jews who had been eyewitnesses and knew the facts about Jesus:

> But those things, which God before had shewed by the mouth of all his prophets, that Christ should suffer, he hath so fulfilled (Acts 3:18).

Exactly as Christ's first advent fulfilled God's promises to His people—promises which the Hebrew prophets recorded centuries earlier in the Old Testament—so His second advent will fulfill in equally precise detail numerous additional prophecies. Therein lies the only source of information we have concerning Christ's return.

With the destruction of the temple and Jerusalem in A.D. 70, the genealogical records were destroyed. Since that time, therefore, it has been too late for any would-be Messiah to prove himself to be a descendant of David. Such inability, however, will not inhibit the Antichrist, for, as we shall see, he will be received, even by Israel, without regard to the Messianic prophecies.

That the Messiah would be a Jew and that His coming would be first of all to His own people is a matter both of history and prophecy fulfilled. That He must come again specifically to His genealogically related people, the Jews, is also plainly stated in the Scriptures. Thus we must come to an understanding of the Messiah's relationship to Israel, and of the role of Israel in both advents, or we cannot gain an accurate insight into either the Rapture or the Second Coming.

CHAPTER 2

The God of Prophecy

I am God, and there is none else; I am God and there is none like me, declaring the end from the beginning, and from ancient times the things that are not yet done, saying, My counsel shall stand, and I will do all my pleasure (Isaiah 46:9,10).

I have even from the beginning declared it to thee; before it came to pass I shewed it thee: lest thou shouldest say, Mine idol hath done them, and my graven image...hath commanded them (Isaiah 48:5).

What does one say to a professed atheist when he demands "proof" that God exists? One could, of course, challenge him to prove that God doesn't exist, and to justify the preposterous scenario that the universe and even the human brain just happened by chance. The life and health of all creatures depends upon the fact that DNA molecules replicate exact duplicates of themselves. Only if the DNA, through chance foul-ups in its mechanism, failed to function properly could evolutionary changes occur.

That billions of intricately designed creatures, each with its proper food, and the delicately balanced ecological relationship between them—to say nothing of the nervous system, eye, and human brain—are the result of a series of chance mistakes in the DNA is too preposterous for belief. Yet those who reject God are left with no other alternative. The consequences of that theory, which is aggressively promoted in America's public schools and media, are not only morally and spiritually destructive, but logically fallacious as well. C.S. Lewis wrote:

> If minds are wholly dependent on brains, and brains
> on biochemistry, and biochemistry on the meaning-
> less flux of the atoms, I cannot understand how the
> thought of those minds should have any more sig-
> nificance than the sound of the wind....

Lewis' simple logic destroys Darwinism. If man is the chance product of impersonal evolutionary forces, then so are his thoughts—including the theory of evolution. Nevertheless, all of today's psychology, whether Christian or secular, rests upon Darwinism. Such was the basis of Freud's atheistic medical model which remains the key element in the attempt to establish a "science of human behavior."

As a result, man came to be viewed as a stimulus-response conglomeration of protein molecules driven by overpowering urges programmed into his unconscious by past traumas. Sin, for which one is morally accountable to God, became a mental illness beyond one's control. No longer a moral problem for which one was personally responsible, wrong behavior could only be corrected by the newly invented ritual of psychotherapy. It was a new ball game with new rules and goals.

Even the Church went along with psychology. For evangelicals, the Bible, though still inerrant, was no longer *sufficient*. Biblical answers to spiritual problems were now perceived as inadequate and were at first supplemented and then replaced by "scientific" diagnoses and cures unknown to prophets and apostles. The *salvation of sinful souls* through Christ alone somehow metamorphosed into the *cure of sick minds* through psychotherapy.

A "Scientific" Explanation?

Christ's mission took on new meaning. His coming to earth was seen as more akin to a heavenly psychiatrist's visit to help us feel good about ourselves than that of a holy God descending among sinners to judge sin and bring salvation. Paul warned that in the last days professing Christians would have "a form of godliness while denying the power thereof" (2 Timothy 3:5). Lip service is still given to the power of the

Holy Spirit and the gospel, but as a practical matter, far more faith is placed in the ritualistic power of psychotherapy to change lives. "Getting in touch with one's feelings" and "understanding oneself" rendered obsolete Christ's supernatural solution to a problem of evil which began with Lucifer's rebellion.

By claiming to offer a "scientific explanation" for human behavior, psychology invaded the realm of soul, spirit, morals, and religion. It thus posed a greater challenge to belief in God and the gospel than had physics or chemistry, which proposed no explanation for the universe or man's existence. Many of this century's greatest scientists have issued grave warnings against trying to mix science and religion. Einstein said, "...scientific theory has nothing to do with religion." Nobel laureate Erwin Schroedinger added, "[Science] knows nothing of...good or bad, God and eternity." Pretending to know what it couldn't, psychology offered a religious science of the mind and claimed to present new evidence for God's existence: the harmony of psychology and Scripture. The truth is that the two are irreconcilable.

Einstein, Schroedinger, and their colleagues were right: Science has nothing to say about God or morals. It can no more prove that God does or doesn't exist than it can prove that one sunset is beautiful and another is not. Moreover, proofs are really beside the point. It is impossible scientifically to prove one's own existence—but who doubts it? Then why is a proof of God's existence necessary? If God really is, then He should be able to make Himself known. And if He can't do that, then whether He exists or not would be irrelevant to practical concerns.

Natural Inability to Know God

Of course, the problem may not be that God isn't making Himself known but that mankind fails to recognize Him when He does so. Even the natural world suggests such a probability. Consider, for example, energy. It is invisible and intangible, though its effects can be seen and felt everywhere. And though those effects bombard us constantly, mankind was for thousands of years unaware of the existence of energy as we now understand it.

The invisible component out of which all things were made remained unrecognized, not because it didn't manifest its presence and power, but in spite of that fact. Its effects were commonly known, but no one was capable of recognizing the presence of energy behind the phenomena it produced and which so abundantly proved its existence. Even today, though we know much about it, no scientist knows what energy is, how it originated, or why it functions as it does. Nor do we know what gravity is, or space, or light or any other basic ingredient of the universe.

Could it not be the same way with God? If He created energy, would He not be even more elusive and incomprehensible than anything He made? To be the creator of all, God (by very definition) would have to be infinite and thus beyond human understanding. He would have to reveal Himself, or we could never know Him. Yet how could He make Himself known to finite beings? Our self-centered ignorance and blindness to truth posed a major difficulty.

How could God make Himself known in such a way that a finite man would be absolutely certain that God was revealing Himself? To ask such a question is not an attempt to avoid the issue. It raises a very practical problem which God, if He exists, would have to overcome and honest skeptics must acknowledge.

From the innermost depths of the atom (which we haven't yet been able to explore) to the furthermost reaches of the cosmos, the intricately organized universe God made adequately reveals His infinite intelligence and power. It is something else, however, for God to manifest His love and will for mankind. To do so, He must make Himself known *personally* in such a way that a finite man would realize beyond a shadow of doubt that the infinite God was revealing Himself. How could an infinite God unveil Himself personally to finite beings?

Suppose God thundered from the sky with an audible voice. How would anyone know for certain that it was God who had spoken? Suppose He made some great display of power. How would it be known that God had acted and that it was not some natural phenomenon? Suppose He made Himself visible in some earthly form? If He came as a man, who would believe that He was God? Yet how could He reveal Himself to finite creatures unless He became one of them?

Suppose, instead, that God manifested Himself in some transcendent form. How could anyone know that it was God and not some highly evolved extraterrestrial visiting earth? How, indeed! Miracles, no matter how spectacular, would not suffice, for skeptics could argue that highly advanced technology seems miraculous to those who don't know how it works. And yet, if God really existed and was the creator of mankind, surely He would want to communicate not only His existence but His will to the creatures He had made and to whom He had given the capacity to know Him.

There Is Only One True God

Here we confront the many religions in the world. Each one claims to follow the revelations of the true god or gods—yet even in their basic concepts of deity there are sharp contradictions. Obviously, contradictory views can't all be right. Hinduism, for example, embraces millions of gods and worships idols which supposedly represent them, because *everything* is god. Islam, on the other hand, denounces idol worship and pantheism/polytheism and claims that Allah is the only true God. Buddhism, in contrast, needs no god.

Allah was, in fact, the name of the chief god in the Kaabah, the pagan temple that Muhammad "purged" by destroying the more than 300 idols contained in it. Muhammad likely kept the name of this ancient pagan moon god and the symbol of the crescent moon because it would be easier to convert idolaters to his new religion if he could offer something with which they were familiar. Muslims see no contradiction in this strategy, nor even in keeping the chief object of worship in the ancient Kaabah, the black stone that Muslims kiss and revere today, even as idolaters did before Muhammad incorporated it into Islamic religious practice.

The God of the Bible states unequivocally: "Before me there was no God formed, neither shall there be after me. I, even I, am the Lord; and beside me there is no saviour" (Isaiah 43:10,11).

He does not simply ignore the gods of other religions. He denounces them all, including Allah, as imposters who actually front for Satan or his demons. The great apostle Paul wrote, "The things which the Gentiles [non-Jews] sacrifice [to their gods], they sacrifice to devils" (1 Corinthians 10:20). Nor is such a denunciation narrow-minded or dogmatic. What could be more important than properly identifying the one true God, and what blasphemy could be worse than suggesting that God is something or someone who He is not?

Some well-meaning people, forgetting that the issue is truth and not wanting to cause offense, insist that the gods of all religions are simply different names for the same being or force. Such an idea, however, is like a man declaring that all women in the world, no matter what their names and individual identity, are one and the same person—and that each of them is his wife. The particular woman to whom he is married would not accept that fraud, nor would the other women to whom he is not married allow him to treat them as though each were married to him.

Irreconcilable Differences

While there are some similarities, the distinctions between the gods of major world religions are far greater than those between individual men and women. The adherents of competing religions take very seriously the identifying attributes of their deities. Thus, it is not generosity but a cynical trivialization of that which is vital and sacred to suggest that the gods of all religions are the same. It is an affront to Muslims to insist that Allah is the equivalent of the many gods in Hinduism; or to tell a Christian that his God, who gave His Son to die for the sins of the world, is the same as Allah, of whom it is specifically stated that he has no son.

To say that all religions are the same denies the meaning of language and is an insult not only to the followers of these religions but to intelligence itself. The difference is particularly glaring when it comes to Christianity. It stands alone on one side of a theological chasm, with all other religions on the other side—a chasm that renders any ecumenical union impossible without destroying Christianity itself.

One cannot deny, for example, the irreconcilable conflict between the belief that Christ died for our sins and rose again (which is the very heart of Christianity) and Islam's blasphemous claim that Christ did not die on the cross, much less for sin, but that someone else died in His place. To sweep such differences under an ecumenical rug (as Roman Catholicism, and specifically Vatican II, seeks to do) is not kindness but madness.

Nor is it possible to reconcile the claim of all non-Christian religions that sin is countered by good works with the Bible's oft-repeated declaration that only Christ, because He was sinless, could pay the penalty for sin, and that to do so He had to die in our place. Of course Christ's claim, "I am the way, the truth and the life; no man comes to the Father except by me" (John 14:6), is the strongest possible rejection of all other religions as satanic counterfeits.

The very subject of this book, the *Second Coming of Christ,* is a belief that is unique to Christianity and separates it from all of the world's religions by a chasm that cannot be bridged by any ecumenical sleight-of-hand. Muhammad never promised to return, nor did Buddha, nor did the founder of any other of the world's religions. Only Christ dared to make this promise, and only He made it credible by leaving behind an empty tomb. That undeniable fact is reason enough to take seriously His assertion that He would return to this earth in power and glory to execute judgment upon His enemies.

Prophecy, Evidence, and the Bible

That the Bible, which provides the historical account of the life, death, and resurrection of Jesus Christ, is unique for this and many other reasons becomes obvious from even a superficial comparison with all other sacred writings. The Hindu scriptures, for example, are obviously mythological. There is no historical evidence that the characters ever existed or that the fantastic tales refer to events that actually occurred. The same is true of much that is recorded in the scriptures of other religions.

Take, for example, the Book of Mormon. Not one pin or coin or the tiniest shred of evidence of any kind has ever been found to verify that the people, much less the events, to which the Book of Mormon refers were real. Not even a mountain or river or any piece of topography or geography described in the Book of Mormon has ever been located. And this in spite of the fact that the Mormon Church has zealously pursued an intensive search of North, Central, and South America in its attempt to find some evidence of the great nations which the Book of Mormon describes as having lived there.

In contrast, the world's museums contain vast stores of evidence of all kinds confirming the historicity of the Bible. Yes, the skeptics have attacked the biblical record; but in *every* case, when the archaeological work has been done, the skeptics have been proved wrong and the Bible right. As only one example, critics at one time denied that the Hittites mentioned in the Bible had ever lived because no record of their existence had as yet been found. Today in Ankara, Turkey, there is an entire museum devoted to the Hittites. Their relics are contained in museums around the world; and their history as we now know it agrees exactly with what the Bible has claimed for thousands of years.

In Israel's public schools the children are taught the history of their people and land directly from the Old Testament. Archaeologists in the Middle East use the Bible as a guide that tells them where to dig for ancient cities. The historical, geographical, and scientific accuracy of the Bible has been vindicated repeatedly as have no other sacred writings.

The Bible was written by men who claim to have been inspired by God and to have recorded the message He wanted them to convey to mankind. So specific are the Bible writers that each claims to have written down, not a paraphrase or a vague recollection, but the very words of God verbatim. Those words speak with convicting power to the human conscience and bear their own testimony (Hebrews 4:12). The Bible claims that just as all men recognize the same moral standards, because God has written His law in their hearts (Romans 2:14,15), so the gospel of Jesus Christ recorded in the Bible bears witness in every conscience as well (John 1:9; 2 Corinthians 4:2).

What About Objective Evidence?

The ardent skeptic, however, insists upon something more objective and convincing. The Bible declares that the universe all around us, so intricately organized and so subjected to precise and ingenious laws that it could not possibly have happened by chance, bears eloquent testimony to God's existence (Romans 1:19,20). Unfortunately, modern man has been misled into believing that science has some explanation for the universe and human life, though this is not the case at all. Sir Arthur Eddington declared, "Ought [i.e., right and wrong] takes us outside chemistry and physics." Schroedinger reminds us: "Whence came I and whither go I? That is the great unfathomable question for every one of us. Science has no answer to it."

The average person, however, has been led to believe that science does in fact have the answers, but that they are too complex for ordinary people to understand. Thus they remain blind to the testimony of creation all around them. One of the beauties of the Bible is that it provides a very simple evidence for God's existence that anyone can easily and fully comprehend. It gives an equally simple and unequivocal way to identify which one of the sacred Scriptures claimed by the world's religions was inspired of God, and Who is the only Savior of the world.

What is this simple yet profound evidence that the Bible offers? It is prophecy fulfilled, an irrefutable verification reserved to the Judeo-Christian Scriptures alone. No honest person can remain an unbeliever after even a brief study of prophecy, as we hope to demonstrate in the pages following.

As we have already noted, prophecy is the missing element in all other sacred scriptures of the world's religions. It is not to be found in the Koran, the Hindu Vedas, the Bhagavad-Gita, the Book of Mormon, the sayings of Buddha, or the writings of Mary Baker Eddy. By contrast, prophecy comprises nearly 30 percent of the Bible.

The God of Prophecy

It is not surprising, then, that the God of the Bible identifies Himself as the One who accurately foretells the future and makes certain that it unfolds as He said it would. In fact, God points to prophecy as the irrefutable evidence of His existence and the authenticity of His Word. The verses at the beginning of this chapter offer an example. Yet the fact that God uses prophecy in this manner is scarcely recognized even by evangelicals.

Prophecy, of course, is the topic we will pursue in the following pages. Our approach, however, will be different from what one usually encounters in books of this nature. There are many individual prophecies in the Bible with which we will not concern ourselves because they lack universal interest and may be argued by skeptics. There are, however, two major topics of prophecy which must be studied if one is to have any understanding of the Bible. They are: 1) Israel; and 2) the Messiah, who would come to Israel and, through her, to the world. These two major topics involve undeniable specific fulfillments of prophecy and they hold the key to the timing of the Second Coming.

The Bible does not waste its time, as philosophers so foolishly have for centuries, in any attempt to provide some academic proof for the existence of God. The God to whom the Bible bears testimony is capable of communicating with mankind and promises to reveal Himself to all who sincerely desire to know Him and earnestly seek Him. "You will seek for me and find me, when you seek for me with all your heart" says the Old Testament (Jeremiah 29:13). The New Testament echoes the same promise: "He [God] is a rewarder of those who diligently seek him" (Hebrews 11:6).

In communicating Himself and His will, God balances subjective evidence with objective proof. The Bible records God's provision of many tangible signs to those who wanted to know Him and His will. To "put out a fleece" is a common expression that is understood worldwide. It comes from Gideon's use of a sheep's fleece to be certain of God's will.

Placing it on the ground overnight, he asked God for two signs: dew on the fleece and not on the ground one morning, then dew on the ground but not on the fleece the next (Judges 6:36-40). God honored his request because Gideon's heart was right and such evidence was necessary for the unusual task to which God was calling him.

That is not to say that God will honor every "fleece" that any person may by whim or stubborn demand lay before Him. Those who neglect to study diligently and heed the Scriptures God has provided and preserved through the centuries need not expect some new word of prophecy or some miraculous sign. Those who make such demands fall into the hands of Satan, who is only too glad to provide the "signs and wonders" they seek and thereby lead them astray.

Israel: Irrefutable Proof

There is a sign God has given to the entire world for all generations. That sign is the land and people of Israel. God speaks of "Israel my glory" (Isaiah 46:13) and refers to her as the one "in whom I will be glorified" (Isaiah 49:3). How would this glorification come about? It could only be by God's specific dealings with Israel before a watching world, after having prophesied precisely what would happen (2 Chronicles 7:20). Referring to the rescue of Israel at Armageddon, the subject of many Old Testament prophecies, Ezekiel 38:23 declares: "Thus will I [God] magnify myself, and sanctify myself; and I will be known in the eyes of many nations, and they shall know that I am the Lord."

The Bible declares that the prophecies it provides concerning Israel supply the irrefutable evidence for God's existence and for the fact that He has a purpose for mankind. History is not merely happenstance. It is going somewhere. There is a plan. Prophecy reveals that plan in advance. And at the heart of that plan biblical prophecy places Israel as God's great sign to the world.

It was to Israel that the Messiah, the Savior of the world, was sent. As predicted by her own prophets, Israel rejected

Him. How ironic that in rejecting Jesus the Jews fulfilled prophecies that identified Him as the Messiah! If we are to understand anything of Christ's Second Coming, then we must gain some insight into Israel's key role as revealed by the Old Testament prophets and by Christ and His apostles.

CHAPTER 3

An Irrefutable Sign

Behold, I will make Jerusalem a cup of trembling unto
all the people round about, when they shall be in the
seige both against Judah and against Jerusalem. And
in that day will I make Jerusalem a burdensome stone
for all people: all that burden themselves with it shall
be cut in pieces....For I will gather all nations against
Jerusalem to battle; and the city shall be taken...then
shall the Lord go forth to fight against those nations
(Zechariah 12:2,3; 14:2,3).

The fulfillment of hundreds of specific prophecies in the
ancient and modern history of the Jewish people is God's
great sign to mankind—a sign that no one can mistake or deny.
God's unique dealings with Israel before a watching world constitute an irrefutable proof that He exists and that He is guiding
history. He is not the god of the deists, but is intimately involved
with earth's inhabitants, for whom He has great love and definite
plans that He will carry through to their conclusion. Both Israel
and her Messiah are vital to God's purpose for mankind.

That God gave Israel her land, took her out of it and scattered
her throughout all the world, then brought her back to it centuries later is a saga unique in the annals of history. It is beyond
the possibility of chance and without ordinary explanation. Her
future in the promised land with the Messiah eventually ruling
the world from Jerusalem on David's throne has been assured by
God. Woe to those who try to revise His plan!

Even before He brought the descendants of Abraham,
Isaac, and Jacob (whom God later named Israel) into the land
of Canaan as He had promised, God warned them through

Moses: "If thou wilt not hearken unto the voice of the Lord thy God, to observe to do all his commandments and his statutes...ye shall be plucked from off the land whither thou goest to possess it. And the Lord shall scatter thee among all people, from the one end of the earth even unto the other...and thou shalt become an astonishment, a proverb, and a byword among all nations..." (Deuteronomy 28:15,63,64,37).

Other prophets continued to plead and warn. Typical are the following: "I will make you to be removed into all the kingdoms of the earth...and I will make the cities of Judah a desolation without inhabitant (Jeremiah 34:17,22)....For, lo, I will command and I will sift the house of Israel among all nations" (Amos 9:9).

In spite of God's guidance, blessing, protection, and patient warnings, Israel repeatedly rebelled against Him. She worshiped the false gods of the nations around her, even as God had foretold she would. Warnings such as those just quoted were repeated many times by the Hebrew prophets as God, reluctant to punish His people, pleaded with them to repent. The day came, however, when He could withhold His judgment no longer.

God's Reluctant Judgment

The people of Israel persisted in their rebellion for nearly five centuries. At last God reluctantly fulfilled His word. Jerusalem and the temple were destroyed by Nebuchadnezzar, then restored and rebuilt, then later destroyed once again. Exactly as His prophets had foretold, God scattered His people, Israel, throughout the entire world (Leviticus 26:33; Deuteronomy 4:27, 32:26; 1 Kings 14:15; Nehemiah 1:8; Jeremiah 9:16, 49:32, etc.). Today, the "wandering Jew" is found in every corner of the earth.

Though God used the nations into which she was dispersed to discipline Israel, all the world will be held accountable for their mistreatment of His people. The Lamb of God, who came in meekness to die for our sins, will return as the Lion of the tribe of Judah to execute judgment.

That Israel was cast out of her land and scattered world-wide exactly as God said represents a fulfillment of prophecy involving so many people, so many nations, and such a lengthy span of time that no one can honestly remain a skeptic, much less an atheist. Jewish history stands as a universally visible monument to God's existence, to the fact that the Bible is His infallible Word, and the Jews are His chosen people.

Approximately 2500 years have passed since the Babylonian captivity and more than 1900 years since the latest Diaspora when Jerusalem was destroyed by the Romans in A.D. 70. During the ensuing centuries the wandering Jews had no homeland. Yet they were never absorbed into the nations among which they had been scattered. These hated, despised, and persecuted people, who had every reason to intermarry and lose their identity, remained an identifiable ethnic unit. That in itself is miraculous. God fulfilled His promise through the prophets to preserve His people in order to bring them back to their land as He had sworn He would.

Those who insist that God is finished with Israel have closed their eyes to specific and numerous prophecies to the contrary. The following is only one example among many:

> Therefore fear thou not, O my servant Jacob, saith the Lord, neither be dismayed, O Israel: for, lo, I will save thee from afar, and thy seed from the land of their captivity....For I am with thee, saith the Lord, to save thee: though I make a full end of all nations whither I have scattered thee, yet will I not make a full end of thee: but I will correct thee in measure, and will not leave thee altogether unpunished (Jeremiah 30:10,11).

Listen once more to what God has said about this people who are of such great significance in His plan of redemption and who are such a visible sign to the world. So important are they that if the natural order in the world is to be preserved, then Israel must be preserved also, as Jeremiah tells us:

Thus saith the Lord, which giveth the sun for a light
by day, and the ordinances of the moon and of the
stars for a light by night, which divideth the sea...the
Lord of hosts is his name: if those ordinances depart
from before me, saith the Lord, then the seed of
Israel also shall cease from being a nation before me
for ever (Jeremiah 31:35,36).

Ten Lost Tribes?

It is often argued that Israel was not preserved but that ten
tribes were lost, carried away captive into Assyria (2 Kings
15:29; 17:6,18). If that is the case, then the Bible is filled with
false prophecies about the 12 tribes being brought back to their
land in the last days. One must believe either this theory or
Scripture—both cannot be true. The prophecies cited above
refer to all of Israel and were spoken by God long after the ten
tribes were supposedly lost.

In fact, the theory of "ten lost tribes" is an anti-Semitic myth.
Space does not permit the detailed discussion which this subject perhaps deserves. However, a careful reading of the history
of Israel in Scripture denies what must be considered a satanic
doctrine, for it destroys in theory (as others have sought to do
in practice) the continuity of Israel. That continuity was repeatedly assured by God and is essential for the major prophecies
of Scripture to be fulfilled in the last days.

There are sound scriptural reasons for rejecting the lost
tribes theory. First of all, the ten tribes were not taken far from
Israel. Why then would they be lost? It is unreasonable to
imagine, with all the ebb and flow of kings and kingdoms in
the ensuing centuries, that none of these people would return
to their land, and that all of them would forget their ethnic
identity. Such a presumed cultural memory loss goes against
everything we know of the persistence of these people to
retain their Jewish heritage. Those who were carried captive
into Babylon returned, so why not those taken a lesser dis-
tance to Assyria?

Secondly, it would be unrealistic to imagine that every last
person was removed. That many remained in the land of Israel

in spite of the Assyrian captivity, even as many remained in Judah during the Babylonian captivity, is evident. For example, many members of the ten tribes of Israel were still living in their land during the spiritual revivals in Judah under King Hezekiah and King Josiah—revivals that occurred one year and nearly 100 years respectively after the carrying away into Assyria.

A year after the Assyrian captivity, Hezekiah called upon those from the ten tribes who had not been taken captive to repent. He sent messengers "throughout all Israel and Judah...saying, Ye children of Israel, turn again unto the Lord God of Abraham, Isaac, and Israel, and he will return to the remnant of you, that are escaped out of the hand of the kings of Assyria" (2 Chronicles 30:6). In fact, we are told that a multitude of people from Ephraim, Manasseh, Issachar, and Zebulun came to keep the Passover in Jerusalem at that time.

Likewise, the revival a century later under Josiah affected many from the ten tribes. We read that there were in existence functioning "cities of Manasseh, and Ephraim, and Simeon, even unto Naphtali" (2 Chronicles 34:6). The Levites even went through the cities of Israel, gathering funds from "Manasseh and Ephraim, and of *all the remnant of Israel*" (34:9, emphasis added) to finance the repairing of the temple in Jerusalem. Multitudes from six of the ten allegedly lost tribes, still in contact with Judah, came to Jerusalem, tender to the call of the prophets to repent and keep the feasts of Jehovah.

Remember Anna, who came into the temple in Jerusalem, just when Joseph and Mary had brought in the eight-day-old Jesus, and identified Him as the Redeemer? We are told that she was "of the tribe of Asher" (Luke 2:36). So here is evidence of a survivor of a seventh tribe of the "lost" ten. We need not say more. Let us accept God's Word on this subject.

A Shameful Chapter in Human History

The persistent and infamous persecution of Jews down through the centuries is undeniable. It also defies any ordinary explanation. Such continual abuse at the hands of their fellow man was a perpetual reminder that, though chosen of God and greatly beloved, they had sinned and were under His judgment. It was also a reminder of something else equally remarkable—that Satan was determined to destroy them.

God had promised that His Messiah, the Savior of Israel and of the world, would come through these people. God's battle with Satan could only be won by the Messiah. He alone could wrest mankind from Lucifer's evil grasp. Consequently, if Satan could destroy Israel there would be no Messiah and Satan would have won the battle for the universe. That there has been not only a supernatural aspect to Jewish (and by Jewish we mean all 12 tribes) persecution but a certain diabolical element, as well, is a matter of history. Even those who call themselves Christians have often been the instruments of Satan in this battle of the ages.

For centuries the Roman Catholic Church, claiming to have taken Israel's place in God's favor, consigned the Jews to ghettos and forced them to wear identifying insignia. Luther persisted in this persecution even after his break with Rome, giving Jews the option of converting to Christianity or having their tongues torn out. The forced "conversion" of Jews in the Roman Catholic Inquisition and at other times in history is well known. It was not until 46 years after her birth that the Vatican acknowledged Israel's right to exist.

Hitler justified his tactics against the Jews on the basis of what the officially recognized Christian church, both Catholic and Protestant, had done for centuries. That highly educated, scientifically advanced and "civilized" nations would single out a group of fellow human beings for extermination is not only incredible but betrays a satanic element. That these people, in spite of such a programmed destruction, would be preserved, retain their ethnic identity, and would even multiply in numbers around the world is almost beyond belief.

Surely God has kept the Jews from genocide and from losing their identity as a national people exactly as He promised. The theory of "ten lost tribes," or of British Israelism, or that the real Jews became the white Europeans and Americans, stands in the fullest contradiction to a major theme and repeated testimony of God's Word.

Miraculous Restoration to Her Land

Even more indicative of God's hand behind the scenes is the fact that, just as the Bible declared, the descendants of Abraham, Isaac, and Jacob have been restored to their ancient land and reborn as a nation in today's modern world (Jeremiah 30:3,10,11; 31:8-10; Ezekiel 11:17; 28:25, etc.). Nearly 1900 years after the last destruction of the nation of Israel and the scattering of her people all over the earth, the nation of Israel came into existence once again in the land that God gave to her nearly 4000 years ago. It is a restoration unique in human history, in fulfillment of numerous and specific prophecies, and it bears the unmistakable imprint of the hand of God. Yet there is an even more astonishing aspect of this story.

The passage quoted at the beginning of the chapter is among the most remarkable in the Bible. It was recorded by Zechariah, under the inspiration of the Holy Spirit, nearly 2500 years ago. To appreciate his prophecy fully, one must remember that at the time the words were uttered Jerusalem was in ruins and the land around it, mostly desert or swamp, was a largely uninhabited wilderness—and it remained that way for centuries. Any chance that Jerusalem could recover its ancient glory, much less that it would be of international importance in today's modern world, was nil.

Under those hopeless conditions, God, through His prophet, made three astonishing declarations: 1) that the day would come when Jerusalem would be the focus of attention for all mankind; 2) that the entire world would at that time tremble in its concern over Jerusalem; and 3) that one day the armies of all nations would gather against Jerusalem to destroy it.

For centuries this prophecy seemed to be a grand mistake that had no rightful place in the Bible. The land of Israel remained largely a wasteland with a few nomads feeding their flocks on its sparse growth and scratching out a bare existence from its arid soil. Zechariah's prophecy could not have come from God but rather from his own madness. So it must have seemed for 2000 years. Yet today, as foretold, Jerusalem, though still of negligible size and in a location of no significance, is the center of international attention. The impossible has happened and for reasons that are still not understood by the world!

"A Cup of Trembling"

Not only is Jerusalem the center of world attention, but just as Zechariah foretold, it has become a "cup of trembling" for a modern world. Whether atheist or believer, Hindu, Buddhist, Muslim, or Jew, all mankind knows that the next world war, when it occurs, will break out over Jerusalem! Could any intellectually honest person deny that only God could have inspired such an incredible prophecy 2500 years in advance?

Smaller than Holland, Israel occupies about one-sixth of 1 percent of the land possessed by the Arabs surrounding her. The latter have the oil and the wealth and influence that goes with it. Israel has nothing: no oil or gas, no precious metals, no great rivers, no high mountains nor the vast fertile valleys they create. Then why the international concern over this postage stamp piece of arid real estate and the four million refugees who have fled there to escape persecution? It makes no sense. Yet the prophets foretold this situation precisely as it exists today.

The major nations of the world have their diplomats working day and night to effect a peace treaty between Israel and her Arab neighbors. Why? Because all mankind knows that the peace of Jerusalem is the key to the peace of the entire world exactly as God said through His prophets!

For centuries such a prophecy seemed the height of absurdity. Yet today, Jerusalem hangs like a millstone around the necks of 6 billion people who cannot escape the necessity of either bringing peace to this despised people or destroying them. Those who favor the latter alternative are growing in numbers and power.

Yes, to some extent, Jerusalem is the focus of attention because it is sacred to Catholics, Muslims, and Jews. But neither Catholics nor Muslims existed when these prophecies were made. Nor does Jerusalem's sacredness to these three religions explain why the whole world is concerned with establishing peace in the Middle East. This false peace will be guaranteed by the Antichrist and will ultimately lead to the most destructive war in earth's history. Sadly, one day soon and precisely as prophesied, all of the nations of the world will bring their armies against Israel to destroy her people.

The Bible's prophecies concerning the Jews, Jerusalem, and Israel are specific, preposterous, and impossible—yet they are being fulfilled to the letter. No honest person faced with these facts can possibly doubt that God is the author of the Bible, the Jews are His chosen people, and Israel is the land God gave them! Woe to those who seek to frustrate the promises which God has given to Israel, His chosen!

CHAPTER 4

God's Chosen People

> I will give it unto you to possess it, a land that floweth with milk and honey: I am the Lord your God, which have separated you from other people. And ye shall be holy unto me: for I the Lord am holy, and have severed you from other people, that ye should be mine (Leviticus 20:24,26).

Whatever one may choose to believe, God's Word declares repeatedly and unequivocally that Israel is His specially chosen people and that they will never lose that singular status. Israel's unique destiny, ordained by God to fulfill His will for mankind, is the dominant theme of Bible prophecy. The prophecies concerning the Messiah are inextricably linked with His people, Israel. It was to Israel, and through her to the world, that the Messiah, Himself a Jew, was to come.

Therefore, a clear insight into the prophecies pertaining to Israel's past, present, and future is foundational to any understanding both of the first advent of Christ and of His promise to "come again." Israel, as we have already noted, is God's prophetic timepiece, the great sign which He has given to the world to prove His existence and to demonstrate that He is in charge of history. Like it or not, the Jews are God's chosen people.

A chosen people? Chosen by God? That favor seems to have brought more than its share of troubles. In *Fiddler on the Roof,* Topol echoes many a Jew's bewildered protest, "How about choosing somebody else!" Obviously that plea won't change the facts. There is no escaping God's purpose or the biblical record.

Refusing to face the overwhelming evidence, skeptics contemptuously dismiss the very suggestion that there could be a special "chosen people." Atheists deny the existence of any God to do the choosing. Nevertheless, that biblical claim, even though widely rejected, has focused attention upon the Jews. In many cases it has brought persecution from those who hate the Jews, as though they were the ones who conceived the idea that God had some special affection and plan for them.

Muslims, on the other hand, insist that it was not the descendants of Isaac but those of Ishmael who were chosen by God. Muhammad's Quraish tribe claimed to trace themselves back to Ishmael and through him to Abraham. Therefore, it is argued, the land of Israel (which Muslims insist was promised to Ishmael) belongs to the Arabs. That Isaac, however, is the true heir was declared unequivocally by God to Abraham (Genesis 17:18-21). The land of Israel belongs to the descendants of Isaac. As for the Koran, it fails even to mention Jerusalem or any part of the land of Israel—an omission which is fatal to Islamic claims at this late date.

Five Distinguishing Characteristics of Israel

Let us take a closer look at this remarkable "chosen people." There is no better place to start than the book of Genesis. There we meet a man named Abram, whom God chose and later renamed Abraham. Both Arabs (through Ishmael) and Jews (through Isaac) claim him as their father. In fact, there is no evidence that the Arabs are descended from Abraham through Ishmael. As Robert Morey has pointed out in his excellent book *The Islamic Invasion:* "The prestigious *Encyclopedia of Islam* traces the Arabs to non-Abrahamic origins." The evidence that Jews are Abraham's descendants, however, is overwhelming. Here is where the story begins:

> Now the Lord had said unto Abram, Get thee out of
> thy country...unto a land that I will shew thee: and
> I will make of thee a great nation...and I will bless
> them that bless thee, and curse him that curseth thee:

and in thee shall all families of the earth be blessed (Genesis 12:1-3).

The Lord thy God hath chosen thee to be a special people unto himself, above all people that are upon the face of the earth (Deuteronomy 7:6).

There are five distinct elements in the covenant God made with Abraham, Isaac, and Jacob (Israel), which set their descendants apart from all other peoples on the earth. Here they are in the order in which they were given: 1) the promise that the Messiah would come to the world through Israel; 2) the promise of a particular land that was given to Israel as a possession forever; 3) the Mosaic law and its accompanying covenants of promise, which defined a special relationship between God and Israel; 4) the visible manifestation of God's presence among them; and 5) the promised reign of the Messiah, on the throne of David in Jerusalem, over His chosen people and over the entire world.

We will defer the first and last promises above, which pertain specifically to the Messiah, until later and deal with the others now. The verses quoted from Genesis 12 contain the first promise of a land that was to be given to Abram and his descendants after him. The next few verses in that chapter record Abram's obedient departure from Ur of the Chaldees, the land of his nativity, where his family had lived in idolatry for many years after the dispersion of the builders of the Tower of Babel. Around the ruins of that tower the city of Babylon was built. It would become the capital of the first world empire, the place of Israel's later captivity, and of great importance concerning Christ's return to this earth, as we shall see.

We very quickly find Abram arriving in "the land of Canaan." Its inhabitants were already known as Canaanites and they possessed the land at that time. This was the land that God identified to Abram as the land which his descendants would possess about 400 years later. Thus it became known as "the promised land" and is still referred to as such. The following are a sampling of God's many confirmations of this special promise concerning the land:

> And the Lord appeared unto Abram, and said, Unto thy seed will I give this land...for all the land which thou seest, to thee will I give it, and to thy seed for ever.

> I am the Lord that brought thee out of Ur of the Chaldees, to give thee this land to inherit it....Thy seed shall be a stranger in a land that is not their's [Egypt], and shall serve them....But in the fourth generation they shall come hither again.

> In the same day the Lord made a covenant with Abram, saying, Unto thy seed have I given this land, from the river of Egypt [in the Sinai desert] unto...the river Euphrates [and there follows a description of the exact territory] (Genesis 12:7; 13:15; 15:7,13-16,18-21).

The same promise is repeated to Abraham's son, Isaac, on more than one occasion. For example: "For unto thee, and unto thy seed, I will give all these countries, and I will perform the oath which I sware unto Abraham thy father...and in thy seed shall all the nations of the earth be blessed" (Genesis 26:3-5). The twin promise of the land and the Messiah is repeated again to Jacob, whom God later named Israel: "I am the Lord God of Abraham thy father, and the God of Isaac: the land whereon thou liest, to thee will I give it, and to thy seed...and in thy seed [i.e., the Messiah] shall all the families of the earth be blessed" (Genesis 28:13,14).

God's Self-Identification

Linking His very name with these promises, the God of the Bible identifies Himself 12 times as "the God of Abraham, Isaac, and Jacob" (Exodus 3:15,16; 1 Chronicles 29:18; Matthew 22:32; Acts 3:13, etc.). He revealed Himself as such to Moses at the burning bush. At the same time, He gave Moses His name,

"Yahweh," which means "I AM THAT I AM." He is the self-existent One whose existence depends upon no other, and upon whom the existence of all else depends. Jesus uses the fact that Yahweh is known as "the God of Abraham, Isaac, and Jacob" to argue for the resurrection:

> But as touching the resurrection of the dead, have ye not read that which was spoken unto you by God, saying, I am the God of Abraham, and the God of Isaac, and the God of Jacob? God is not the God of the dead, but of the living (Matthew 22:31,32).

"God" is not a name but a generic term that could apply to any god. Therefore, the God of Abraham, Isaac, and Jacob gives us His name. It is "Yahweh." Thus He is distinguished from all the gods of the world's religions. Yahweh is definitely not Allah for many reasons. Their character is exactly the opposite. Yet the highest officials of the Roman Catholic Church—in Vatican II and elsewhere—declare that the God of the Muslims and of the Christians is one and the same. Even evangelicals, trying to be broadminded and ecumenical, are suggesting that Muslims worship the same God as do Christians. Nothing could be further from the truth!

Here again we find clarification through an understanding of Israel's role. Allah is surely not "the God of Abraham, Isaac, and Jacob" but their sworn enemy who desires the extermination of their descendants! Allah is a proper name—a name that existed long before Muhammad invented the anti-Israel and anti-Christian religion of Islam. Allah was, as we have already noted, the name of the moon god, which was represented by the chief idol in Mecca's Kaabah. Hence the symbol of the crescent moon. For all of Islam's rejection of idolatry, Allah had a long pre-Islamic history as a pagan god represented by an idol—certainly not the God of the Bible at all!

The gods of the heathen, represented by idols, are consistently and repeatedly denounced in the Bible and those who worship them are condemned by Yahweh's prophets. Never is there the least hint or suggestion that any such god is or could be an unwitting representation of Yahweh. Indeed, Paul, as we've noted, declares that those who worship idols really worship the demons who identify themselves with them.

"Chosen" by an "Impartial" God?

Even among Christians there is increasing controversy over whether Israel any longer has a special place in God's plans. This controversy is accompanied by a growing rejection of the biblical teaching that the land of Israel belongs to the Jews. Some argue that for God to choose Israel would mean that He was unfairly playing favorites. After all, the Bible says that God is "no respecter of persons" (Acts 10:34).

Such impartiality on God's part was not easily revealed to Peter, for the Jews (and the early Christians were all Jews) considered all Gentiles to be without hope under the law of Moses. It took miraculous signs to convince Peter that the gospel was not only for Jews but for the Gentiles also. Even many Christians today cannot believe that God loves every person and desires that all should be saved, though the Bible teaches it plainly: "For God so loved *the world*…who will have *all men* to be saved….The Father sent the Son to be the Saviour *of the world*" (John 3:16; 1 Timothy 2:4; 1 John 4:14, emphasis added).

How can God's impartiality be reconciled with the idea of a chosen people? God made it very clear on a number of occasions that it was not "respect of persons" that caused Him to choose Israel. He chose them *in spite of their unworthiness and unattractiveness,* not because He found them more appealing than other peoples. In fact, they were rebels who deserved nothing but judgment. It was these unworthies in whom He decided to demonstrate His love, grace, and mercy to the world. Listen as He speaks to Israel through His prophets:

> The Lord did not set his love upon you, nor choose you, because ye were more in number than any people; for ye were the fewest of all people: But because the Lord loved you, and because he would keep the oath which he had sworn unto your fathers [Abraham, Isaac and Jacob], hath the Lord brought you out [of Egypt] (Deuteronomy 7:7,8).

This is a rebellious people, lying children, children that will not hear the law of the Lord: which say...to the prophets, Prophesy not unto us right things, speak unto us smooth things, prophesy deceits (Isaiah 30:9,10).

Son of man, I send thee to the children of Israel, to a rebellious nation that hath rebelled against me: they and their fathers have transgressed against me, even unto this very day (Ezekiel 2:3).

God's Unsearchable Grace

The Bible repeatedly says that the Jews, like all mankind, are rebels who are unworthy of anything except judgment. Even so, God blesses Israel by grace without any merit on her part because of His promises to Abraham, Isaac, and Jacob. Moreover, this grace is made possible by the Messiah's redemptive death. The contradiction between the Bible and the Koran could not be clearer on this point.

Although Allah is called "the Merciful Compassionate One," he is, in fact, compassionate only with a few, merciless with most, and has no basis for mercifully forgiving the sinner. In contrast to the biblical gospel of God's grace, Islam's salvation is by works and is merited by keeping the law. The Koran has no concept of divine mercy and grace and the penalty for man's sin having been paid in full by the Redeemer.

The Koran declares that Muslims receive God's blessing, not by grace, but because they are worthy: "Ye are the best of Peoples, evolved for mankind, enjoining what is right, forbidding what is wrong, and believing in Allah" (Sura 3:110). This same verse goes on to call the Jews "perverted transgressors." Sura 4:52,53 calls the Jews the people "whom Allah hath cursed...[who] have no one to help [them]."

It is commonly argued today, even by evangelicals, that the return of millions of Jews to their land is merely a chance happening of history without any prophetic significance. Surely God would not have brought the Jews back to Israel, it is argued, because they aren't worthy of it. A large percentage of them are atheists or agnostics and nearly all have rejected their Messiah. Many are humanists, materialists, New Agers.

Certainly Israel has not always acted in perfect righteousness toward the Arab Palestinians or toward her neighbors. With such a litany of sins to her credit stretching back to ancient times, how could Israel enjoy God's special blessing?

Grace and Promise

Israel's imperfections are beside the point. As the verses we've cited and hundreds like them in the Bible attest, Israel has been rebellious from the very beginning. Her present condition is nothing new. God has punished Israel for her sins. The worst punishment, however, lies ahead during the Great Tribulation, which will culminate in the battle of Armageddon. Yet the promises to Abraham, Isaac, and Jacob remain and will be fulfilled by God's grace. For if God's blessing comes only to those who are worthy of it, then all mankind is doomed. For as the Bible reminds us, "all have sinned" (Romans 3:23; 5:12).

There is no way for a sinner to pay for his own sins. Even one violation of the law puts the lawbreaker in a hopeless condition before God. Keeping the law perfectly in the future (even if that were possible) could never make up for having broken the law even once in the past. Obviously, there is no extra credit given for perfect compliance with every precept, for that is exactly what the law demands. Thus, good deeds can never obtain God's forgiveness for past sin.

The debt must be paid by One who is without sin and who is able to bear the judgment that the guilty deserve. Such is God's solution to evil—and to pay that debt was the primary mission of the Messiah. It was through His death for our sins that He judged and destroyed Satan. Hence, the good news of the gospel: "For by grace are ye saved, through faith, and that not of yourselves, it is a gift from God" (Ephesians 2:8).

Part of God's punishment upon Israel in the past was to scatter her people throughout all nations. He is now bringing them back to their land in unprecedented numbers, not because they merit it but because of His promise to Abraham, Isaac, and Jacob to do so. It has been a modern phenomenon far exceeding the original exodus of their ancestors from Egypt into the promised land.

A Promise for the "Last Days"

Of particular amazement to the world was the collapse of communism and the shredding of the Iron Curtain. One major bonus has been the resultant astonishing flood of Jews pouring back into Israel by the hundreds of thousands from the former Soviet Union—a land that formerly refused to allow them to leave.

What a sight it was to watch the daily influx of grateful immigrants arriving at Tel Aviv's Lod airport from all parts of the world, but especially from the northern land of Russia! It was deeply moving to see many of them kiss the ground when they exited the plane, weeping for joy.

An observer of this uniquely emotional scene who was familiar with the Hebrew prophets could not help but recall the promise God made 2500 years ago and which He said He would fulfill in the last days:

> For thus saith the Lord: Sing with gladness for Jacob, and shout among the chief of the nations: publish ye, praise ye, and say, O Lord, save thy people, the remnant of Israel. Behold, I will bring them from the north country, and gather them from the coasts of the earth, and with them the blind and lame, the woman with child and her that travaileth with child together; a great company shall return thither. They shall come with weeping, and with supplications will I lead them: I will cause them to walk by the rivers of waters in a straight way, wherein they shall not stumble: for I am a father to Israel, and Ephraim is my firstborn. Hear the word of the Lord, O ye nations, and declare it in the isles afar off, and say, He that scattered Israel will gather him, and keep him, as a shepherd doth his flock....Therefore they shall come and sing in the height of Zion, and shall flow together to the goodness of the Lord (Jeremiah 31:7-12).

Why was this promise to be fulfilled in that period of time called "the last days"? The reason is obvious and of great importance to our subject. The Second Coming could not take place without Israel having become a nation once again in her own land—for it is to Israel that Christ returns in the midst of Armageddon, to rescue her from the enemies who are intent upon exterminating her.

How close are we to that day? The fulfillment at this particular time in history of the many ancient prophecies that immigrants would flood into Israel in the last days is a major sign of the nearness of Christ's return.

Yahweh does not violate His promises. If He failed to keep His Word, whether to bring blessing or judgment, His character would be tarnished and His holy name dishonored. As He often said through His prophets concerning His intention to bring Israel back into her land in the last days: "I do not this for your sakes, O house of Israel, but for mine holy name's sake" (Ezekiel 36:22); "Thou art my servant, O Israel, in whom I will be glorified" (Isaiah 49:3).

What a great and convincing "sign" is Israel's return to her land after 2500 years! Today, in fulfillment of prophecy, the eyes of the world are upon that seemingly insignificant and tiny piece of arid real estate. She is, exactly as foretold, a "cup of trembling" for all nations—a trembling concerning what may happen there and to the entire world as a result.

Can anyone honestly compare the prophecies concerning Israel with her history and remain an atheist? Or can anyone deny that Jesus Christ is the only Savior? His advent, prophesied by the same Spirit-inspired mouthpieces for God, is intimately connected to Israel and her tortured history of dispersion and return to her land.

The other great theme of biblical prophecy is the Messiah who was to come through and to Israel. Those specific and numerous prophecies concerning Christ's coming, and their fulfillment in the life, death, and resurrection of Jesus of Nazareth, provide conclusive identification of Jesus as the Christ. They also constitute a further irrefutable proof for the existence of the God who inspired the Hebrew prophets.

CHAPTER 5

An Unlikely Prophetic Scenario

> The assembly of the wicked have inclosed me: they pierced my hands and my feet....They part my garments among them, and cast lots upon my vesture [robe] (Psalm 22:16,18).

> They gave me also gall for my meat; and in my thirst they gave me vinegar to drink (Psalm 69:21).

It was the night of April 9, A.D. 32, a Wednesday. The scene was the "last supper" and Jesus was alone with the 12 who comprised the inner circle of His disciples. Only three days earlier, on Sunday, April 6—a day now celebrated as Palm Sunday—the acclaim awarded Jesus of Nazareth had reached a crescendo. Having raised Lazarus from the dead, He had ridden into Jerusalem that day, not as one would expect of a hero, but astride a donkey colt. Nevertheless, throngs of people, having heard of Lazarus' resurrection, lined the approach to the Holy City to welcome Him. Waving palm branches and shouting for joy, the multitudes had hailed Him as Israel's long-awaited Messiah. Few, if any, in that joyous crowd realized that they were fulfilling a prophecy of about 500 years earlier:

> Rejoice greatly, O daughter of Zion; shout, O daughter of Jerusalem: behold, thy King cometh unto thee: he is just, and having salvation; lowly, and riding upon... a colt the foal of an ass (Zechariah 9:9).

Following that astonishing event Jesus had remained day after day in the vicinity of Jerusalem as though He were presenting

Himself in a new way to Israel. He had never before lingered at Jerusalem in this manner. It was extremely dangerous to do so, because the rabbis were determined to arrest and kill Him. Now, however, He seemed to have thrown away all caution. Though secreting Himself in a safe place at night, He returned each day to walk among the people and teach in the temple.

Unable to take Jesus into custody because of the crowds of admirers surrounding Him at all times, the increasingly frustrated rabbis were confounded as they watched His popularity grow by leaps and bounds. It was, of course, a time of excited, almost breathless, anticipation for Christ's disciples. The establishment of His kingdom was obviously at hand!

Alone with their Lord now, in the upper room, the 12 could scarcely contain their elation. Surely the One whom they had followed for more than three years was about to assert His right to rule on David's throne. The rabbis could never stop Him now, for the people were behind Him in overwhelming numbers.

A Frightening Turn of Events

The hour for which His inner circle of disciples had been waiting so long had come at last. So they thought, but how wrong they would soon discover themselves to be! In a seemingly impossible and frightening turn of events, their Master would in a few hours be arrested, condemned to death, mockingly crowned with thorns, and crucified like a common criminal. Dreams shattered, the disciples would flee in shame and fear for their own lives.

During His brief earthly ministry, Christ had repeatedly foretold His rejection and death at the hands of Israel's religious leaders. He had also declared publicly that He would rise from the dead after three days and had pointed His hearers to the Old Testament prophets who had already declared the same concerning the Messiah. Still, no one had understood. Peter had even rebuked Him for holding such a negative thought: "Be it far from thee, Lord: this shall not be unto thee" (Matthew 16:22,23). Instantly had come Christ's stern rebuke: "Get thee behind me, Satan!"

The prophets had clearly declared that the Messiah, when He came, would be rejected by His own people, crucified, and raised again from the dead. Yet neither the rabbis, who studied the Scriptures daily, nor the disciples, to whom Christ had tried to explain these things, comprehended what the prophets had foretold. Had they understood their own Scriptures, many of the religious leaders might have realized that Jesus of Nazareth was indeed the Messiah. Certainly the disciples would have acted differently had they grasped the messianic prophecies.

Today a similar confusion surrounds the Scriptures that pertain to Christ's return to planet Earth. Even among evangelicals there is not only disagreement on the subject but blindness to many of the pertinent prophecies. Consequently, an indifference prevails toward the most staggering event in history—an event which is much nearer than most Christians suspect.

That the prophesied Messiah, instead of ruling on David's throne as expected, would be rejected by His own people and killed was completely alien to the thinking of Christ's disciples. It was as though they hadn't even heard His words when He tried to tell them so. And now, in this last intimate moment with His faithful few before the cross, the Lord sought to explain further the purpose of His pending crucifixion. "I am going away to prepare a place for you," He told them.

Here were words whose meaning they understood but which did not fit their expectation. Going away? At the moment of triumph when all Jerusalem was hailing Him as the Messiah? It didn't make sense. Going where? Why? What about the kingdom?

Confusion Concerning the Kingdom

Visible consternation reflected from the anxious faces gathered about the table. What about the Davidic kingdom the Messiah was supposed to reestablish? Christ had promised that they would reign with Him on 12 thrones, judging the 12 tribes of Israel. He couldn't go away now! Was He having second thoughts—perhaps even preparing them for some disappointment? Had they been deceived? Too disturbing to face, the thought was drowned in the irrepressible flood of self-centered ambition and optimism.

Again it was the disciples' lack of understanding of what the prophets had so clearly declared that created such costly confusion. Ultimately, their lack of discernment would cause them to be unfaithful to Christ at the very time when they should have been most loyal to Him. How could they have been so ignorant of what their own Hebrew prophets had foretold concerning the messianic kingdom!

To the chagrin of the disciples sharing the "last supper" with their Lord, that kingdom in which they eagerly anticipated playing a leading role would have to await its appointed time. Though that time was revealed in the Scriptures and known to Christ, His followers and the rabbis were abysmally ignorant of such prophecies. That very night Jesus, the prophesied King of Israel, would be led away in apparent helpless defeat to be condemned to death at a mock trial. The disciples, disillusioned and shattered, would all forsake Him. Fervent pledges of loyalty and love forgotten, they would flee to protect their own lives.

Betrayal and Cowardliness in the Inner Circle

Knowing all that would transpire, Christ solemnly warned the 12 that they would all desert Him. He even quoted the prophecy that foretold their cowardliness: "Smite the shepherd, and the sheep shall be scattered" (Zechariah 13:7; Matthew 26:31)—a prophecy which none of them understood even when He pointed it out to them.

Peter, the most outspoken in swearing his fidelity ("I will lay down my life for thy sake"—John 13:37), was given special attention by the Lord. Jesus told him plainly: "Simon, Simon, behold, Satan hath desired to have you, that he may sift you as wheat: but I have prayed for thee, that thy faith fail not.... [Nevertheless] the cock shall not crow this day, before that thou shalt thrice deny that thou knowest me" (Luke 22:31-34).

Again the words were incomprehensible. That rugged fisherman, convinced that he knew his own heart, insisted that he would die before he would be unfaithful to the One he so fervently loved. So said all of the other disciples as well. In spite of their good intentions, however, they would prove the prophets right that very night. The entire spectacle would transpire exactly as it had all been written centuries earlier in surprising detail under the inspiration of the Holy Spirit.

Jesus knew all that would happen, even what the prophets had not foretold, for He had inspired them. Significantly, He told His disciples, "I tell you before[hand]...that, when it is come to pass, ye may believe that I am *he*" (John 13:19). The word "he" is in italics and does not appear in the original. Jesus was declaring once again that He was Yahweh, the I AM of Israel, who "declares the end from the beginning, and from ancient times the things that are not yet done" (Isaiah 46:9,10).

Nor did Christ hide from this inner circle the awful treachery within their own ranks. Once again He showed the disciples that He was the God of Israel by revealing the secret intentions of the one who would betray Him. Sorrowfully, He challenged the shallowness of their commitment and under- standing with this shocking declaration:

> Verily I say unto you, One of you which eateth with me shall betray me....The Son of man indeed goeth, *as it is written of him;* but woe to that man by whom the Son of man is betrayed! good were it for that man if he had never been born (Mark 14:18-21).

After that horrifying pronouncement, the disciples should have allowed no one to leave the room until the culprit had confessed and repented! Instead, this prophetic utterance by their Lord elicited only the briefest flurry of concern among the disciples. Each one with seeming innocence and sincerity asked, "Lord, is it I?" Christ answered Judas in the affirmative. Incredibly, none of the others seemed to notice.

Almost immediately the disciples' selfish ambitions came again to the fore and they returned to their argument over who would be the greatest in the kingdom. Surely it would be inau- gurated very shortly! So they thought. And why not? The crowds that were daily shouting Christ's praises would insist upon it.

"As it is written of him"! That all-important reference by the Lord to what the prophets had said seemed to mean nothing to any of those present. Inexcusable blindness to the prophetic Scriptures would be costly not only to the betrayer but to all of the disciples.

A Pawn in Satan's Hands

Judas was too full of his own secret aspirations to bother with arguing about his place in the kingdom. Why waste time on a dream that was not to be? Judas had inside information that Jesus was not going to take David's throne after all. The rabbis would see to that—with no small help from him. The crucial time had come to betray his Master to the religious leaders for crucifixion.

Intoxicated with the greedy anticipation of what he would do with 30 pieces of silver, the traitor muttered an excuse and slipped out into the night. The whole idea of a messianic kingdom was a grandiose delusion. In spite of the seeming miracles Jesus had performed, it was only a matter of time until this One whom so many had followed in the mistaken belief that He was the Messiah would be hunted down and arrested by the rabbis. So why not help them, since they were willing to pay handsomely? Why let that money go unclaimed or to someone else?

Judas was a man bereft of conscience. At first he had fought the temptation to steal from the small fund that came from occasional donations and which he had volunteered to keep track of and to guard. But after yielding that first time, the second theft came much easier, then the third and the fourth. It was not long until stealing, and lying to cover up, had become a challenging and seemingly rewarding way of life.

Satan had found his instrument; Judas was now a pawn in his hands. It couldn't be so wrong to realize a tidy profit by hastening what was surely inevitable. So he told himself once again as he made his furtive way to the rendezvous that would make him rich—and seal his soul's doom.

The name Judas would ever after be synonymous with treachery and betrayal. What a pitiful figure he was, driven by greed, inspired by Satan. And all the while he was oblivious to the fact that both his infamous deed and his tragic end lay before his very eyes in Scripture. David had written, "Yea, mine own familiar friend, in whom I trusted, which did eat of my bread, hath lifted up his heel against me" (Psalm 41:9).

Judas had prided himself on the sweet deal he had negotiated. It had not been easy, but he had succeeded in driving the haggling, skinflint rabbis up to 30 pieces of silver—a fabulous retirement nest egg.

Overlooked by the betrayer were the staggering words of the prophet Zechariah: "So they weighed for my price thirty pieces of silver...a goodly price that I was prised at of them" (11:12,13). That Judas would in bitter remorse, but too late, throw that blood money back at the rabbis' feet; that they would use it to buy a field for burying the destitute (Zechariah 11:13); and that he would kill himself (Psalm 55:12-15) had also all been foretold.

The Kingdom—Key to the Puzzle

The other disciples were oblivious to the historic drama in which they would play such cowardly roles. Each continued unabashedly to boast of his own qualifications for highest ranking, next to Christ, in the kingdom—a kingdom about whose advent and timing they were so terribly mistaken. They, like the rabbis, were heedless of the very Scriptures they read daily. Numerous prophecies, which they should have known, indicated clearly that the Messiah would not ascend to David's throne at His first coming, as they were so eagerly expecting. How their entire outlook and conduct would have changed had they but understood the prophets!

Disillusioned with predictions offering dates for the Rapture, most of those who call themselves Christians today have little interest in prophecy. Consequently, misunderstanding similar to that of the disciples concerning the timing and establishment of the kingdom now prevails in the Church. In fact, confusion regarding the kingdom of God is prevalent even among those who retain a deep interest in the return of Christ. Yet the kingdom, as we shall see, is a key part of the puzzle. Without it there would be no Second Coming. The prophets made that abundantly clear.

The first coming of Christ nearly 2000 years ago fulfilled specific prophecies concerning the kingdom of God—prophecies that had been a matter of record in the Old Testament for centuries. So must His Second Coming, which will also fulfill additional prophecies about that kingdom provided in the New Testament. The fact that everything prophesied concerning Christ's first appearance took place exactly as foretold provides absolute confidence that all of the prophecies concerning His return will also surely come to pass.

What those prophecies are, both in the Old and New Testaments, which foretell the Second Coming and the establishment and other details of the kingdom—and why they have been neglected, overlooked or misunderstood—is a fascinating study. Nor is it just an academic inquiry, but one of great practical value, as we shall see.

Strange Proof of Being the Messiah

On that shameful night of His betrayal, Jesus knew exactly what Judas had planned and what the rabbis were determined to do. In obedience and in love, and to procure our redemption, He would take that bitter cup from His Father's hand and pay the debt we owed to Infinite Justice for our sins. Ironically, Israel's religious leaders were unaware of the fact that their evil designs against Christ would prove Him to be the Messiah. In arresting and condemning Him to be crucified, they would unwittingly be fulfilling precisely what God had decreed and what the Hebrew prophets they claimed to honor had foretold.

Completely overlooking what they should have seen in their own Scriptures, the rabbis would think that in crucifying Him they had destroyed this One whom they so passionately hated. In fact, through death He would destroy Satan and break forever his evil power. Yes, even that unbelievably brilliant strategist, who had inspired Judas to betray his Lord, had no better insight into the Old Testament prophecies. Though he could quote the Bible, as he had when tempting Jesus in the wilderness, Satan did not understand it either. "That old serpent, the Devil" (Revelation 12:9) would be caught by surprise by the stunning defeat he was about to suffer.

Hanging naked upon a cross as a condemned criminal, jeered and taunted by the rabbis and rabble, Jesus of Nazareth, ex-carpenter and itinerant preacher, would seemingly be stripped of all messianic pretense. His ignominious decease would look like hopeless defeat to His disenchanted and cowardly disciples. Instead, by fulfilling specific prophecies, His crucifixion would prove conclusively that Jesus was the Christ. Blind to this fact, the seemingly victorious powers of darkness would gloat in obscene anticipation of taking over the world and the universe. Surely God's Son had failed in His rescue mission to planet Earth!

In reality, that humiliating and seemingly tragic death would be Christ's triumph. It would be the glorious fulfillment of the purpose for which the Son of God had been incarnated as a man into this world. As the old hymn says:

> By weakness and defeat,
> He won the victor's crown;
> Trod all His foes beneath His feet,
> By being trodden down.
> He Satan's power laid low.
> Made sin, He sin o'erthrew.
> Bowed to the grave, destroyed it so—
> And death, by dying, slew!

Christ had explained His mission to His disciples a number of times, but to no effect. They were so obsessed by their own self-centered anticipation of wielding great power in the messianic kingdom that His words fell without meaning upon their ears. Though His crucifixion would fulfill Scripture authenticating Him as the Messiah, to His disciples as well as to the rabbis it would seem to prove the opposite.

"We thought He was the Messiah, but of course He couldn't have been because they killed Him!" So went the pathetic lament of the two on the road to Emmaus (Luke 24:19-21). They were only expressing the embarrassing and humiliating disillusionment felt by all of the erstwhile disciples of Christ who were now in hiding. How could they have been so deceived by this messianic pretender? Perhaps the rabbis were right after all that no prophet could come out of Galilee (John 7:52).

Their champion was dead. That was proof enough. As it is today, even among many who call themselves Christians, so it was then—the cross did not fit human concepts of greatness and power.

CHAPTER 6

Victory by Defeat

Except a corn of wheat fall into the ground and die, it abideth alone: but if it die, it bringeth forth much fruit....Now is the judgment of this world: now shall the prince of this world [Satan] be cast out. And I, if I be lifted up from the earth [on a cross], will draw all men unto me [either to salvation or judgment] (John 12:24,31,32).

Let us go back and take a closer look at events leading up to Christ's crucifixion. We want to see the faith-inspiring correlation between what the prophets foretold and what actually transpired. Particularly, we want to have burned into our hearts and minds how a failure to understand the Old Testament prophecies caused the religious leaders and Christ's own disciples to dishonor God and fail to recognize who the Messiah was and why He came. That lesson should provide sufficient incentive for each of us to take another careful look at prophecy with renewed interest and appreciation.

For months the scribes, Pharisees, and Sadducees had been plotting to kill Jesus. Fearful of losing their positions and authority and encouraged by satanic enticement, Israel's religious leaders were blinded to the truth by pride and self-protective jealousy. Their hearts were filled with envy and hatred toward this One who defied their traditions and who spoke truth with an authority that pierced their hardened consciences like a sword. Had they truly been willing to know and do God's will, they would have understood His Word (John 7:17). Without that willingness to submit to His truth, no one can understand the Scriptures.

It was common knowledge by now that Jesus of Nazareth had healed multitudes of every kind of disease, made the lame walk, opened the eyes of the blind, even raised the dead. Those public miracles, witnessed by so many, could not be denied. No wonder the self-centered religious leaders both hated and feared Him. His growing popularity with the masses threatened to put them out of business. They were serving themselves instead of God and His people. As John tells us:

> Then gathered the chief priests and the Pharisees a council, and said, What do we? for this man doeth many miracles. If we let him thus alone, all men will believe on him: and the Romans shall come and take away both our place and nation.

> ...Caiaphas...said unto them, Ye know nothing at all,...it is expedient for us, that one man should die...and that the whole nation perish not (John 11:47-50).

This Crafty Imposter

How could the rabbis justify even to themselves such malice? It was quite easy, as rationalization always is. The miracles had to be an elaborate trick with the aid of unknown accomplices. This Jesus of Nazareth was such a crafty, slippery impostor. Whomever the Sanhedrin hired to engage Him in public debate in order to expose Him as a fraud was made to look abjectly foolish. How had He acquired such knowledge and brilliance? He confounded their best lawyers with an ease and wisdom that was obviously far beyond anything being taught in their rabbinical schools—or in any other centers of learning on this earth.

This audacious Nazarene had even said that His kingdom was "not of this world." What did that mean? Was He deliberately baiting them? Multitudes were treating Him as though He were indeed a king. The situation had become so explosive that the Romans might very well step in suddenly with military force. Something had to be done!

Intoxicated by the seeming miracles—especially by His apparent ability to feed thousands of followers with a few loaves and fishes—the impetuous populace was murmuring against Caesar and hinting that this Jesus ought to be installed as King of the Jews. His followers, now numbering in the thousands, were under His hypnotic spell. Falling for His staged triumphal entrance into Jerusalem, they had openly hailed Him as the Messiah. Threats by the religious leaders to excommunicate anyone who even so much as whispered such heresy had failed to stifle the insidious rumors or to stem the growing tide of His popularity.

In opposing this Galilean and being made out to be fools for their trouble, the rabbis had lost the respect and attention of the common people. Even the children swarming around Him in the temple were crying, "Hosanna to the son of David" [i.e., Messiah]. When the chief priests and scribes reproved Him for accepting such praise, Jesus had boldly replied: "Yea, have ye never read, Out of the mouth of babes and sucklings thou hast perfected praise" (Matthew 21:16)?

Those who had once obeyed with reverence the edicts of the ruling Sanhedrin now ignored them. Instead, they hung with rapt attention on every word of this upstart Nazarene, as though He were God Himself—which, indeed, He blasphemously claimed to be. That had been the last straw! Surely now they had legal cause under the Mosaic law for a public execution. No one could complain.

He Claimed to Be God!

"Unless you believe that I AM [that was the name with which God revealed Himself to Moses!] you will die in your sins, and where I go you cannot come" (see John 8:21-24). Absolute blasphemy, to be sure, but what did He mean by "where I go you cannot come"? He kept throwing in these strange ideas as a diversionary tactic. So blinded were the rabbis by self-interest that their consciences were dulled to the voice of truth when He spoke in their very midst.

The statements He made about Himself were staggering: "I AM the Bread of Life come down from heaven" (John 6:33-35);

"I AM the light of the world, he who follows me shall not walk in darkness" (John 8:12); "I AM the door, by me if any man enter in he shall be saved" (John 10:9); "I AM the Son of God" (John 10:36); "I AM the resurrection and the life...he who believes in me shall never die" (John 11:25,26). Anyone else who persisted in making such incredible claims would be dismissed as insane—but not this man. He spoke these words with an authority that couldn't be challenged. The rabbis had tried.

This cunning rabble-rouser deliberately used the words "I AM" in a way that not only outraged but dumbfounded and frightened the scribes and Pharisees. There could be no doubt that He was claiming to be God. Yet He cleverly avoided boasting about it, as one would expect some egomaniac to do. He made His dignified and seemingly sincere claim to deity with His use of "I AM" in exactly the same way Yahweh had revealed Himself to the prophets. One was afraid to stand near Him when He made these brazen declarations for fear lightning would strike or the ground would open up to swallow Him as it had Korah and his followers (Numbers 16:32)!

"Before Abraham was, I AM" (John 8:58). There it was again! On that occasion even the common people within earshot had been so scandalized that they had joined the rabbis in taking up stones to kill Him. Yet He walked unscathed through their midst, and they were powerless to stop Him. And now the rabble were thoroughly convinced and on His side. The Romans were complaining about the restlessness among the people! What could be done? Multitudes were treating Him as though He really were the Messiah!

How dare any man in his right mind make such grandiose claims for himself—even that he was God! Yet this obviously pious and otherwise seemingly humble Galilean was no self-deluded simpleton. He knew the Scriptures better than anyone! Israel's cleverest lawyers had tried to trip him up with trick questions about the law of Moses, and He had turned the tables on them every time. He had to be eliminated for the good of the nation.

A Frustrated Manhunt

Where had He gotten His education? Certainly not in their rabbinical schools, which He had never attended—yet the people reverently called Him "Rabbi!" It was galling and infuriating for the religious leaders to hear a title they had labored so long to earn applied admiringly to this uneducated Galilean. Without any conscience at all He accepted such adulation: "Ye call me Master and Lord: and ye say well; for so I AM" (John 13:13). He seemingly had no compunction about applying God's unspeakable name to Himself!

This carpenter-turned-itinerant-preacher was an enigma. He was no mere reckless liar—far worse than that. There was no mistaking the fact that He knew exactly what He was saying and obviously believed His grandiose claims, for He pronounced them with great conviction. "Destroy this temple, and I will raise it up in three days!" He was an incurable braggart as well as a blasphemer of the most impertinent kind.

Such flagrant defiance of the law demanded the death penalty. That just verdict had been secretly agreed upon by the authorities long ago—but how to take Him when admiring mobs surrounded Him at all times was the problem. Jesus of Nazareth had headed the list of "most wanted" criminals for so long that it had become an embarrassment. Even the temple guard who had been sent to arrest Him returned empty-handed, mumbling helplessly, "Never man spake like this man" (John 7:46).

Why was He still at large? His arrest and death had been sought diligently for months, but no one had been able to lay a hand upon Him. And now, at last, here was the chance they had so long awaited—a stroke of good fortune. He would not elude them this time!

A Break for the Sanhedrin

One of Christ's own inner circle had surprised the rabbis with an opportunity they had never expected. Judas had told them that, for some strange reason, unlike His past caution, Jesus was staying on at Jerusalem. It would be a simple matter to lead a band of soldiers to an isolated night rendezvous where they could take Him all alone without the protection of the crowd that always surrounded Him in the city.

Although the rabbis had nothing but contempt for that greedy traitor, they were only too glad to use him to their own ends. He had driven a hard bargain. Thirty pieces of silver was a large sum—but more than worth it to the Sanhedrin. Before the night was over, with Judas guiding them to Jesus' hiding place and with no admiring rabble flocking around to protect Him, they would arrest this blaspheming troublemaker and turn Him over to the Romans for execution. He would die like the common criminal He was. At long last they would be rid of Him.

What a relief it would be when this great impostor was out of the way and the people were once more under their power. Oh, yes, He had said He would rise from the dead the third day—claimed that was what He meant about raising up the temple, that He was referring to the temple of His body. So be it. They would seal the tomb and set a guard so the disciples couldn't steal the body and claim a resurrection. This lie would be His last—the final proof that would explode the myths surrounding Him and break the spell that held even His most ardent followers. That charlatan would soon be forgotten, like so many pretenders before him who had gathered a following only to die in disgrace, their disciples scattered in disillusionment.

So the Sanhedrin thought. It was not, however, the connivings of Judas and the rabbis that determined the shameful events of that dark night and the following day. The plotters were oblivious to the fact that they were the unwitting instruments of God's will. Christ's mock trial and crucifixion, which the rabbis thought proved their power over Him, would prove instead what they so furiously denied—that He was indeed the Messiah.

All According to God's Plan

Prophecies by the dozens, recorded centuries before by Israel's acknowledged prophets, were being fulfilled to the letter by those who sought His death. Every move the religious leaders made added one more proof that Jesus of Nazareth was the Christ. That astounding fact, when at last he understood it, would be Peter's dramatic revelation in his first sermon on the Day of Pentecost. The betrayal, Pilate's sham judgment, and the crucifixion had already been decreed by the "determined counsel and foreknowledge of God" (Acts 2:23) long before the world was even created (Ephesians 1:4; 1 Peter 1:20). All would occur exactly as the prophets had foretold.

How could the future be known and revealed before it happened? Surely such an outrageous idea had to be a myth! Astrologers deceitfully used ambiguous phrases that could apply to almost any occasion or event. Likewise, the words of the Hebrew prophets contained in the Scriptures were often so cryptic that they could be interpreted in many ways. So why waste valuable time on such vain speculations?

Such skepticism toward prophecy caused it to be a neglected topic in the Israel of that day. Prophecy is likewise largely in disfavor even in the evangelical church in our time, and because of similar unbelief. Yet the words are clear for those hungry to know God's revealed will and wise enough to seek and obey it. To them He unfolds the future, as Daniel was told: "None of the wicked shall understand [prophecy]; but the wise shall understand" (Daniel 12:10). As we shall clearly see, there is no more exciting and enlightening topic to study than prophecy!

The very Scriptures the rabbis read with such pomp and ceremony in the synagogues each Sabbath plainly declared the horrendous outrage against heaven which they were determined to carry out. The perpetrators of the most heinous crime in the history of the universe were acting out the fulfillment of prophecy and were not even aware that they were doing so. What terrifying judgment they were bringing upon themselves—judgment that could have been avoided had they but known and heeded the prophets!

The Enigma of Two Comings

Isaiah, the prophet who had written so much about the Messiah's endless reign of perfect peace, had also declared unequivocally that He would be "despised and rejected" (Isaiah 53:3) by Israel and even slain (53:8,9). How could He be killed, and yet reign over the promised kingdom? The contradiction seemed impossible to reconcile, so the prophecies of His rejection and death were simply ignored. Of course, if these prophecies referred to *two comings* of the Messiah—one in weakness as the "Lamb of God" (John 1:29) to die for our sins, the other in power and glory as the "Lion of Judah" (Revelation 5:5)—then the contradiction disappeared.

Such a likelihood, however, never occurred to the Jews in Christ's day, causing them in ignorance to fulfill the Scriptures by crucifying their Lord. In like manner most Christians today reject the possibility that *two comings* for Christ yet remain in the future. We shall see that, after examining all the relevant prophecies and comparing them carefully one with another, there is no other conclusion one can logically reach.

David, greatest of Israel's kings, upon whose throne the Messiah would eventually reign, had foretold the same astonishing rejection of the Messiah by His own people (Psalm 22:6,7). He had even described the manner of His death—that this Holy One would be crucified (Psalm 22:16). That prophecy was inspired of God and written into Scripture many centuries before this method of execution had been adopted by the Romans as a means of putting down uprisings following their conquests. David and the other prophets had to be divinely inspired, for who but God could know the future so far ahead and with such accuracy?

There was more. The God who inspired David to prophesy the crucifixion had also promised him that the Messiah would be his descendant and would reign on the Davidic throne in Jerusalem: "I will set up thy seed after thee...and I will establish...the throne of his kingdom for ever" (2 Samuel 7:12-17). To be despised and rejected by Israel and crucified—and yet to reign over His people in Jerusalem? Clearly both could not occur at the same time.

Surely Messiah had to come *twice* to fulfill two such divergent prophecies. And since His reign would never cease, He had to be crucified the first time, rise from the dead—and at a later coming ascend to David's throne. For the learned rabbis not to recognize that fact was inexcusable.

Victory in Apparent Defeat

The cross was Christ's triumph—a victory that would establish His kingdom through apparent defeat. Through death He destroyed "him that had the power of death, that is the devil" (Hebrews 2:14). That same victory over sin and over the forces of darkness is now available to Christ's followers. It comes for them, as for their Lord, not by bravado nor with the guarantee of immunity from suffering, but by way of meekness, submission to the Father's will, and apparent defeat in the death of the cross. As Jesus said, "If anyone will come after me, let him deny himself, and take up his cross and follow me" (Matthew 16:24).

Not that Christians must all die on literal crosses, though martyrdom has been the fate of many. The flagellation of the flesh accomplishes nothing. Victory is in *His* cross, not in some other cross one might bear. Christ alone could pay the full debt for sin. Through faith in His substitutionary death upon the cross for all mankind, those who believe are eternally set free from sin's penalty. It is a gratuitous gift of God's grace.

And what of sin's power to deceive and enslave? Freedom from both sin's penalty and power come in the same way— through embracing His death as one's very own. When Christ took our place, God's justice required His death. Those who believe He died in their place acknowledge that they justly deserved the death penalty and confess that they have died in Him. Sin no longer has any power over those who are dead, nor does this world hold any enticements for them.

At the "last supper"—in another world long ago and far away it now seemed—Christ had explained that He was going to return to His Father's house in heaven. That was the place from whence He had come and to which He had promised to take them. First, however, He must return to the Father alone, leaving them to tell the world of His death for sin and His resurrection.

Why must He go away? These were troubling words which, once again, they did not understand. They were still expecting the kingdom to be established momentarily.

All too soon that incredibly marvelous 40 days after His resurrection which Christ spent with His own to restore their faith came abruptly to an end. Suddenly and without any warning He left them. The disciples watched in astonishment as, with hands outstretched in blessing, Christ rose from this earth and disappeared far above them in a cloud. His last words moments before had been: "Ye shall receive power, after the Holy Ghost is come upon you: and ye shall be witnesses unto me both in Jerusalem, and in all Judaea, and in Samaria, and unto the uttermost part of the earth" (Acts 1:8).

The Promise of a "Second Coming"

As the disciples gazed upward in bewilderment, two angels stood by them and announced that He would return to that very place on the Mount of Olives from which He had just ascended. Moreover, He would come again in the same manner in which He had left: in a visible descent from the heavens. Other Scriptures make it clear that He will come in glory and power and "every eye shall see him" (Revelation 1:7). The exact words of the angelic messengers were: "This same Jesus, which is taken up from you into heaven, shall so come in like manner as ye have seen him go" (Acts 1:11).

"Science fiction?" some would ask. No! In fact, it is a scenario far more amazing than that. Nor should this angelic declaration have been startling or new to the disciples. The prophet Zechariah had already stated it clearly, including the fact that this One who would return to the Mount of Olives was God:

> Then shall the Lord [Yahweh] go forth, and fight against those nations [surrounding Jerusalem at Armageddon]....And his feet shall stand in that day upon the Mount of Olives, which is before Jerusalem (Zechariah 14:3,4).

The prophet Zechariah adds this interesting commentary in the next verse: "And the Lord my God shall come, *and all the saints with thee.*" There can be no doubt that Zechariah 12–14 refers to the return of the Messiah at Armageddon to rescue His people Israel from those who have them surrounded with overwhelming force and are about to annihilate them. Clearly this is the same event which John reveals in Revelation 19. One whose name is "The Word of God" (v. 13)—surely the same One to whom we've already referred, who has been the expression of God from the beginning (Isaiah 48:16)—Christ Himself, comes to Armageddon accompanied by "the armies which were in heaven."

The Necessity of a Previous "Rapture"

The heavenly "armies" which John says will accompany Christ must be the "saints" of whom Zechariah writes. There can be no doubt that both passages describe the same event. Jude tells us that this coming of the Lord in power and glory was foretold by Enoch thousands of years earlier: "And Enoch also, the seventh from Adam, prophesied of these, saying, Behold, the Lord cometh *with ten thousand of his saints,* to execute judgment upon all" (Jude 14,15).

It is clear, then, that the "saints" of all ages, which would certainly include all Christians, accompany Christ from heaven when He returns to the Mount of Olives at His Second Coming. It takes no genius to conclude that for His saints to come back to earth with Christ *from heaven* they must have been taken up there previously. We are faced, therefore, with the inescapable conclusion that Christ, sometime prior to the Second Coming, takes all those who have believed in Him (the resurrected dead and the transformed living) to heaven.

Many Christians will never die physically. Their resurrected Savior has promised that when He returns to raise those believers who have died, He will catch away from this earth all living Christians as well and transform their physical bodies to be like His resurrected body of glory. That occasion is called the Rapture, which simply means an ecstatic catching away. It is a promise which is absolutely unique. Neither Muhammad,

Buddha, nor any other of the founders of the world's religions ever dared even to make such an offer. Dead men don't "come again."

Paul, who was not with the original disciples when the Lord spoke to them of His return, became the chief authority on the subject. Indeed, the fact that Paul who had not known Christ on earth became the chief authority on Christianity is one of the powerful proofs of Christ's resurrection. He wrote most of the epistles, rebuked Peter publicly for straying from Christ's teachings (Galatian 2:14), and the other disciples, including Peter (Acts 15:12; 2 Peter 3:15-16), acknowledged his inspiration and authority. Paul certified that he had been personally instructed by the risen Christ:

> But I certify you, brethren, that the gospel which was preached of me...I neither recieved it of man, neither was I taught it, but by the revelation of Jesus Christ (Galatians 1:11,12).

Paul provided details about the Rapture which none of the other apostles explained. He described it in these words: "And the dead in Christ shall rise first: then we [Christians] which are alive and remain shall be caught up together with them in the clouds to meet the Lord in the air: and so shall we ever be with the Lord" (1 Thessalonians 4:16,17).

It is clear from the Scriptures that Christ's promised return involves two distinct events. At the Rapture, Christ comes *for* His saints to catch them up from this earth. At the Second Coming, He comes *with* His saints from heaven to rescue Israel and execute judgment upon Antichrist and his followers. These two events will be separated by seven years, a period during which the Antichrist will be in control of this earth. Biblical justification for this belief will become overwhelming as we proceed.

CHAPTER 7

The "Blessed Hope"

Let not your heart be troubled: ye believe in God, believe also in me. In my Father's house are many mansions: if it were not so, I would have told you. I go to prepare a place for you. And if I go and prepare a place for you, *I will come again, and receive you unto myself,* that where I am, there ye may be also (John 14:1-3).

What overpowering emotions stirred within the disciples as they watched their Lord disappear into heaven, then heard from the angels the promise of His return to the Mount of Olives! Their thoughts must have gone back immediately to what Christ had told them at the last supper. That solemn occasion was taking on more significance each day as their understanding deepened. On the eve of His betrayal Christ had given them similar assurance of His return with the words, *"I will come again."* Yet there seemed to be a puzzling contradiction.

Christ had declared that He was going back to His Father's house, from whence, after a short while, He would return to take them up there as well to be with Him forever. His promised return would be for a specific purpose: *"I will receive you unto myself."* They had understood Him to mean that He was going to take them to heaven, to His Father's house, *"that where I am, there ye may be also."* So His coming again had to be for the purpose of catching them up to heaven to be with Him.

Yet the angels, when they said He would come back to the Mount of Olives, had made no mention of anyone being taken to heaven. If that were indeed the purpose of His coming, it surely wouldn't be necessary for Him to return all the way to this same place outside Jerusalem. He could catch His followers up to meet Him far above the earth. That He would indeed do so was the revelation that the Holy Spirit would later speak through Paul who, at this time, was the sworn enemy of Christ and His church.

Moreover, the prophet Zechariah had said that when the Messiah's feet stood upon the Mount of Olives He would bring with Him from heaven "all the saints" (Zechariah 14:5). Rather than taking anyone to heaven at that time, He would come back to earth to rescue Israel when she would be surrounded by the armies of the world gathered to destroy her. In fact, the Messiah would destroy those armies and immediately set up His millennial kingdom over which He would reign from David's throne in Jerusalem.

There seemed to be a glaring contradiction. Christ's return to do battle with Israel's enemies at Armageddon didn't sound at all like His promise to take His own to heaven. Something wasn't right. And if they were going to rule with Him in Jerusalem, how could they have been taken to heaven? There was apparently much they still didn't understand.

Presumably the disciples saw the apparent inconsistency and puzzled over it. Most Christians today don't even recognize the seeming contradiction, much less know how to reconcile it. Let us, however, defer that problem for the moment.

The "Blessed Hope"

Christ's promise had been unequivocal: *"I will come again, and receive you unto myself; that where I am there you may be also!"* For the first time, having watched Him caught up to heaven, the disciples found hope in those electrifying words which they had never understood before. Surely their resurrected Lord would return very soon to take them to His Father's house. In fact, He had said, "Ye shall not have gone over the cities of Israel until the Son of Man be come" (Matthew 10:23). That couldn't take long!

To make up for past failures they would show Him how quickly their assigned task could be accomplished—perhaps in a few weeks, surely not longer than a few months. He was sending the Holy Spirit from heaven to empower them to be His witnesses. The sooner they completed that important work the sooner He would return to take them to His Father's house in heaven as He had promised.

With Christ's *I will come again!* still fresh in memories, the early Christians eagerly waited and watched for their Lord's return. He had said that they were not of this world, but that He had chosen them out of it. Paul would soon write under His Lord's inspiration: "For our conversation [citizenship] is in heaven; from whence also we look for the Saviour, the Lord Jesus Christ: who shall change our vile body, that it may be fashioned like unto his glorious body" (Philippians 3:20,21). The world held little interest for these citizens of heaven. They were homesick for the Father's house, longing to be with their Lord in that eternal haven of rest.

Hated, persecuted, and killed by Rome, the early Church took comfort in the belief that Christ might return at any moment to rescue His followers from their trials. Paul called the anticipation of an imminent Rapture "that blessed hope" (Titus 2:13), and indeed it was for those early believers who went through "fiery trials" and "rejoiced at being partakers of Christ's sufferings" (1 Peter 4:12,13). How they longed to leave this world to be with Him!

As the weary weeks became years, however, and the years multiplied into decades, and finally centuries passed, the vast majority of those who claimed to be Christ's followers gave less and less thought to that "blessed hope." The promise of Christ's return was first neglected and then forgotten. Finally it was lost in the maze of new interpretations and heresies that began to multiply.

Attitudes and outlook changed. Citizenship in heaven had proved to be too nebulous a concept. Something more tangible was desired. Being despised on this earth, hated, persecuted, and killed, as their Lord had been, no longer seemed a necessary accompaniment of true Christianity. Perhaps this world had something to offer after all. Perhaps the church could even take the leadership in political affairs and transform the world, establishing the kingdom in Christ's absence. A more accommodating attitude toward secular society might even make the unsaved more receptive to the gospel—especially if they realized that becoming a Christian needn't mean persecution or even much of a change in one's way of life.

The First "Vicar of Christ"

The steadily worsening apostasy took on a hitherto unimagined dimension with the ascent to power of a new Emperor in A.D. 313. He was a brilliant military strategist and general named Constantine. He also had a genius for political organization and realism. Constantine faced the fact that almost three centuries of persecuting Christians had not stamped out that strange sect. Instead it had grown until nearly one out of every ten citizens in the empire was among that despised band.

Tertullian's remark that the blood of the martyrs was the seed of the Church, inexplicable though it might be, had proved to be true. People apparently wanted something more than pleasure and profit. Only firmly held convictions worth dying for could make life worth living.

These "followers of the way," as they were called in those early days of the Church, even prayed for the Roman emperors and other magistrates and soldiers who persecuted and killed them! Why not take advantage of that exemplary loyalty to kings and kingdoms which seemed to be a part of this strange religion?

The Christians were conscientious, hard workers. They didn't get drunk or rebel against the government. Insurrection was not in their natures. Then why not encourage them, give them full rights? Perhaps their philosophy of industry and fidelity would spread to other citizens. The empire would be much the better for it if the numbers of Christians multiplied. The new policy was a very pragmatic one.

To further this strategy, Constantine himself claimed to have become a Christian, though he continued, as Pontifex Maximus, to head the pagan priesthood and to preside over the pagan holiday ceremonies. Of course, that was his duty as emperor and it was excused in view of his encouragement of the building of Christian churches. A new day of tolerance had dawned.

Worshiped as God, the emperor was the head of the empire's official religion. Now that Christianity was recognized along with the old paganism, Constantine assumed leadership of the Christian Church. In doing so, he took the title Vicar of Christ. Posing as the Church's greatest friend and benefactor, and perhaps even doing so sincerely, Constantine became its destroyer.

Christ had refused Satan's offer of the kingdoms of this world if He would but bow down to him. In a moment of weakness, a Church weary of persecution accepted the same offer from Satan, this time presented through the Roman emperor. It was the beginning of centuries of what would be known as the Church's "Babylonian captivity."

Augustine lamented that those who were now inside the Church were "drunkards, misers, tricksters, gamblers, adulterers, fornicators, people wearing amulets, assiduous clients of sorcerers, astrologers...the same crowds that press into the churches on Christian festivals also fill the theatres on pagan holidays." For many Christians, however, it was a welcome change to go from being despised, hated, hunted, and killed, to being popular and even leaders in the world.

Once it had meant almost certain persecution and possible death to heed the gospel. There had been little need to worry about false professions of faith under those circumstances. Now it was just the opposite. False professions were more the rule than the exception.

The Church Marries the World

In the new order of things under Constantine, it had become a great advantage to be a Christian. One had to attend one of the growing number of Christian churches to get anywhere in business, politics, and even in the military. Conversions of convenience multiplied as church attendance soared.

Corruption quickly reached to the top in the Church. The empire's best-paying jobs with the most worldly prestige and influence were in church leadership. Constantine encouraged the growth of an ecclesiastical system that he could use to his own ends. It attracted men whose ambitions were not to gain reward in the world to come but in the present one.

Many who rose to power within the Church hierarchy were master politicians who knew how to use Christian terminology but knew not Christ. As Will Durant put it in *The Story of Civilization,* the paganism of Rome "passed like maternal blood into the new religion, and captive Rome captured her conqueror. While Christianity converted the world, the world converted Christianity." What a tragic commentary! Such was the birth of Roman Catholicism, which would dominate the scene from that moment on.

The Church that was supposed to be the bride of Christ, awaiting eagerly the return of her Bridegroom to take her to heaven, had tired of waiting for Him and married the world instead. Now occupied with building an earthly kingdom over which she could reign in an adulterous partnership with kings and emperors, the Church lost its hope of heaven and began to look upon itself as the replacement for God's earthly people, Israel. Forgotten were admonitions such as this from the Lord:

> Lay not up for yourselves treasures upon earth, where moth and rust doth corrupt and thieves break through and steal: but lay up for yourselves treasures in heaven, where neither moth nor rust doth corrupt, and where thieves do not break through nor steal: for where your treasure is, there will your heart be also (Matthew 6:19-21).

In disobedience to her Lord, the Church became the wealthiest institution on earth and gloried in her earthly treasures. Much of the wealth was acquired by selling salvation. Every sin had its price for "forgiveness." The greater and more numerous the sins the wealthier the Church of Rome became. Crosses and altars that supposedly depicted the sacrifice of Christ were gilded with gold. Bishops, cardinals, and popes, who claimed to be the successors of barefoot fishermen disciples, lived lifestyles that shamed even secular kings. The perversion of the Church that began with Constantine continued to worsen through the centuries, giving us today's Roman Catholicism.

During the Dark Ages and for centuries thereafter, Roman Catholicism was recognized by secular governments as the only true Christian Church. The popes had their armies, fought numerous wars (sometimes against each other), made political alliances with princes, kings, and emperors, over whom they gradually asserted their power. Emperors trembled at the threat of excommunication by a pope, for only heretics doubted that outside the Church there was no salvation. To be excommunicated meant eternal damnation without any hope—and that threat gave the Church almost absolute power.

Rome became "that great city, which reigneth over the kings of the earth" (Revelation 17:18). Her rule was not by military might, for the Roman legions were no more. Her power to rule the world was wielded by a religious hierarchy that claimed to have inherited the keys to the kingdom given by our Lord to Peter. For centuries Roman Catholicism was the hand inside the glove of secular authorities, who even executed those whom she pronounced heretics. Thus Rome disclaims any responsibility for the martyrs of the infamous Inquisition, for the actual executions were, in most cases, carried out by the state.

Hope of the Rapture Is Lost

There was no longer any reason for Christ to return. Claiming that Constantine had given them his authority, the popes ruled with an iron hand over what they conceived to be "the kingdom of God" come to earth. To this day the popes proudly bear Constantine's three religious titles: Pontifex Maximus, Vicar of Christ, and Bishop of Bishops.

These titles, together with imperial power, the early popes claimed, had been conferred upon them by Constantine himself. To support that assertion the Church circulated a document known as *The Donation of Constantine*. Today it is recognized, even by Catholic historians, to have been a deliberate forgery. That such a document was needed is more than sufficient proof that the doctrine of papal succession, upon which today's popes rely as proof of their supreme spiritual authority, was a much later invention.

The Rapture is unknown in today's Roman Catholicism. In fact, it is specifically contradicted by the twin Catholic dogmas of purgatory and indulgences. Although down through the centuries there have been many relatively small groups of evangelical believers independent of and persecuted by Rome, they, too, for the most part lost the hope of the Rapture.

Depending upon how much they have suffered in this life, good works accomplished, indulgences earned, faithful Catholics must spend varying and unknown lengths of time in purgatory suffering for the sins for which Christ also suffered. That unbiblical teaching eliminated the promise, "The dead in Christ shall rise first: then we which are alive and remain shall be caught up together with them...to meet the Lord in the air" (1 Thessalonians 4:16,17). A simultaneous resurrection of the "dead in Christ" and all living believers caught up together with them in the Rapture would be impossible. All of the dead would not have finished purgatorial sufferings, and the living would not even have been there as yet.

The Reformation did little to recover any hope in Christ's promise, "I will come again and receive you unto myself." The Rapture is generally denied or has little importance among Reformed groups such as Presbyterians and Lutherans. There seemed to be good reason to avoid that teaching due to past fanaticism surrounding it. The best proof that the hope of an imminent Rapture was not biblical was found in the fact that Christ had not yet come.

Unfortunately, when the "blessed hope" of Christ's imminent return has been revived periodically in the last two centuries, the excitement created here and there has usually developed into date setting, causing the Rapture to become an object of derision. Voluntarily divested of their earthly possessions, cruelly deluded, white-robed zealots have more than once waited in vain on hilltop or rooftop while the promised hour came and went. Such fanatical anticipation has always subsided once again into disillusionment and forgetfulness.

An Understandable Apathy

The "blessed hope" became prominent in evangelical thought in the 1970s and early 1980s with the publication of Hal Lindsey's *The Late Great Planet Earth* and other books attempting a biblical treatment of the Rapture. Then came *Eighty-eight Reasons for [the Rapture to occur in] 1988* followed by *Eighty-nine Reasons for 1989.* The flurry of excitement turned to disappointment and disillusionment when Christ failed to Rapture His Church in September of either of those years as the author had assured readers the Scriptures promised. Then came *1994?,* by Harold Camping, and a similar delusion.

In between, a Korean "prophet" declared that the Rapture would occur on October 28, 1992. Many of his followers around the world, but especially in Korea, quit their jobs and gave away their possessions to await the promised event. The day passed with everyone still on earth, leaving the deluded believers embarrassed and ashamed. Shortly thereafter the leader was indicted for converting to his own use about four million dollars of the church's funds. It seemed that he used much of the money to buy bonds whose maturity date far exceeded the day he had set for the Rapture!

In the wake of such excited anticipation and then disappointment, greater disillusionment than ever smothered the legitimate hope of Christ's imminent return. The Rapture and Second Coming are now looked upon as topics to be avoided by the vast majority of Christians—and, it would seem, with good reason. The gospel, too, because it was clearly preached by these date setters, has come in for increasing mockery.

Today there are about 1.8 billion people around the world who call themselves Christians and claim to believe God's Word. Most of them, however, as one might suspect after the passage of so much time, give little thought to the Lord's return. His promise *"I will come again!"* is still in the Bible and remains a tenet—if a vague, unimportant, and controversial one—of the Christian faith. That it musters little genuine interest, much less hope, is not surprising considering the fact that nearly 2000 years have passed since our Lord spoke those words.

Who can say how many more years or centuries may go by before that promise is fulfilled? After all, the Bible says that with God a thousand years is like "yesterday when it is past, and as a watch in the night" (Psalm 90:4). By that reckoning, Christ has only been gone a few hours. So it could be thousands of years yet before His return. And what difference does it really make? That is the vital question we must confront in all honesty.

CHAPTER 8

Reconciling Contradictions

> When shall these things be [the destruction of the
> temple]? and what shall be the sign of thy coming,
> and of the end of the world? And Jesus answered [in
> the next 28 verses He gives numerous signs and then
> He says]…when ye shall see all these things [signs He
> has given], know that it [the Second Coming] is near,
> even at the doors. Therefore, be ye also ready: for in
> such an hour as ye think not the Son of man cometh
> (Matthew 24:3,33,44).

What contradictions are these! Can it be? On the one hand,
Christ declares that His coming will follow immediately
upon the heels of multiple and unusual signs widely scattered
around the globe: wars, pestilences, famines, earthquakes, a time
of trouble (the Great Tribulation) such as the world has never
known nor ever shall know again. There will be supernatural
occurrences in the sky: a darkened sun and moon and "the sign
of the Son of man," visible to all. These signs will be apparent to
everyone on the earth. There will not be the slightest doubt in
anyone's mind that Christ's coming is at hand, "even at the doors."
No one will be taken by surprise.

On the other hand, Christ with no less clarity declares that
His coming will catch almost everyone by surprise.

The contradiction could hardly be more blatant. Quite easy
to reconcile, is the answer some give. Only the Christians will
heed the signs. Didn't Paul say, "But ye, brethren, are not in
darkness, that that day should overtake you as a thief" (1 Thessalonians 5:4)? Those who are spiritually blind, however, won't
recognize the signs, and they are the ones who will be caught

by surprise. So goes the argument, but it doesn't fit the Word of God.

Cataclysmic Events that Will Terrorize the World

The signs Christ and the apostles and prophets mention are not of such a subtle nature that it would take any spiritual discernment at all to recognize them. On the contrary, the signs are so overwhelming that they can't be overlooked or ignored by anyone. The Second Coming takes no one on earth by surprise.

The events leading up to Christ's return to the Mount of Olives are so unprecedented and universally calamitous that the whole world knows the time has come for the prophesied face-to-face confrontation between Christ and Antichrist. The Bible declares that "the beast [Antichrist], and the kings of the earth, and their armies" will gather together at Armageddon to make war with Christ (Revelation 19:19). They know that the fatal hour has arrived for the final showdown.

Consider again the signs of His return which Jesus enumerates in Matthew 24. Then read the terrifying description of the incredible devastation occurring on earth which is mentioned already in chapter 6 of Revelation. Forget the mind-boggling destruction mentioned elsewhere. At this early stage in the Great Tribulation one-fourth of the earth's population has been killed. That's more than 1.5 billion people! Natural disasters beyond imagination assault this beleaguered planet. Catastrophic meteor showers rain down upon the earth, accompanied by gigantic earthquakes and volcanic upheavals of such magnitude that "every mountain and island [moves] out of their places." Every person on the earth realizes that God's wrath is being poured out from heaven. Proud leaders are so terrified that they cry out to the mountains and rocks to fall upon them to hide them from God's fierce anger (Revelation 6:15-17).

No, Christ does not warn us to be "ready" because we might otherwise not have the godly discernment to recognize the subtle spiritual signs that will herald His coming. Those signs will be physical and of such magnitude that they can't be overlooked or ignored by anyone, no matter how spiritually blind.

An Inescapable Contradiction

Christ warns us to "watch" for an entirely different reason. He will come at a time when mankind, confident and complacent—and a sleeping church (Matthew 25:5)—will least expect Him: "At such an hour as ye think not the Son of man cometh" (Matthew 24:44). There will have been no conclusive, physical signs. Therefore, the disasters mentioned above could not yet have occurred. God's judgment is the last thing the world of that day will be expecting. There will be no advance warning. It will be like the calm before a hurricane—but in this case there will be no sense of a storm impending.

Jesus warned that He would come when conditions would be like those just prior to the flood: "They did eat, they drank, they married wives...until the day that Noah entered into the ark and the flood came and destroyed them all" (Luke 17:27). His coming will occur at a time of business as usual, of pleasure, of optimism for the future. Just as it was immediately before the flood, the last thing the world will expect is judgment from God.

Surely Christ is not describing the Second Coming in the midst of Armageddon! Normal business conditions, complacency and surprise could only apply to a previous coming—the Rapture. At the time of the Second Coming mankind has endured perhaps four years of God's wrath and is expecting more. This world is in ruins and teetering on the brink of total destruction.

For Christ's coming to be without warning and to catch everyone by surprise it must occur *before* the time of great disaster He refers to in Matthew 24. He comes *before* God pours out His wrath upon earth as described in Revelation. Otherwise He could not say that His coming would be at a time similar to the days of Noah just before the flood.

Yet, just as clearly, He declared that He would come *after* these horrible disasters have wreaked their awful toll and *after* God's wrath has been poured out for several years upon this earth. These catastrophes will be the signs which Christ says will herald His coming. Moreover, His coming will not take place until all of these events have occurred, so that no one will have any doubt that His coming is "at the doors."

All of mankind will know that He is about to descend from heaven, because of the unmistakable signs that herald His return. So Jesus declared in unequivocal language. Yet just as clearly He warned that there would be no signs at all to signal His coming. It will occur when conditions on earth make it seem, even to His own, that He surely wouldn't be coming then: "in such an hour as ye think not." That's when He will come!

The contradiction seems inescapable: He comes when there have been no warning signs, yet He comes after all of the signs have been displayed to a terrified world; He comes like a thief when no one would expect Him, yet He comes when everyone will expect Him.

Two Separate Events: The Rapture and the Second Coming

How can Christ come immediately following unmistakable signs which are intended to warn of His coming—and at the same time come as a thief in the night when few if any of His followers would expect Him? How can He come "when they say peace and safety" (1 Thessalonians 5:3) and at the same time come in the midst of Armageddon, the most destructive war the world has ever known? How can the saints be *caught up from earth to heaven* to dwell with Christ eternally and at the same time come with Him *from heaven* to execute judgment upon this earth?

How can two scenarios that are so contrary to one another both be true? There is only one possible answer to that question. Obviously, these diametrically contradictory descriptions of His coming cannot refer to the same event.

We saw that what the Old Testament prophets said of Christ's coming could not fit into one time frame and one event. Thus two comings of the Messiah were required, though the prophets didn't say so directly. There was no excuse for

Christ's contemporaries not to realize that fact. Likewise it is inexcusable today not to realize that what the Bible says of His return simply cannot fit into one time frame and one event.

There must be two separate comings of Christ, both still future, which occur at two distinctly different periods of time. There is no other way to reconcile the otherwise contradictory statements in Scripture concerning Christ's return. According to Christ's own words, the conditions on earth at one coming will be the exact opposite of those at His other coming.

It is impossible to combine in one event and in the same time frame an ecstatic catching away of all believers *to* heaven with the descent of Christ and all believers *from* heaven to rescue Israel at Armageddon. The Second Coming takes place *after* the incredible devastation of earth, called the Great Tribulation, which the Bible predicts for that time. The Rapture takes place *before* the Great Tribulation. The whole world will know that the Second Coming is about to take place. No unbelievers, and even very few Christians, will be expecting the Rapture when it occurs.

The Second Coming, which is the climactic event of the Great Tribulation, will occur in the midst of Armageddon. The armies of the world will have conquered much of Israel and will be pressing their attack against Jerusalem. They will be intent upon effecting what Hitler called the "final solution to the Jewish problem"—the enraged extermination of every Israeli and probably of all Jews on planet Earth (Zechariah 12).

Threatened with total destruction, Israel, in desperation, will undoubtedly retaliate with nuclear weapons. The entire human race—indeed, all life on this planet—will be in danger of annihilation as this nuclear exchange escalates. Christ referred to that moment with these solemn words: "And except those days should be shortened, there should no flesh be saved [alive]" (Matthew 24:22). He will have to intervene, not only to save Israel, but to preserve life itself on earth.

Yes, a Secret Rapture!

Clearly, the Rapture and the Second Coming must be two separate events. The Second Coming, occurring at the end of

the Great Tribulation and in the midst of Armageddon, will surprise no one. The Rapture, occurring at a time of normalcy and
complacency, will catch the world and a sleeping church by
surprise.

Millions of Christians—and quite likely all infants—will suddenly vanish from earth, but how or why will not be known by
the world. Nor will those left behind believe that Christ has
caught away those who have disappeared and taken them to
His Father's house in heaven. A seemingly plausible explanation (which we will discuss later), will be provided by the
Antichrist, who will take over world leadership at that time.
His hypothesis will satisfy the world, but it will be a lie.

Several times Christ's coming is likened to that of a thief
who creeps in when all are asleep. Peter writes: "The day of the
Lord will come as a thief" (2 Peter 3:10); and Paul adds, "as a
thief in the night" (1 Thessalonians 5:2). A thief deliberately
comes in such a time and manner that no one is aware of his
presence. He secretly takes what he is after and leaves without
anyone's knowledge.

In like manner, the Rapture will be a secret snatching away
of a prize from this earth. Christ declared: "Behold, I come as
a thief" (Revelation 16:15). Secretly, like a thief, Christ will take
out of this world His church. The world will not know it is
happening until suddenly millions are missing. Those who
complain that a "secret Rapture" isn't biblical need to look at
such Scriptures again.

No Signs for the Rapture

We not only see from Scripture that the Rapture (Christ
coming *for* His saints) takes place first, followed seven years
later by the Second Coming (*with* His saints for Israel). We also
see that there will be no signs for the Rapture, no warning that
it is about to occur. The signs are for the Second Coming.

When Christ comes secretly to catch His saints up to
heaven, the world will be living in self-complacency and pleasure, seemingly on the way to solving its ecological problems
and establishing perpetual international peace. Any thought of
the Rapture will be widely ridiculed. Even few Christians will

expect that long-promised event, although it should be their hope. One could say that such is already the general attitude even in the evangelical Church. How many are eagerly watching and longing for Christ to take them to heaven?

As we shall see in the following pages, many of the signs of the Second Coming are already in the world today. Others are clearly on the horizon, casting their long shadows in our direction. There can be no doubt that the props are being set in place and the curtain is about to rise on the final drama in human history. The principal actors, including the Antichrist, are waiting in the wings, eager to effect their will. In fact, they will play their roles precisely as the prophets have foretold.

The final act, called "the day of the Lord" (1 Thessalonians 5:2), must begin with the Rapture, for that time period is ushered in "as a thief in the night." The Second Coming cannot mark the beginning of "the day of the Lord," for it comes as no surprise. It is essential to understand that all the signs the Bible gives pertain to the Second Coming.

No signs precede the Rapture. It can only be that coming which will take place without warning, when the world and even most Christians least expect it. Everything on this earth will be changed after that event. The Rapture could occur at any moment. That has always been the case.

The reasons to expect our Lord now, however, are more compelling than ever. How close are we? Today's sleeping Church, sinking ever deeper into apostasy, is one of the primary marks of the nearness of Christ's return. The signs of the Second Coming are building, and the Rapture must precede that event by seven years. Surely we are very close.

CHAPTER 9

Signs of the Times

> When ye see a cloud rise out of the west, straightway ye say, There cometh a shower; and so it is. And when ye see the south wind blow, ye say, There will be heat; and it cometh to pass. Ye hypocrites, ye can discern the face of the sky and of the earth; but how is it that ye do not discern this time? (Luke 12:54-56).

There can be no doubt that Jesus Christ, who is God, came to this earth as a man through a virgin birth, lived a perfect, sinless life, died for our sins, and rose from the dead the third day. Historically these events are firmly established. We have, however, an even more powerful witness. That Christ came to this earth in the past is not only a matter of history. It is also a matter of fulfilled prophecy. Consider what that means.

Christ's first coming nearly 2000 years ago, as we have already seen, fulfilled dozens of specific prophecies made by the Hebrew prophets and recorded centuries earlier in the Old Testament. So will the Rapture of His Church and His Second Coming fulfill even more details of the prophetic blueprint. Furthermore, these events are not independent of one another, but part of an overall plan of God. They all fit together like pieces in a jigsaw puzzle. Each event can be understood only in relation to the whole.

Here we confront another aspect of the uniqueness of Christ that sets Him apart from all others. No prophecy foretold the coming of Buddha, Confucius, Muhammad, or any other of the leaders of the world's religions. Muslims suggest that Christ's statement, "I will send you another Comforter," foretold the coming of Muhammad. However, that claim doesn't fit by any stretch of the imagination.

Christ said that the Comforter would "come from the Father" (John 14:26; 15:26). Yet Muhammad denied that God was a father or had a son. Christ said of the Comforter, "He dwelleth with you and shall be in you" (John 14:17). So the Comforter, who was already with the disciples more than 500 years before Muhammad was born, obviously could not have been Muhammad.

Christ came once, nearly 2000 years ago. The how and where of His coming and all that He suffered and accomplished was exactly as the prophets foretold. He is coming again, and very soon. That coming, too, in every detail, will be exactly as prophesied.

Prophecy Provides Foolproof Identification

Why were such prophecies given? There are at least two fairly obvious reasons. First of all, prophecy indicates that the God who created us has not lost interest in His creatures nor has He lost control of events. He is in charge of history and will see that it works out according to His plan. That plan involves His people, Israel. It also involves the Messiah and the Church. God wants us to know His plan in advance and has revealed it through His prophets.

Secondly, at His comings there must be no doubt as to the identity of the Messiah. Antichrist, as we shall see, will try to pass himself off as the Christ. The deception will be clever and persuasive. Those who know prophecy will be armed in advance with the facts that unmask Satan's most brilliant deceit.

All that was needed to identify Christ at His first advent, and all that will be needed to identify Him when He comes again, has already been stated by the prophets. That overwhelming proof of His identity provides absolute assurance of our salvation. Of equal importance, we can share with others the proof prophecy provides. It is the most powerful means of convincing unbelievers and of introducing them to the Savior.

There is another important significance of prophecy which is not as readily accepted. God wants us to know the signs of the times that reveal the nearness of Christ's return. We have seen how neglect and ignorance of prophecy caused both the secular and religious authorities to crucify Christ at His first advent. In view of today's neglect of prophecy, there is every reason to expect a comparable confusion when Christ comes again. To prevent such tragic misunderstandings—for those who are willing to take a fresh look at the Messianic prophecies—is a major purpose of this book.

As we have seen, Israel's religious leaders of that day were blind to the fact that the Messiah would be rejected by His own people and crucified. The same was true, until after the resurrection, of even Christ's closest followers. They were blind also to the fact that when Christ made that solemn promise, *"I will come again,"* it was one more proof that He was the Savior.

As we have already seen, a most vital part of the testimony of the Old Testament prophets was that the Messiah must come more than once. Centuries beforehand, the Hebrew prophets had given their stamp of authenticity to the electrifying words which the disciples would find so incomprehensible: *"I will come again."*

After These Many Centuries—Why Now?

Christ's declaration, however, confronts us with a dilemma. After the passage of nearly 2000 years, He has not come as He promised. Succeeding generations of believers have watched and waited and have gone to their graves without seeing their earnest hopes and prayers realized. Why should we be any more likely than they to see this promise fulfilled in our time?

How close are we? Is it presumption even to ask that question? Some Christians think so. However, since so much has been revealed by the prophets, might it not be that the answer even to this question is contained in the very prophecies which the rabbis overlooked and which we neglect today? Surely the possibility of discovering an answer to that burning question makes the careful study of what the prophets had to say more than worthwhile.

Those thrilling but as yet unfulfilled words, *"I will come again,"* must be taken in the context of all of Scripture. Let us not forget that the One who made that promise had come to fulfill specific, detailed, and numerous Old Testament prophecies. Everything He said and did and all that man did to Him was only the culmination of what the prophets had long before declared.

Yet there can be no doubt that Christ left this earth without fulfilling all messianic prophecies. Thus He must return, and He must do so exactly as the prophets have foretold. The disciples' perspective of prophecy was too narrow. There was a much larger picture they did not comprehend. We must beware of missing it as well. If we are to understand when and why and for whom Christ will return, then we must see His promise to do so in the full context of God's eternal plan.

God had taken great care to inspire His prophets and guard His Word to provide His people with sufficient means of recognizing the time of the Messiah's first advent. Would He not inspire His prophets to give similar insight into the Rapture and Second Coming as well? We believe that He has, and we will substantiate that from Scripture.

Jesus indicted Israel's religious leaders for failing to recognize the signs of the times in which they lived: "Ye hypocrites, ye can discern the face of the sky and of the earth; but how is it that ye do not discern this time?" (Luke 12:56). Apparently they were responsible to know the signs given in Scripture, to recognize when they were present, and to conduct themselves accordingly. That same accountability is ours today.

"Signs" of His Coming?

As far as most Christians are concerned, when Christ comes He comes, so why not let it go at that? After all, there's nothing that can be done either to hasten or delay that day. Raising children, holding the family together, earning a living, and preparing for retirement leave little time even to think about an event that will not likely happen in one's lifetime. Fear of repeating past fanaticisms and follies seems reason enough to avoid focusing any attention upon Christ's return. Reason enough, that is, until one reads the words of Jesus more carefully.

One cannot escape the fact that Christ and His apostles gave definite signs to watch for that would herald the nearness of His return. Why give these signs if some generation at some time in the future was not expected to recognize them and know that His Second Coming was, as He Himself said, "near, even at the doors"?

Yes, but if the Rapture occurs seven years prior to the Second Coming, then those signs are not for us. So it would seem. Yet Christ commanded His own to watch for His coming and warned against being caught by surprise at His return—and surprise could only apply to the Rapture. Are we faced again with a contradiction, and this time one that cannot be resolved?

We may be certain that the answers are to be found if we desire to know them and diligently search His Word. Jesus also said, "And when these things begin to come to pass, then look up, and lift up your heads; for your redemption draweth nigh" (Luke 21:28). When these things *begin...look up*. The commencement of the signs cannot herald the Second Coming, for that event cannot occur until the signs are all complete. Therefore, with this statement, Christ can only be referring to the Rapture.

When Jesus, in response to His disciples' request for signs of His return, enumerated a long list of events (wars, rumors of wars, pestilence, earthquakes, famines, etc.), He also used that same word, *begin*. He made this interesting comment: "All these are the *beginning* of sorrows" (Matthew 24:8). The Greek word Jesus used for "sorrow" is most interesting as well. It referred especially to a woman's birthpangs.

Jesus is apparently revealing that these signs will *begin* to occur substantially ahead of the Second Coming. They will increase in frequency and intensity like birthpangs. Moreover, it would seem that these signs *begin* prior to the Rapture. Then how could the Rapture come as a surprise? Because these signs when they begin, will by their very nature be phenomena that have always been known on the world scene: earthquakes, famines, pestilences, wars.

Fanaticism and date setting are folly. It would seem to be at least equal folly, however, to ignore Christ's warnings about being caught by surprise. We are responsible, as every generation before us has been, to know the signs of His coming and to determine whether they are present and what they mean in our day. No matter that others have misinterpreted Scripture and mistakenly set a time for Christ's return, only to be proved wrong. We are responsible to know the signs and to apply that knowledge biblically.

Though past generations have so consistently misinterpreted the Scriptures, is it possible that we now possess the insight they lacked? Isn't such a suggestion the very height of conceit? It could be, except for one obvious but overlooked fact, which we will discuss later. As we shall see, ours is the first generation to whom certain special signs Christ foretold could possibly apply!

Christ's Total Mission Is the Key

In our attempt to understand the full meaning of Christ's promise, "I will come again"—and to establish how close we are to that event—we must examine the full range of biblical prophecies. It is not enough merely to look at Christ's own words and the events and teaching of the apostles that followed His departure from earth. The Old Testament prophets foretold not only His first advent, but His Second Coming as well.

It is to the Old Testament, then, that we must first of all turn to begin our investigation. Nor shall we have proceeded far in this careful study until we will be forced to conclude that prophecy is the backbone of God's Word. Without prophecy the Bible would lose much of its uniqueness and power to convince the searching soul.

God has stated unequivocally: "Surely the Lord God will do nothing, but he revealeth his secret unto his servants, the prophets" (Amos 3:7). If we would know God's secrets and understand all that He has planned, then we must study what He has spoken through His prophets. For it is through the prophets that God has declared His eternal purpose—and even the details of how He will work it all out for our good and His glory.

Christ's crucifixion and departure from this earth were not the unfortunate results of an aborted mission but the successful completion of *phase one*. Thus, His promise to return was the pledge to finish the remainder of a task which the prophets had laid out in no uncertain terms. The mission that brought the Messiah to this earth was much larger than His disciples imagined.

Christ's purpose in coming back again will be to bring to a grand conclusion His total objective. Consequently, we must understand God's plan from eternity past to eternity future or we cannot possibly reach a valid conclusion from the Scriptures concerning the timing of His triumphant return in power and glory to the scene of His rejection and crucifixion.

Chapter 10

A Most Amazing Prophecy

In the first year of Darius...I Daniel understood...that [the Lord] would accomplish seventy years in the desolations of Jerusalem. Seventy weeks [of years] are determined upon thy people [Israel] and upon thy holy city [Jerusalem]...to bring in everlasting righteousness, and to seal up the vision and prophecy, and to anoint the most Holy [i.e., for Messiah's reign to begin]....From the going forth of the commandment to restore and to build Jerusalem unto the Messiah the Prince shall be seven weeks, and threescore and two weeks (69 weeks of years equals 483 years)...[Then] shall Messiah be cut off [i.e., slain] (Daniel 9:1,2,24-26).

Imagine setting the date for Christ's triumphal entry into Jerusalem 500 years before the event and being accurate to the very day! Daniel did that. In fact, this and his many other prophecies are so astonishing that the book of Daniel has been a chief target of determined skeptics for more than 100 years. Somehow Daniel had to be exposed as a fraud.

Critics have insisted that Daniel's prophecies must have been made after the fact. Otherwise, one would have to admit that God, as Daniel claimed, had given him a personal revelation of future world events hundreds of years before they happened. Such an admission would be intolerable for any skeptic to be forced to make.

If the prophecies of Daniel could not be discredited, the cause of atheism would suffer an irreparable blow. Therefore, the book of Daniel has been examined and attacked relentlessly.

It has withstood every assault and demonstrated conclusively that it is God's Word. Mankind is left with no excuse for rejecting the Bible and the message it brings.

Daniel's Many Remarkable Prophecies

To deal with the many prophecies of Daniel is beyond the scope of this writing. The four world empires—Babylonian, Medo-Persian, Grecian, and Roman—are foretold, including numerous details concerning each. For example, the succession of the Medo-Persian empire by the Grecian empire and the division of Alexander the Great's Grecian empire into four parts is prophesied (8:20-22). That division is again mentioned in 11:4. The next 16 verses give amazing details of the wars of Ptolemy (the Grecian general who took possession of Egypt after Alexander's death) and his successors against the Seleucids of Syria. That prophecy climaxed with details concerning Seleucid ruler Antiochus Epiphanes (11:21-36), a type of Antichrist. Incredibly, one reads history written in advance!

Daniel, too, in the two legs of the image, foretells the division of the Roman Empire into eastern and western kingdoms (Rome and Constantinople). In its feet and ten toes, signifying ten kings, the revival of the Roman Empire under ten heads in the last days is foretold. Daniel also prophesies the coming of the Antichrist and that he will rule over the revived Roman Empire (9:26). He further foretells that Christ (the "stone cut out without hands"—4:34,44,45), at His Second Coming, will destroy the Antichrist and this last world empire and establish His millennial reign.

Interesting as Daniel's many prophecies are, we must confine ourselves to those which pertain directly to the Messiah's first advent, to the Rapture, and to the Second Coming. So remarkable are this great prophet's insights concerning the coming Messiah that had Christ's critics understood only one verse in Daniel they would have been compelled to change their entire outlook toward Jesus of Nazareth.

As we have seen, Christ's contemporaries, from the rabbis to the disciples, were confused about the kingdom. They imagined that it was to be set up in their time. And because Jesus didn't liberate Israel from Rome and reign as king on David's throne but was crucified instead, even the disciples were convinced, at that point, that He couldn't possibly be the Messiah. John the Baptist suffered from the same misconception. From prison he voiced his doubts that Jesus was the Christ. The reason for those doubts sheds light upon a similar confusion today concerning the kingdom.

A Great Prophet—Yet Ignorant of Prophecy

It seems impossible that John the Baptist could have been so mistaken. This man had been chosen by God for a very special mission, and one which he had completed magnificently. John had even been "filled with the Holy Spirit" before his birth. While still in the womb, he had leaped with joy at Mary's announcement to her cousin Elizabeth that she was with child of the Holy Spirit. Though unborn, John had supernaturally reacted with joy to the news that Mary would give birth to the Messiah, the One whom John was to introduce to Israel.

John knew his mission, and as certainly as he knew his own identity he knew that Jesus was the Christ. When the Pharisees sent officers to ask whether he believed himself to be the Messiah, he "confessed, I am not the Christ....I am the voice of one crying in the wilderness, make straight the way of the Lord" (John 1:19-24). In quoting from Isaiah 40:3, John claimed to be the fulfillment of that prophecy. He not only knew his mission by revelation from God, but he had visible and miraculous confirmation:

> And John bare record, saying, I saw the Spirit descending from heaven like a dove, and it abode upon him [as Christ came up out of the water after John baptized him]. And I knew him not [until that time]: but he [God] that sent me to baptize with water, the same said unto me, Upon whom thou shalt see the Spirit descending and remaining on him, the same is he....And I saw, and bare record that this is the Son of God (John 1:32-34).

This fiery and fearless messenger of God not only knew that Jesus was the Messiah, he revealed insights unknown to Israel's religious leaders into what that meant: "Behold the Lamb of God, which taketh away the sin of the world" (John 1:29). In spite of his calling and knowledge, however, the day came when he sent two of his disciples to ask Jesus, "Art thou he that should come? or look we for another?" (Luke 7:19).

What could possibly have brought this man, who was so in touch with and inspired of God, to the place where he would ask a question evidencing such unbelief? On this very occasion, though John had expressed great confusion, Jesus said, "There is not a greater prophet than John the Baptist" (Luke 7:28). Then how could he doubt that Jesus was the Messiah?

The answer is very simple. John suffered from the same misunderstanding as all the rest—that the Messiah would set up His kingdom and rule on David's throne the first time He came. That being the case (as he thought), why was he, John, in prison about to have his head cut off? If anyone deserved to reign in that kingdom, surely it was he, the one who had proclaimed Jesus to be the Messiah and had introduced Him to Israel. Yet Jesus seemed powerless to deliver him from King Herod, the very monarch who would have to be deposed for the Messiah to take David's throne. It didn't make sense—unless Jesus was not the Christ after all.

Had John known only one of the verses from Daniel to which we have referred, he would have understood that the time was not right for the Messiah to set up His kingdom. That verse also presents one of the prophecies whereby we know for certain that the Roman Empire must be revived. It is the culmination of Daniel's interpretation of Nebuchadnezzar's dream about the strange image with a "head of fine gold, his breast and his arms of silver, his belly and his thighs of brass, and his legs of iron, his feet [with ten toes representing ten kings] part of iron and part of clay" (Daniel 2:31-33).

In the Days of Those Kings

Inspired of God, Daniel explained that the four parts of the image, each of a different substance, represented four world kingdoms:

> Thou, O king [Nebuchadnezzar]...art this head of gold. And after thee shall arise another kingdom [Medo-Persian] inferior to thee, and another third kingdom [Grecian] of brass, which shall bear rule over all the earth. And the fourth kingdom [Roman] shall be strong as iron (Daniel 2:37-40).

We see these four world kingdoms again in chapter 7, where further details about each of them are given. There they are depicted as four beasts. The fourth (Roman) has ten horns and we are told what they signify: "The ten horns out of this kingdom are ten kings that shall arise" (Daniel 7:24). That these ten kings pertain to the future revived Roman Empire is evident from the fact that no such division of that empire ever occurred in the past.

The interpretation that the ten toes of the image signify ten kings yet to arise is also clear from the explanation Daniel gives in his interpretation of the image in chapter 2. Finally, he declares in that key verse (2:44): "And in the days of these kings [represented by the ten toes] shall the God of heaven set up a kingdom, which shall never be destroyed: and [it]...shall break in pieces and consume all these kingdoms, and it shall stand forever."

Inasmuch as the Roman Empire was never ruled by ten kings or co-emperors, it must be revived under ten heads for this prophecy to be fulfilled. Certainly there were not ten kings ruling the empire in the days of Jesus. Therefore, on the basis of this one verse, the rabbis, the disciples, and so great a prophet as John the Baptist should have known that it was not time for the Messiah to set up His kingdom. Daniel 2:44 is very explicit that the millennial kingdom will not be established except "in the days of these kings." No reasonable interpretation can be adopted to change that simple fact.

That the Roman Empire, as already noted, was divided into two segments, as depicted by the two legs of the image, is a matter of history. The division was also religious and continues to manifest itself to this day in the separation between Roman Catholicism and Eastern Orthodoxy. This breach will more than likely not be healed until the Antichrist inaugurates his new world religion. That we are, however, already moving rapidly in that direction seems evident. It is also clear from numerous Scriptures that religion will play as important a role in the revived Roman Empire as it did in the ancient one. The close partnership between the popes and emperors will of necessity have its parallels in the key role to be played by the Roman pontiff in assisting the Antichrist in his reign.

Seventy Years and Seventy Weeks

Verse 26, quoted from Daniel 9 at the beginning of this chapter, gives another reason why the Messiah would not set up His kingdom the first time He came to earth: "And after threescore and two weeks [adding that to the previous 7 makes 69 times 7 equals 483 years from the command to rebuild Jerusalem] shall Messiah be cut off [i.e., slain]." So Daniel, too, like David, Isaiah, and Zechariah indicated in plain language that Messiah would be killed the first time He came. There was no excuse for anyone in Christ's day who was at all familiar with the Scriptures to misunderstand this oft-repeated prophecy.

Let us take a closer look at these verses. The ninth chapter of Daniel is one of the most amazing passages in Scripture. It begins with Daniel gaining insight (from reading the prophecy of Jeremiah) into a very precise and important date that was immediately on Israel's horizon. The Babylonian captivity was to last exactly 70 years. After that period had been fulfilled, the Jews would be free to return to their land. This was good news indeed for the captives!

The reason for this precise period of 70 years was no mystery. God had made a covenant with Israel, a binding contract that carried a penalty for its violation. Yahweh had done His part, but Israel had failed to fulfill her obligation. Therefore God's judgment came upon her as He had warned it would from the beginning. He had been patient, but at last the time for judgment had come:

> And the Lord hath sent unto you all his servants the prophets, rising early and sending them; but ye have not hearkened, nor inclined your ear to hear. They said, Turn ye again now every one from his evil way...and dwell in the land that the Lord hath given unto you....Yet ye have not hearkened unto me, saith the Lord; that ye might provoke me to anger.... Therefore...this whole land shall be a desolation [and ye] shall serve the king of Babylon seventy years. And when seventy years are accomplished, I will punish the king of Babylon (Jeremiah 25:4-14).

What had Israel violated? When God first brought the descendants of Abraham, Isaac, and Jacob (Israel) into the promised land, He instructed them: "Six years thou shalt sow thy field...but in the seventh year shall be a sabbath of rest unto the land, a sabbath for the Lord: thou shalt neither sow thy field nor prune thy vineyard" (Leviticus 25:1-7). Every seventh year all Hebrew slaves were also to be released and debts owed by Hebrews to one another were to be forgiven (Exodus 21:2; Deuteronomy 15:12). Jeremiah reminded his people even as the invading armies of Nebuchadnezzar were in the process of executing God's retribution:

> Thus saith the Lord, the God of Israel; I made a covenant with your fathers in the day that I brought them forth out of the land of Egypt, out of the house of bondage, saying,...let ye go every man his brother an Hebrew, which hath been sold unto thee...when he hath served thee six years, thou shalt let him go free from thee: but your fathers hearkened not unto me, neither inclined their ear (Jeremiah 34:13,14).

For 490 years Israel had failed to obey these ordinances of the seventh-year sabbath. She had neither let the Hebrew slaves go free nor allowed the land to lie fallow. Thus, she owed God 70 years (490 divided by 7) of sabbaths that she had failed to keep. With the Babylonian captivity came Israel's bitter restitution. For 70 years the Jews would themselves be slaves, and the land would enjoy the 70 sabbaths that were owing to God.

Prophecy Is Like the Weather

Upon learning the reason for the Babylonian captivity and how long it would last, Daniel does something that many find strange today. He doesn't "claim" this promise. No "positive confession" from him! Nor does he immediately send word to the captives that their sentence is about to end and that they will soon be on their way home and all they need to do is "claim their blessing." Instead, he addresses God in earnest prayer, confessing the sins of his people and calling upon God to restore them to their land.

Why ask God to do what He has already said He would? Yet isn't that what prayer is all about? It isn't so simple as "claiming" a promise. For God's promises to be fulfilled, we must call upon Him to do so and meet the required conditions. Ask Him to do what He has promised? What else can we ask? Surely we dare not ask God in prayer to do anything that is against His will. Yet how many Christians attempt to use prayer to persuade God to fulfill their own desires!

Daniel's reaction was so unlike what we see among Christians in our time. Judging from today's attitudes, one could say of prophecy what Mark Twain used to say of the weather: "Everyone talks about it but nobody does anything about it!" The purpose of prophecy is not only to tell us in advance what will happen, but to move our hearts to prayer, repentance, and readiness to play our part in its fulfillment.

An important part of the role we are to play is to engage in earnest prayer for God to fulfill in our day the prophecies He has made. Especially we should be in prayer for the return of Christ. "And the Spirit and the bride say, Come....Surely I come quickly. Even so, come, Lord Jesus" (Revelation 22:17,20).

Four Hundred and Ninety Years Once Again

While Daniel is praying, God sends the angel Gabriel to inform him of something that he could not have known from Jeremiah's prophecy: Divine judgment upon Israel will not be complete at the end of the 70 years. The 490 years of disobedience will be paid for in an additional way. That length of time must be endured once more by Israel before the Messiah will set up His kingdom.

Gabriel announced to Daniel that another period of precisely 490 years (70 weeks of years) lies ahead for the people of Israel and for Jerusalem before Messiah will ascend to David's throne. It will include "the time of Jacob's trouble" (Jeremiah 30:7), the climax of God's judgment upon Israel immediately preceding the Second Coming. Thus an understanding of these 70 weeks of years is essential if we are to gain insight into the timing for the Rapture and the Second Coming.

To interpret this prophecy correctly, we must not forget that the 70 weeks of years are specifically stated to be "determined upon thy people [Israel] and upon thy holy city [Jerusalem]." To attempt to apply this 490-year period in any other way than that which is so plainly stated—to the Church, for example—would do offense both to the Bible and common sense.

The Church did not come into existence until 483 of the 490 years had already passed. Thus this period of time and this prophecy could not possibly have applied to the Church. The end of the 490-year period would have come a mere seven years into the Church's history had the last week run its course immediately following completion of the 69 weeks which ended with Christ's prophesied crucifixion. By that reckoning, the 490 years ended more than 1960 years ago and could have no more significance for Israel today than for the Church. The mathematics seem quite simple. Yet Christ did not ascend to David's throne at His first advent, nor has He returned to do so. Nor did the next seven years following Christ's ascension to heaven see the culmination of the prophecies that were to be completed in the last week.

The 490 years (70 weeks) could not possibly have ended because the Messiah has not yet established His millennial kingdom. Daniel 9:24 is explicit: "to bring in everlasting righteousness, and to seal up the vision and prophecy, and to annoint the most Holy [i.e. for Messiah's reign to begin]. If the 70 weeks have ended, then a major part of Bible prophecy has been proved false. No Christian can accept that for a moment; not because our faith in the Bible is blind, but because we have carefully examined it and know it to be the infallible Word of God. There can be no mistakes or failed prophecies. We must, therefore, seek another interpretation.

Inasmuch as the relevant prophecies have not been fulfilled, we can only conclude that the 490 years (70 weeks of years), for some reason, have not yet ended. Clearly this important prophetic period was interrupted after Christ's death so that the last week (of years) has yet to run its course. In fact, Daniel does divide the 70 weeks into segments: "From the commandment to restore and to build Jerusalem unto the Messiah the Prince shall be seven weeks, and threescore and two weeks...and after threescore and two weeks shall Messiah be cut off." The last week of the 70 is clearly separated from the rest.

Establishing a Precise Date

So the 70 weeks are divided as follows: 7 weeks, 62 weeks, and 1 week. Why? The first 7 weeks of years (49) is most likely distinguished from the rest because it was that exact period of time (from the beginning of the 70 weeks) until Malachi, in 397 B.C., penned the last of the Old Testament. To understand the 62 weeks (which added to the 7 makes 69) and the one week remaining, it is necessary to go back to the time when these 70 weeks began.

Daniel is very specific. The 70 weeks (490 years) was to be measured "from the going forth of the commandment to restore and to build Jerusalem." So this period begins, not with the rebuilding of the *temple* under Zerubbabel, but from the later authorization Nehemiah received to rebuild *Jerusalem*. The Bible itself establishes for us with exactitude this most important date.

Nehemiah was in the service of King Artaxerxes in the winter palace of the Persian monarchs at Shushan. This was the same place where Daniel received one of his most important visions (8:2). The reconstruction of the temple had been completed about 70 years before, yet nothing had been done to rebuild the city. The people living in its ruins were poor and few in number. Concerned for his homeland, Nehemiah asked some friends who had just returned from Jerusalem how the Jews were faring there. We pick up the story in his own words:

> And I asked them concerning the Jews...and concerning Jerusalem. And they said unto me, The remnant that are left of the captivity there in the province are in great affliction and reproach: the wall of Jerusalem also is broken down, and the gates thereof are burned with fire. And when I heard these words, I sat down and wept, and mourned certain days, and fasted, and prayed before the God of heaven (Nehemiah 1:2-4).

Nehemiah determines to petition the king for authorization to rebuild Jerusalem. And he asks God to give him favor with the king to grant this request. That prayer was answered. Nehemiah even tells us precisely when the authorization was granted and thereby gives us the date we need to apply Daniel's prophecy:

> And it came to pass in the month Nisan, in the twentieth year of Artaxerxes the king...I said unto the king, If it please the king...that thou wouldest send me unto Judah, unto the city of my fathers' sepulchres, that I may build it....So it pleased the king to send me; and I set him a time. (Nehemiah 2:1-6).

The reign of Artaxerxes Longimanus began in 465 B.C. Thus the twentieth year of his rule was 445 B.C.—the date from which to count the 69 weeks of years unto the coming of the Messiah.

In A.D. 32, exactly 69 weeks of years (483) by the Hebrew calendar from the time Nehemiah received authorization to rebuild Jerusalem, Jesus Christ rode into that "City of David"

(Luke 2:11 and 45 other times) from which He will one day rule the world. That triumphal entry is now celebrated as Palm Sunday. It was Nisan 10, the very day the Passover lambs were taken out of the flock to be observed for four days, that the "Lamb of God" (John 1:29) presented Himself to Israel. Four days later "Christ our Passover" (1 Corinthians 5:7), exactly as prophesied, was crucified as the Passover lambs were being slain (John 19:14).

For the investigation of the facts pertaining to both dates and for the calculations of the time elapsing between them we are indebted to Sir Robert Anderson. The data is given in detail in his book, *The Coming Prince*. As head of the criminal investigation division of Scotland Yard, Anderson was certainly a man well-qualified to conduct an accurate investigation into this prophecy.

What an incredible prophecy! The God who watches over history declared 500 years in advance not only that a specific event would occur but that it would happen on a particular day! Try to imagine the many related circumstances and happenings which also had to fit into place! That Daniel foretold 500 years in advance the precise day when Christ would make His triumphal entry into Jerusalem has been fully established. That amazing fact requires the most stubborn skeptic to become a believer. No honest person can deny the evidence.

When Stones Would Cry Out

Why would Daniel's statement "unto the Messiah the Prince" signify Christ's entry into Jerusalem? Why not His birth? There are a number of reasons. His birth was known to very few. Certainly there was no announcement to Israel that the Messiah had been born. It was too soon for that. Even during His public ministry, Christ told His disciples not to reveal that He was the Messiah (Matthew 16:20). The reason for the prohibition is obvious. The Messiah could only be revealed to Israel on the precise day foretold by Daniel and in the manner described by the prophet Zechariah.

Whether Jesus was the Messiah would not be established by a majority vote on the part of the Jews. Nor would it be by the persuasiveness of His disciples. The Old Testament prophecies had to be fulfilled to the letter. On no other basis was the Messiah to be identified. Therefore, the Messiah could not be revealed until the appropriate time and in the manner prophesied. Had Christ allowed His disciples to proclaim Him as the Messiah before that time, it would have been proof that He was in fact not the Messiah!

By the time this special day, April 6, A.D. 32, arrived Christ had fulfilled many of the necessary messianic prophecies. All that remained was the triumphal entry into Jerusalem foretold by Zechariah, to be followed by the cleansing of the temple, His betrayal, crucifixion, and resurrection. Those climactic events would occur in that very week, as Christ alone knew.

As Jesus rode into Jerusalem on a borrowed donkey— something He had never done before—hundreds, perhaps even thousands, of His disciples lined the small, winding road leading down from the Mount of Olives. It was a spontaneous yet prophesied demonstration. Throwing out their clothes for the beast to walk upon, the enthusiasts waved palm branches over Christ's head and hailed Him as the Messiah. To the Pharisees, the cries of the mob were blasphemous.

Never before had Christ been greeted publicly by a huge crowd in this manner. Their unlikely response to His entrance into Jerusalem, not on a white horse and brandishing a flashing sword but on this humble beast, was itself the fulfillment of prophecy: "Rejoice greatly, O daughter of Zion; shout, O daughter of Jerusalem: behold, thy King cometh unto thee: he is just, and having salvation; lowly, and riding upon an ass" (Zechariah 9:9).

Amazingly, the crowd, without knowing it, was doing exactly what Zechariah had foretold. Very likely no one present that day knew Zechariah's prophecy, much less related it to Jesus and what was happening. The Pharisees were scandalized that the people were calling Him the Son of David, which meant the Messiah. They ordered Jesus to rebuke His disciples, to which He replied: "I tell you that, if these should hold their peace, the stones would immediately cry out" (Luke 19:40). This was the "coming of the Messiah the Prince" (Daniel 9:25) on the precise day Daniel had prophesied and in the very manner Zechariah had foretold! Those prophecies were being fulfilled to the letter!

A Passover plot? How much money would it have taken to pay this entire multitude to go through these motions! Had Christ arranged for His friend Lazarus to die and thereby bring Him back to Jerusalem just in time for this remarkable occasion? Following the precise timing of the events of the last few days before the crucifixion as given to us in the Gospels is fascinating.

After messengers came telling Jesus that His good friend Lazarus was sick, "He abode two days still in the same place" (John 11:6) before going to Bethany. It would be largely in response to the resurrection of Lazarus that the crowds would line the approach to Jerusalem a few days later to hail Jesus openly for the first (and last) time as the Messiah. The exact day for that climactic event to occur was of the utmost importance.

So the Bible does set dates after all. The precise day on which the Messiah would reveal Himself to Israel and then be rejected and slain by His own people is only one of the specific dates given in Scripture. As we have already noted, the exact date of the Second Coming can be known as well.

CHAPTER 11

"The Prince That Shall Come"

> And the people of the prince that shall come shall destroy the city and the sanctuary....And he shall confirm the covenant with many for one week: and in the midst of the week he shall cause the sacrifice and the oblation to cease (Daniel 9:26,27).

> And his power shall be mighty, but not by his own power: and he shall destroy...the mighty and the holy people...And through...peace shall [he] destroy many: he shall also stand up against the Prince of princes; but he shall be broken without hand (Daniel 8:24,25).

Precisely 70 weeks of years, beginning Nisan 1, 445 B.C., must roll by to fulfill all that has been foretold by the prophets concerning Israel and Jerusalem. Of course, we are long past A.D. 39 when that period of 490 years of 360 days each should have ended. We know that 69 of these weeks of years (483 years) went exactly according to schedule and ended in A.D. 32. Daniel clearly stated that at that precise time Messiah would come, but instead of reigning He would be slain. And so it happened.

As foretold, the 69 weeks of years were climaxed by Christ being hailed as "the Messiah the Prince"—then four days later being denied His kingdom, mocked with a crown of thorns, and crucified. Thereafter Jerusalem and the temple were to be destroyed once again, this time by the people of the Antichrist, "the prince that shall come." That prophecy also was fulfilled exactly as Daniel declared it. But what of the other prophecies? What happened to the last week?

The climax of these 70 weeks is described by Daniel as "to make an end of sins...to seal up the vision and prophecy, and to anoint the most holy" (9:24). That would include, of course, the Messiah reigning as King of kings over His worldwide millennial kingdom from His father David's throne. That seat of authority is in the City of David where God has chosen to place His name (Deuteronomy 12:11,21, etc.; 1 Kings 11:36; 14:21, etc.). Fulfilled at last would be the promises which God had repeatedly made to His ancient chosen people, Israel, through His prophets.

That Christ is not yet physically present and reigning in Jerusalem as promised—that He isn't even reigning there and over this world invisibly—is obvious. There are those who suggest that He is reigning from heaven now and that in this way the promise to Israel has been fulfilled. One need hardly argue that Christ is not in control of this world as the Scriptures promise He will be one day. The daily news attests to that fact, as does our everyday experience. We are, quite obviously, not yet in the millennium, in spite of the claims of the post-millennialists.

It is certain that the 70 weeks could not have expired without the promises all being fulfilled. God would be proved a liar if that were the case. Something has caused a delay. If those weeks had continued one after the other without interruption, they would have ended seven years (one week of years) after Christ's death and resurrection. Obviously they did not. Even the destruction of Jerusalem and the temple which Daniel foretold did not occur within the 70-week period.

The Gap Between the Sixty-Ninth and Seventieth Weeks

It is of great importance that 38 years expired after Messiah was "cut off" in A.D. 32 until "the city and the sanctuary" were destroyed in A.D. 70. Had that destruction occurred within seven years (a week of years) of Christ's death, there might have been some excuse for thinking that Daniel's 70 weeks had run their course even though Christ is obviously not yet reigning visibly. No one, however, can dispute the fact that the week of years (seven years) immediately following Christ's death did not see the fulfillment of Daniel's prophecy. Even those who claim all was fulfilled in A.D. 70 must admit a gap of at least 31 years between the end of the sixty-ninth and the beginning of the seventieth weeks, and with no reason for it.

From Daniel's wording it is clear that the last week of the 70 was not to follow immediately on the heels of the sixty-ninth. "The prince that shall come" (i.e., Antichrist) could not be on the scene until after the destruction of Jerusalem. Yet he will be here during the seventieth week. It is, in fact, for that last seven years that he makes "a covenant with many."

We have given many reasons why the seventieth week has not yet become history. For example, far greater tribulation than occurred in A.D. 70 has befallen both Jews and Christians in the past century. Certainly Antichrist has not yet arrived on the world scene to make his "one week" covenant with both Israel and the world ("with many"), allowing the temple to be rebuilt, broken that covenant in the midst of the week as Daniel foretold (9:27), and caused the temple sacrifice to cease.

Surely Nero, who some claim was the Antichrist, did nothing of the kind. Furthermore, the events Christ foretold in the Olivet discourse which were not associated with the A.D. 70 destruction of Jerusalem (the Second Coming, the instantaneous gathering by angels of the "elect" from every corner of earth, etc.), have assuredly not happened as yet. There can be no doubt that the final week leading up to Messiah's reign has not yet run its course.

A Divine Suspension

What has happened to this missing week? We can only conclude that for some reason God has not allowed it to proceed to its prophesied conclusion. The events that Daniel foretold in detail for the 69 weeks all happened right on schedule, but none of those things that were to occur thereafter took place except the destruction of the temple and Jerusalem. The progress of prophesied events suddenly halted at the end of the sixty-ninth week and has remained in abeyance to this day. Recognizing this fact is extremely important when it comes to determining how close we are to the Rapture and the Second Coming.

We know for certain that if the seventieth week had followed directly after the other 69—or even at any other time since—all of the prophecies of Daniel 9:24-27 would have been fulfilled. In fact, none of the events which were to take place during that final week has occurred. Apparently the seventieth week has been deferred because the time has not yet come for those particular events of that crucial period of God's dealings with Israel to take place. Why that should be the case is of vital concern, as we shall see.

That these events so important to Israel and Jerusalem have not yet occurred cannot be argued. This parenthesis in God's prophetic calendar is undeniable. Thus far the events foretold to take place in that final week of years are all absent from history. We can understand at least one reason for the delay.

Everything that is to occur in that seven-year period revolves around a man who has not yet appeared on the scene. Daniel refers to this central character as "the prince that shall come." Prior to the ascension to David's throne of "the Messiah the Prince," this other "prince" must establish Satan's counterfeit of the Kingdom of God. It is for this denouement that the seventieth week has been reserved.

"The Prince That Shall Come"

Who is this man who, though not the Messiah, will play such a key role in Israel's future? We are given a number of clues. It is said that the people of this prince will destroy Jerusalem and the temple. When Daniel wrote this, Jerusalem and the temple had already, in 586 B.C., been laid in ruins by Nebuchadnezzar. Daniel could only have referred, therefore, to a future destruction. In His day, Jesus also foretold that same devastation after the disciples showed Him Herod's temple and boasted of its beauty: "And Jesus said unto them…verily I say unto you, There shall not be left here one stone upon another, that shall not be thrown down" (Matthew 24:2).

We know that such a ferocious leveling was executed upon the temple and Jerusalem in A.D. 70 by the Roman armies under the command of Titus. Was Titus, then, "the prince that shall come"? No, because he failed to do what the prophecy ascribes to this prince. Daniel's words are clear: "And he [the prince that shall come] shall confirm the covenant with many for one week." What covenant and what week could this be?

It takes little insight to answer the second part of the question. Since Daniel had just finished relating the events that would occur during the 69 weeks, one can only conclude that this week which he mentioned next must be the seventieth week. Then how could the people who destroyed Jerusalem and the temple more than 1930 years ago be "the people of the prince that shall come," a man who must be on earth during this yet future seven-year period?

A Revived Roman Empire

In the only possible answer to that question, we have one more reason why the Roman Empire must be revived in the last days. It was the armies of Rome that destroyed "the city and the sanctuary." The people of this empire are to be the people of this coming prince. The people of a prince are his subjects; thus he will rule the Roman Empire. Inasmuch as he did not rule it in the past, he must rule it in the future. For that to happen, the Roman Empire must be revived. There is no way to escape this conclusion.

It is clear that, although there will be some important similarities, the Roman Empire will not be revived in exactly the same form in which it existed in the past. We have already noted that it will function under ten kings who will apparently each have control over a part of it. Such a division was unknown to the ancient Roman Empire. This coming prince will be over these ten vice-rulers and will govern the whole empire, for all of its people shall be his people. In fact, this last world empire will encompass all nations, as we shall see.

A Rebuilt Temple

What could be the provisions of this "covenant" to which Daniel refers, and with whom does the coming prince make it?

We know it is "for one week," the seven-year conclusion of Daniel's 70 weeks of years. We may also reasonably deduce that it involves sacrifice and oblations, for "in the midst of the week he shall cause the sacrifice and the oblation to cease." One would suspect that this "prince" has guaranteed such worship for the seven years, then goes back upon his word. Other Scriptures confirm this assumption.

Since the entire 70 weeks pertain to Israel and Jerusalem, we can only conclude that this covenant involves the temple in that "holy city," the only place where "sacrifice and oblation" could be offered by Jews. We know definitely from other Scriptures that the temple will yet be rebuilt in Jerusalem. This *will* happen even though it seems next to impossible at the present time due to the Dome of the Rock, Islam's third holiest shrine, being situated on the temple site.

Daniel's statement that the covenant will be made "with many" instead of "with Israel" accurately reflects today's international scene. The entire world is concerned about Jerusalem and through the United Nations is involved in the current peace negotiations between Israel and the Arabs. Any arrangement for the rebuilding of the temple in the future will have to be made with "the many" and not simply with Israel. Again we see the accuracy of prophecy.

The existence of the temple during Daniel's seventieth week is required by a number of other prophecies as well. Take, for example, what Paul declares concerning the Antichrist: "Who opposeth and exalteth himself above all that is called God, or that is worshipped; so that he as God sitteth in the temple of God, shewing himself that he is God" (2 Thessalonians 2:4).

Such blasphemy would surely qualify as the "abomination that makes desolate" (see also Daniel 12:11), which Daniel attributes to the "prince that shall come." Daniel also makes it clear that this coming prince will engage in a final battle with Christ and will be destroyed (8:25). He must, therefore, be the Antichrist. There are also other reasons for reaching this conclusion.

The Antichrist on the Scene

The Messiah is called the Prince (9:25). This one, then, who takes the designation of prince (9:26), would seem to be a pretender to the title of Messiah the Prince. Does the Antichrist pretend to be Christ? Indeed, he does. In spite of portrayals by Hollywood and even Christian writers and preachers of the Antichrist as an obviously evil ogre, the Bible presents a different picture. Far from being terrorized, the entire world, at least at first, will *worship* him (Revelation 13:8)—surely an indication of genuine attraction and even affection.

The prefix "anti" is derived from the Greek. One ordinarily thinks of it as meaning "opposed to" or "against," which is true. However, it also means "in the place of" or "a substitute for." The Antichrist will indeed oppose Christ, but in the most diabolically clever way it could be done: by pretending to be Christ and thus subverting Christianity while posing as its leader. Anything less would not be worthy of Satan's genius.

Among the last days signs Christ gave that would herald the nearness of His coming, our Lord included this warning: "For many shall come in my name, saying, I am Christ; and shall deceive many" (Matthew 24:5). These numerous counterfeit Christs would seem to be preparing the world for the arrival of the real Antichrist on the scene. Are these claimants rivals? Not really. They present to the world the concept that *everyone* is the Christ. Such a belief, until recently, was largely unknown outside of the Orient, yet it is one of the key notions in today's New Age movement.

The "God" of Atheism

A number of cults, such as Unity School of Christianity and the Church of Religious Science, teach the same lie. They assert that the only thing that distinguished Jesus from the rest of us was His attainment to a "higher state of consciousness" known as "Christ consciousness." Whoever attains this Christ consciousness becomes a Christ just like He was. When enough of mankind—a "critical mass"—reach that state, the world will be transformed. Such is a major hope of the New Age.

That the Antichrist will present himself as one who has attained to this state (and he will have the satanic/psychic powers to prove it—2 Thessalonians 2:9,10) seems apparent from Paul's description of Antichrist's reasons for exalting himself as "God." Paul wrote that this man of lawlessness "opposeth and exalteth himself above all that is called God or that is worshipped." Clearly, he is anti-God. He is, in fact, an atheist. Yet he claims to *be* God. That he is not claiming to be the God of the Bible, however, is quite clear, for he actually rejects the very concept of such a God. He is a humanist who exalts himself as a man (and thus potentially all mankind) to the place of gods.

The insight Jesus gave us into this impostor agrees with what Paul had to say, as of course it must. Christ spoke of the Antichrist in these terms: "I am come in my Father's name, and ye receive me not: if another shall come in his own name, him ye will receive" (John 5:43). So the Antichrist doesn't acknowledge any relationship to, or dependence upon, the Father as Jesus did. He needs no one but himself and claims to be a self-realized man who has acquired godlike powers. He comes in his own name. His religion is the exaltation of self, which began with Satan (not surprising, since Antichrist is the human embodiment of Satan)—and the world will love him for this celebration of self.

While the Antichrist will be universally worshiped, Jesus tells us that Israel will feel a special kinship with him and will accept him as her Messiah, her Savior. After all, he brings about the rebuilding of the temple in Jerusalem. Morever, he will apparently bring peace to Israel and through her to the world.

Peace in the Middle East, established by the Antichrist, will become the key to a New Age that will dawn for all mankind, a New World Order. So the world will think, until the bubble bursts.

CHAPTER 12

The Church Must Be Removed

And now ye know what withholdeth [prevents] that he [Antichrist] might be revealed in his time. For the mystery of iniquity doth already work; only he who now hinders will hinder, until he be taken out of the way. And then shall that Wicked one [Antichrist], be revealed, whom the Lord shall consume with the spirit of his mouth, and shall destroy with the brightness of his coming (2 Thessalonians 2:6-8).

Though the Antichrist will somehow bring about a peaceful solution to the conflict between Israel and her Arab neighbors, it is a peace which he will himself violate when he leads the armies of the world to attack Israel. Unaware, because of their disregard of their own Scriptures, of what lies ahead, God's chosen people will fall into Satan's trap.

Israel will imagine that this charismatic world leader's ability to establish peace proves him to be the Messiah. Their covenant with this evil one who will turn out to be their deadliest enemy will lead to the time of greatest distress the Jews as a people have ever known. The prophets called it "the time of Jacob's trouble" (Jeremiah 30:7).

Destroyed by "Peace"

Stand on any street corner in Jerusalem these days and ask passersby, "Do you believe the Messiah will come?" Nearly every Israeli will respond with a resounding, "Yes!" Then ask, "How will you recognize Him?" Again nearly every Jew inhabiting

Israel will reply with a naivete born of hope, "He will bring peace!"

Most Jews justify their rejection of Jesus as the Messiah by His failure to bring universal peace. After all, the prophets said that the Messiah would establish a kingdom of perpetual peace and reign from David's throne. Jesus didn't do so. Therefore, He couldn't be the Messiah. The lie is as simple as that. It could only deceive those who are ignorant of prophecy.

The world at large is not aware that peace with God, which has definite conditions, is the only basis for peace among men. Blind to the prophecies that the Messiah would first of all die for the sins of the world to reconcile mankind to God, today's Jew is ripe for the false peace of the Antichrist. Israel's leaders are heedless of Daniel's solemn warning: "He shall magnify himself in his heart, and by peace shall destroy many" (8:25).

Israel's Spiritual Blindness

We will come back to consider more carefully the events that must take place in this final seventieth week of that period prophesied by Daniel, and the timing of the Second Coming as affected thereby. For the moment, however, we need to consider why this week has not yet run its course and when it might do so. The answer to these questions is crucial to an understanding of the timing of the Rapture and Second Coming.

We have emphasized the fact that the time period of 70 weeks of years pertains only to Israel, and especially to Jerusalem. It involves God's dealings with His ancient people. The purpose is apparently to bring them to repentance and full reconciliation to Himself and His will so that the Messiah can reign over them. In order for this to happen, the spiritual eyes of these people must be opened.

It is important to recognize, therefore, that the Bible declares that blindness has come upon Israel, and why this is so. This blindness prevents most Jews from realizing that relationship with God enjoyed by Abraham. The apostle Paul, a former Pharisee, agonized over Israel's separation from God and from the blessings that God desires for her through the Messiah. We share Paul's deep pain for his people as he confides:

> I have great heaviness and continual sorrow in my heart. For I could wish that myself were accursed from Christ for my brethren, my kinsmen according to the flesh: Who are Israelites; to whom per-taineth...the promises; Whose are the fathers, and of whom as concerning the flesh Christ came, who is over all, God blessed for ever (Romans 9:2-5).

Israel had been in apostasy and heedless of God's warnings through His prophets for centuries before Paul wrote these words. From what Paul, inspired of the Holy Spirit, has to say in this and other epistles, however, it is apparent that a milestone has been passed for Israel. The Messiah has "come to his own and his own received him not" (John 1:11). They have crucified their Creator, crying, "His blood be on us and on our children" (Matthew 27:25). The die has been cast. Something radical has changed between God and His ancient chosen people.

Israel's Fall and World Redemption

Paul calls it Israel's fall. It is not, however, permanent. God is not finished with her. She will one day be restored, but not until the Messiah returns to rescue her at Armageddon. In the meantime, the Gentiles are the beneficiaries of what has happened. Paul puts it like this:

> I say then, Have they [Israel] stumbled that they should fall [permanently]? God forbid: but rather that through their [temporary] fall salvation is come unto the Gentiles....Now if the fall of them be the riches of the world, and the diminishing of them the riches of the Gentiles; how much more their fulness? (Romans 11:11,12).

Since Israel's fall, God has begun to deal directly with the Gentiles in grace and on a grand scale heretofore unimagined.

The prophets "inquired" about this great salvation and even angels don't yet understand it (1 Peter 1:10-12). Most astonishing is the fact that it came about because Israel crucified her Messiah! Nevertheless, she will be held responsible for that infamous deed with which Peter boldly indicted the inhabitants of Jerusalem in his second major sermon:

> The God of Abraham, and of Isaac, and of Jacob, the God of our fathers, hath glorified his Son Jesus; whom ye delivered up, and denied him in the presence of Pilate when he was determined to let him go. But ye denied the Holy One and the Just, and desired a murderer to be granted unto you; And killed the Prince of life, whom God hath raised from the dead; whereof we are witnesses (Acts 3:13-15).

The crucifixion of Christ was a heinous crime for which Israel has been and will be severely punished. Amazingly, however, through her rejection and crucifixion of her Messiah salvation came to the rest of mankind. Christ had to die to pay the debt for the sins of the whole world. The tragedy is that it was His own chosen people who put Him to death. Remember, Pilate found Him innocent and desired to release Him.

Wonder of wonders, the spear that pierced His side drew forth the blood that saves. The blood that flowed from nails contemptuously and wickedly driven into His hands and feet, from thorns mockingly pressed upon His brow—that blood was the price of our redemption (Ephesians 1:7; Colossians 1:14). Israel's rejection of her Messiah brought salvation to the Gentiles. The disciples had a difficult time believing this at first, but eventually they came to understand it.

The Times of the Gentiles

With Israel's rejection of her Messiah, a new era dawned. Jesus called it "the times of the Gentiles"—a time which, He said, must continue until "fulfilled." Only then would Jerusalem be liberated from Gentile influence (Luke 21:24). The duration of "the times of the Gentiles" coincides with the length of time during which Israel will be blind to the gospel and to the fact that she crucified her Messiah. Here is Paul's further explanation:

> For I would not, brethren, that ye should be ignorant of this mystery, lest ye should be wise in your own conceits; that blindness in part is happened to Israel, until the fulness of the Gentiles be come in. And so all Israel shall be saved: as it is written, There shall come out of Sion the Deliverer, and shall turn away ungodliness from Jacob (Romans 11:25,26).

Just before His death, Jesus Christ told His disciples that He was forming a new entity which had never existed before. He called it His Church. In response to Peter's confession that He was the Messiah (Christ), Jesus declared: "On this rock I will build my church, and the gates of hell shall not prevail against it."

Until that time, God's people consisted only of Jews. Their relationship to Him was defined by the Mosaic covenant. After Christ's crucifixion for the sins of the world, there would be an entirely new entity composed of both Jews and Gentiles—the Church. Paul explained it like this:

> Wherefore remember, that ye being in time past Gentiles in the flesh…without Christ, being aliens from the commonwealth of Israel, and strangers from the covenants of promise, having no hope, and without God in the world: But now in Christ Jesus ye who…were far off are made nigh by the blood of Christ. For he is our peace, who hath made both [Jew and Gentile] one….Having abolished…the law of commandments…for to make in himself of twain [Jew and Gentile] one new man, so making peace; And that he might reconcile both unto God in one body by the cross….Now therefore ye are no more strangers and foreigners, but fellowcitizens with the saints, and of the household of God; And are built upon the foundation of the apostles and prophets, Jesus Christ himself being the chief corner stone (Ephesians 2:11-20).

Peter's Fallibility

Roman Catholics insist that Peter is the rock upon which the Church was founded. Yes, Jesus did say to Peter, "On this rock I will build my church, and the gates of hell shall not prevail against it, and I will give unto thee the keys of the kingdom of heaven" (Matthew 16:18,19). Out of that simple statement (basically the same as He made to all the disciples in Matthew 18:18,19 and John 20:23) Rome has manufactured a papal office, papal infallibility, apostolic succession, a magisterium which alone can interpret Scripture, a celibate priesthood to whom confession must be made and which alone can administer grace through seven sacraments, and much more. One can examine Christ's statement with a microscope and never find justification for such embellishments.

It is beyond the scope of this writing to engage in a detailed argument against Rome's errors. If Peter was appointed by Christ at that time as the first pope—and if all popes are infallible—one would never have suspected it from Peter's performance. The "first pope" immediately denied the faith! And if Peter did not receive "papal infallibility" from Christ at that moment, then when did he?

Moments after Jesus commended Peter for confessing that He was the Christ, that impetuous ex-fisherman insisted that Christ need not die on the cross. Here was a blatant denial of the central doctrine of Christianity. "Get thee behind me, Satan," was Christ's immediate rebuke. The papal system was off to an incredibly poor start.

In the very next chapter we find Peter, James, and John on the mount, where Christ was "transfigured" before them, thus giving them a glimpse of His coming resurrection glory. Moses and Elijah appeared there with Christ. In another hasty declaration that was far from infallible, Peter lowered Jesus to the level of a prophet, saying, "Let us build here three tabernacles, one for thee, one for Moses and one for Elijah." Immediately God's voice from heaven rebuked this newly appointed "first pope." On this occasion Peter had denied the uniqueness and deity of God's only begotten Son, who is far above any prophet, including Moses and Elijah.

Later Peter denied that he even knew Jesus when confronted by servants in the palace of the high priest as Christ was being condemned to death. Rome excuses the sins of the popes (among them some of the most inhuman monsters to walk this earth) with the trite saying, "There is a difference between infallibility and impeccability." Popes are allegedly infallible when they make a declaration on faith or morals to the entire Church, even though they deny Christ with their lives—a concept unknown in Scripture and the early Church. Yet all three of the grievous denials of truth and of Him who is the truth, pronounced by Peter and which we have just mentioned, pertained to "faith and morals." Most assuredly they were also stated to the entire Church, for they are in the canon of Scripture.

The Only Rock

It is Christ who builds His Church. He is its head and also its foundation. We have already seen how, in the Old Testament, Yahweh makes it very clear that He alone is the Savior. He also declares with equal clarity and finality that He alone is the Rock: "For who is God except Yahweh, or who is a rock except our God?" (Psalm 18:31). Certainly not Peter! All through the Old Testament, Yahweh is called "the rock" of our/my/his salvation. That God is the *only* Rock is reiterated many times: Deuteronomy 32:4; 2 Samuel 22:2; 23:3; Psalm 18:2; 28:1; 42:9; 62:2,6,7; Isaiah 17:10, etc.

Paul argues that Jesus Christ was the Rock of Israel during her wilderness travels (1 Corinthians 10:4), thus claiming that He is Yahweh. Inasmuch as God throughout the Old Testament declares that He is the only Savior, our Lord and Savior Jesus Christ, in order to be the Savior, had to be God come in the flesh. The same is true concerning the Rock upon which the Church is built: It could only be God Himself. Jesus is that Rock, for He is God. Peter could not take that place, nor did he aspire to do so.

Jesus referred the rabbis to the messianic prophecy in Psalm 118:22,23: "The stone which the builders [i.e., Israel's religious leaders] rejected has become the chief cornerstone" (NKJV). Christ clearly implied that He was the fulfillment of that Scripture, and the rabbis knew it and hated Him for it.

Peter boldly indicted the rabbis with Christ's crucifixion and then applied this same prophecy to Christ: "Jesus Christ of Nazareth, whom you crucified...is the stone which was set at nought of you builders, which is become the head of the corner" (Acts 4:11). Again, in his first epistle, Peter identified Jesus Christ as the "chief corner stone" upon which the Church is built (1 Peter 2:6,7). In rejecting this stone, Israel has been set aside while God builds something new upon it.

It is over this Rock upon which the Church is built that Israel has stumbled and fallen. Isaiah foretold this fall: "And he [the Messiah] shall be...a stone of stumbling and for a rock of offense to both the houses of Israel [i.e., Judah and Israel]" (Isaiah 8:14). Both Peter (1 Peter 2:8) and Paul (Romans 9:33) quote this Scripture and apply it to Christ and to Israel's fall through rejecting Him.

Here we have the two closely related reasons why Daniel's seventieth week has not run its course. The sixty-ninth week ended with Israel's rejection and crucifixion of her Messiah. Out of that rejection came salvation to the world—a salvation that God had planned from eternity past. The way to a new relationship to God was opened to all mankind. Out of Israel's fall, the Church was formed as a composite body of both Jews and Gentiles.

The Church Must Be Removed

Since that time, the Church has been God's focus in this world. She is the instrument of evangelism, bringing the gospel message to all peoples, including Israel. For nearly 2000 years the Church has been the light of the world, calling upon sinners to repent and to be reconciled to God, and warning that a day of judgment is coming. During this time, Israel was set aside, a wandering people without a homeland, scattered among all nations, under God's judgment, but not forgotten by Him.

In 1948, Israel became a nation once again. We have already commented upon what a miracle that was, and upon the even greater miracle that Jerusalem is now the focus of world attention and concern. Has Daniel's seventieth week begun to run its course at last with the restoration of Israel to her land? Obviously not, for she has been there far longer than seven years and Christ has not yet come back to reign in Jerusalem. Clearly the continued presence of the Church on earth stands in the way of Israel becoming the exclusive focus of God's dealings.

Daniel's seventieth week is a period of seven years. Numerous definite prophecies must be fulfilled during that time. When will those events begin to take place? There were two related occurrences which caused the seventieth week to be held in abeyance: 1) Israel's rejection of her Messiah, and 2) the formation of the Church. Suppose Israel turned to Christ. Would that restart God's timeclock? No.

In fact, Scripture is very clear that Israel will not recognize that Christ is her Messiah until the end of the seventieth week, when He appears to rescue her at Armageddon. The prophets were very specific on that point. Therefore we know that, in itself, Israel's continued rejection of Christ does not stand in the way of a resumption of the final week determined upon Israel and Jerusalem.

The presence of the Church, then, must be the hindrance to God's final dealings with Israel. Could the Church be removed, leaving the focus upon Israel once again? Yes, and that is precisely what will happen. One can draw no other conclusion except that the Church, whose formation marked the suspension of the seventieth week, must be removed before those final seven years can run their course. And this removal is exactly what Christ has promised.

Here we have a most powerful argument from Scripture for the Rapture of the Church to take place prior to the beginning of Daniel's seventieth week. A mid-tribulation or pre-wrath Rapture won't do. This last week can't even commence until the Church, whose formation caused its suspension, has been removed. Indeed, she must be removed for a number of other reasons as well.

CHAPTER 13

The Rapture

In my Father's house are many mansions....I go to prepare a place for you. And...I will come again and receive you unto myself; that where I am there ye may be also (John 14:2,3).

For the Lord himself shall descend from heaven with a shout...and the dead in Christ shall rise first: then we which are alive and remain shall be caught up together with them in the clouds, to meet the Lord in the air: and so shall we ever be with the Lord (1 Thessalonians 4:16,17).

Behold I show you a mystery; We shall not all sleep [die], but we shall all be changed, In a moment, in the twinkling of an eye, at the last trump...the dead shall be raised incorruptible and we shall be changed (1 Corinthians 15:51,52).

We're soon departing from this old world of sin and sorrow! One glad day Christians will be caught up bodily and alive into heaven! The souls and spirits of those who had previously died believing in Christ, having been consciously with Him in the interim, will come with their Lord from heaven to rejoin their glorious resurrected bodies. Those alive at the time of His return, their bodies instantly transformed as well, will be caught up together with the saints of all ages to meet Christ somewhere above planet Earth. From there He will personally escort this innumerable throng into the presence of His Father in heaven, as He promised.

We've read the Bible passages describing this event scores of times and assent to it all in our heads. Unfortunately, for all too many of us, the truth hasn't penetrated our hearts and has little effect upon our lives. Somehow, the breathtaking reality of the Rapture—and the awesome fact that it could occur at any moment—doesn't break through. It all seems like a tale that's been told so often that it has lost its meaning and the power to move and motivate us.

What initial enthusiasm the promise once aroused has been dampened by the realization that Christians have been hoping for centuries for Christ's return to catch them up into heaven and it hasn't happened yet. Why should it occur in our day? Yes, why indeed? There are good reasons.

Christ *could* have come at any moment in the past, but He didn't. However, our generation has indications that no previous one has ever had that our Lord's promised return *must* be very soon. Israel's return to her land after 2500 years and the fact that the nations of the world are at last seriously attempting to bring peace between Arabs and Jews are only two of those new indicators unknown in past generations.

Unique to Christianity

The Rapture is a word to which some critics object because they say it isn't in the Bible. In fact, it is in the Latin translation of 1 Thessalonians 4:17. The Latin *rapturos* means an ecstatic catching away, as does our English word. In any language, that is exactly what the Bible declares will occur when Christ returns to take His own to His Father's house of many mansions. Such was our Lord's promise, and He will not fail to keep it.

The hope of the Rapture is a teaching which is unique to Christianity. On that basis alone, it is a far more important doctrine than most Christians acknowledge. For anything that lessens Christianity's uniqueness weakens its foundation and increases the danger of confusion and compromise.

Prior to Christ's first coming nearly 2000 years ago nothing was known of the Rapture. Paul, therefore, calls it a "mystery" now revealed. Although Enoch and Elijah were caught up alive into heaven, those were exceptional cases which gave no such hope to the average believer in Old Testament times. While Buddhism, Hinduism, Islam, and other world religions offer some kind of heaven after death, none holds out the prospect of being caught up to heaven alive. Christ alone, the Conqueror of death, made that promise to those who would believe in Him.

A Promise Never Made Before

No wonder Paul called the Rapture "that blessed hope" (Titus 2:13). This is not some optional or even peripheral teaching. It is so interwoven with our faith that it cannot be extricated. As we shall see in the last chapter, Paul considered the hope of our appearance with Christ in glory to be the major motivation for godly living. Even in teaching concerning the remembrance of our Lord in His death, partaking of the bread and the cup, Paul noted that it was to be done only "till he come" (1 Corinthians 11:26). This hope lies at the very heart of Christianity.

No, we are not suggesting that one must believe in the Rapture in order to be saved. It is not part of the gospel. We are saved by believing that Christ died for our sins, was buried, and rose from the dead the third day. Those who belong to Christ will be taken to heaven at the Rapture whether they believe in this event or not. But if we do not take seriously Christ's promise to catch us up to heaven, why should we believe anything else He said?

Consider the impact of Christ's words: "I will come again and receive you unto myself, that where I am, there ye may be also"! The promise He gave His disciples at that time was not that they would go to heaven when they died, though that was true. Christ was specifically declaring that the day was coming when He would personally return to take all believers together at one time, the living and the dead whom He would resurrect, to His Father's house in heaven. Such a promise had never been made before!

Paul elaborates upon this unique and mysterious coming event and explains it in more detail. The foundation of this hope, however, remains Christ's personal promise—and the occasion of that promise must be remembered to put it in proper perspective. The promise of the Rapture was made on the night of His betrayal, at the same time and as an integral part of His revelation to His disciples that He was going to the cross. Surely the cross was what He meant by "I go to prepare a place for you." It was not a matter of furnishing heaven for our arrival, but of paying the penalty for our sins so that heaven could receive us.

The Most Thrilling Fruit of the Cross

Heaven is at the very heart of Christianity. Christ didn't come, as some teach, to restore us to the garden paradise that Adam lost, but to prepare us for heaven. He didn't come to remodel this old creation, but to make a new one! Therefore the great task of the Church is not to rescue this world from destruction (it will be destroyed) or to improve society, but to call sinners out of the world to become citizens of heaven who watch and wait for their Lord's return to take them there. Our hope is not in insurance policies and a retirement condominium, but it is eternal in the heavens—from whence we are expecting our Lord to return at any moment and catch us up to meet Him in the air.

Christ's shameful death upon the cross (where He endured not only man's evil but God's judgment upon sin), was not intended to set an example of noble ideals and self-sacrifice for the rest of us to follow as we attempt to avert ecological disaster and return the earth to its Edenic state. Far from it! He redeemed us from the curse of the law—a law which required banishment from God's presence for our sin—and He made it possible for us to enter where Adam had never been! Adam and Eve knew the temporary companionship of God when He came down to walk in the garden in the cool of the evening. We have, through the Holy Spirit's indwelling, a more intimate companionship 24 hours a day, and are to dwell with God in His heavenly home eternally!

Sin entered Eden's paradise. It can never enter God's new universe. Though created perfect and innocent, Adam and Eve could sin and as a result died and brought death upon their descendants. We are new creatures created in Christ Jesus over whom sin and death have lost their power. Adam and Eve could be, and were, expelled from Eden. We will never be expelled from heaven. Our Lord Jesus Christ, who is God and man in one person, brings to us a new and indissoluble union between God and man when He comes to live in our hearts—and He will never leave or forsake us (Hebrews 13:5).

Our catching up out of this world and into heaven is the ultimate goal of our redemption. It is the most thrilling fruit of the cross that Christ could share with His disciples the night of His betrayal. To paraphrase His words: "In my Father's house are many mansions and I want to take you there. That's why I'm going to let them crucify me, and I'll bear God's wrath upon sin for your sakes."

The disciples were excited at the prospect of reigning with Him on earthly thrones—and someday they will. He was more concerned, however, for them to understand that He was going to take them to His Father's house in heaven. Only from heaven could they return with Him to rule on the earth in His millennial kingdom. We must all be taken to heaven first, for it is from heaven that the saints come with Christ to rule with Him in His kingdom. Let that fact grip us!

Not of This World

Here again we see a significant difference between Israel and the Church. Those who say that the Church has taken the place of Israel and now has all of the promises that applied to the chosen people (but not their curses!) have really made a bad bargain. Israel was promised a land and a kingdom on this earth. The Church has been promised a home in heaven—and to have the run of the entire universe, a new one which God will make when the present one is destroyed. One perceives the tremendous excitement and joy in Paul's heart as he penned the following verses—a small sample of the many that promise this marvelous heritage:

For our conversation [literally, citizenship] is in heaven; from whence also we look for the Saviour, the Lord Jesus Christ: Who shall change our vile body, that it may be fashioned like unto his glorious body, according to the working whereby he is able even to subdue all things unto himself (Philippians 3:20,21).

Therefore let no man glory in men. For all things are yours; whether Paul, or Apollos, or Cephas [Peter], or the world, or life, or death, or things present, or things to come; all are yours; And ye are Christ's; and Christ is God's (1 Corinthians 3:21-23).

Christ spoke continually of heaven. He encouraged those who were persecuted for His sake, "Rejoice and be exceeding glad: for great is your reward in heaven" (Matthew 5:12); and He counseled all of His hearers to lay up treasure not on this earth but "in heaven" (6:10). To those who would faithfully follow Him, Christ promised a great reward "in heaven" (19:21). Clearly heaven was on His heart day and night and the predominant theme in all He taught. His goal was to take the redeemed there to be with Him forever.

Heaven was the place from which Christ came and to which He returned. To the unbelievers He said, "I go my way, and ye shall seek me, and shall die in your sins; whither I go, ye cannot come." When they asked what He meant, He replied, "Ye are from beneath; I am from above: ye are of this world; I am not of this world" (John 8:21-23). To Pilate He said, "My kingdom is not of this world" (John 18:36).

To His own Christ declared,

If ye were of the world, the world would love his own: but because ye are not of the world, but I have chosen you out of the world, therefore the world hateth you. Remember...the servant is not greater than his Lord. If they have persecuted me, they will also persecute you (John 15:19,20).

And He taught them to pray, "Our Father which art in heaven" (Matthew 6:9), committing themselves into His hands and working for His eternal kingdom—a kingdom not of this world.

Exchanging Earthly Rewards for Heavenly

Ours is a "heavenly calling" (Hebrews 1:3). We have been "blessed with all spiritual blessings in the heavenly places in Christ" (Ephesians 1:3); and it is in heaven that God has reserved for us "an inheritance, incorruptible, and undefiled and that fadeth not away" (1 Peter 1:4). Indeed, our hope is in heaven (Colossians 1:5) where our names have been written (Luke 10:20). No wonder, then, that our resurrection bodies are "spiritual" (1 Corinthians 15:44) and "heavenly" (v. 49; 2 Corinthians 5:2), suited for living in God's presence.

The joy in heaven will be so great eternally that we will need new and glorious bodies to appreciate and express it. Heaven is often thought of as a solemn place of pomp and protocol. We forget what David knew: "In thy presence there is fulness of joy; and at thy right hand are pleasures for evermore" (Psalm 16:11).

Christ endured the cross "for the joy set before him" (Hebrews 12:2), a joy He wanted to share with us in heaven. To know that joy, however, we must share the shame and reproach of His cross. Did He not say, "Follow me"? How can we expect to take a different path to heavenly joy than our Lord? The writer to the Hebrews commended the believers for joyfully accepting "the spoiling of your [earthly] goods, knowing in yourselves that ye have in heaven a better and an enduring substance" (10:34).

Why would anyone willingly follow a path leading to persecution and even death unless the reward for doing so was much greater than the loss endured? Surely heaven's reward infinitely surpasses anything earth can offer. Paul understood and wrote: "For our light affliction, which is but for a moment, worketh for us a far more exceeding and eternal weight of glory; while we look not at the things which are seen, but at the things which are not seen: for the things which are seen are temporal; but the things which are not seen are eternal" (2 Corinthians 4:17,18). As the hymn says, "It will be worth it all when we see Jesus. Life's trials will seem so small when we see Christ!"

Two Distinct Events

In previous chapters we have given a number of reasons why the Rapture and the Second Coming are two distinct events, one occurring at the beginning and the other at the end of Daniel's seventieth week. Christ must first of all come *for* His saints to rapture them *to heaven,* or He could never come *with* His saints *from heaven* to rescue Israel at Armageddon.

The Rapture will occur when least expected; the Second Coming takes place only after all the signs have been given and everyone should know that Christ is about to return in glory and power. The Rapture comes in the midst of peace (1 Thessalonians 5:3); the Second Coming in the midst of war (Revelation 19:11-21). One simply cannot put into one time frame and one event the mutually exclusive statements made in the New Testament about the Rapture and the Second Coming.

"But that means there are still two comings of Christ!" is the protest of many. "Show me in the New Testament where it says there are yet two comings!" The response is rather obvious: "Show me in the Old Testament where it says there are two comings." Of course, it doesn't say so, but, as we have already commented, the conclusion was inescapable. The Messiah was not only going to reign, He was going to be killed. One could not put into one time frame and one event what the Old Testament said about the coming of the Messiah. Failure to understand the two comings caused multitudes to reject Jesus.

The same is true today: There are many who call themselves Christians who will end up following the Antichrist, thinking he's Christ. The reason for their confusion is basically the same as it was the first time Christ came. They will be focusing upon and even seeking to build an earthly kingdom and will be unprepared to be taken to heaven. Failure to understand that the Rapture and the Second Coming are two different events separated by seven years lies at the heart of this confusion.

That these are two distinct events is also clear from Christ's own words. "I will come again and receive you unto myself that where I am there ye may be also" is a personal pledge only for His own. This is what Paul spoke of when he said, "So shall we ever be with the Lord." That is what the Rapture is all about, Christ catching up His bride to present her to His Father. The Second Coming has an entirely different purpose: to rescue Israel in the midst of Armageddon and to destroy Antichrist and his evil world empire.

That longed-for and ecstatic meeting of the heavenly Groom with His bride and His escorting her to His Father's house can hardly take place at the same time He comes with the armies of heaven to destroy the Antichrist and his forces in battle. The promise that we will be caught up to meet Christ in the air and ever thereafter be with Him does not fit the equally valid promise of His descent to the Mount of Olives to rescue Israel. Nor can the intimacy of Christ meeting His redeemed of all ages who already know and believe in Him be confused with the "every eye shall see him" display of power as He reveals Himself at Armageddon to those who have rejected Him.

The One-Event Theory

Some argue that there is indeed a way for both the Rapture and the Second Coming to be one and the same event. We have already shown that the Rapture comes at a time of peace, the Second Coming in the midst of war; the Rapture comes when one would least expect it, the Second Coming only after all the signs have been fulfilled and there could be no doubt that Christ was right at the door. Thus the two events could not possibly occur at the same time. However, inasmuch as a contrary belief is growing in popularity among evangelicals (ignoring the reasons we've just given why it can't be true), let us consider the explanation that is given for putting these two diverse events into one time frame.

It is suggested that as Christ is on His way from heaven to the Mount of Olives, He pauses momentarily above the earth and catches us up to meet Him. We then join the armies of heaven and return to earth with Him. In addition to the reasons we've already given, there are a number of other problems with this view, the most obvious being that the language of Scripture doesn't support it.

In the verses quoted at the beginning of this chapter, Jesus promises to "come again" to take us to His Father's house. That is the whole meaning of what He says. One could never extract from this passage that He doesn't return to take us to His Father's house after all but merely catches us up to join Him in the air on His descent to the Mount of Olives. Moreover, this view allows no time for certain events which must take place after the Rapture and before the Church is ready to return to earth with Christ.

Preparing a Bride for War

Surely the first event in heaven after our Lord takes us there will be the Judgment Seat of Christ (2 Corinthians 5:10; 1 Corinthians 3:12-15). We must all give an account to our Lord for every action or failure to act, for every idle word and secret thought. How long that will take we don't know. Certainly it won't take place hovering above earth as a momentary pause on our Lord's descent to the Mount of Olives, but in the presence of the Father.

After the Judgment Seat of Christ has done its cleansing work and He has wiped all tears from our eyes, for there will be tears both of grief and joy, surely the Groom will want to spend some time with His bride, the now glorified Church. He will have much to tell us! It hardly seems the way to treat a bride to catch her up momentarily and then bring her abruptly back into the middle of the most massive and destructive war in earth's history. Bride and Groom will spend time together in the Father's house.

In Christ's day the Jewish bride was taken to the father's house where the two were in seclusion in the honeymoon quarters for seven days. Christ must have had that custom in mind when He promised to take His bride to His Father's house. Here we have that last week again, the seven years of the tribulation period. At the end of that week, in Revelation 19, just before Armageddon, we find the marriage supper of the Lamb taking place. For that event (and clearly as a result of the Judgment Seat of Christ when all that defiled one's life on earth has been purged—1 Corinthians 3:12-15), the bride is clothed "in fine linen, clean and white...[which] is the righteousness of saints" (Revelation 19:7-9).

More Compelling Reasons for a Pre-Tribulation Rapture

In Revelation 19:11, we find Christ coming to earth at Armageddon to rescue Israel, further described in Ezekiel 38 and 39 and Zechariah 12–14. He is accompanied by "the armies which were in heaven...clothed in fine linen, white and clean." We just saw His bride, the Church, identically clothed six verses earlier, so there is every reason to believe that she, composed of the saints of all ages, comprises at least a large part of these armies. There is not a word here about angels coming with Christ (though there is in 1 Thessalonians 1:7), but we are told that "all the saints" accompany Him to the Mount of Olives (Zechariah 14:5).

The saints could hardly be part of the armies in heaven had they never been to heaven. Nor could they accompany Christ from heaven had they not been taken up there previously. Again we find compelling evidence that the Rapture of the Church must take place some time prior to Armageddon. We have already given one powerful reason why it will take place seven years earlier: Since it was the formation of the Church that caused the seventieth week not to follow directly after the end of the sixty-ninth, the Church must be removed from earth for that week to begin to run its long-delayed course.

No less compelling a reason is the fact that without some absolutely unprecedented cataclysmic global disaster the world will never, no matter how great and ingenious the efforts, be unified under one head. Jews and Arabs must be reconciled. Muslims and Hindus must stop their bloodshed; and "Christians" must be united with those of all religions. Ethnic and tribal hatreds and jealousies of many centuries standing must be removed.

What could possibly end nationalism, jealousy among nations, and warring between rival ethnic and religious groups? What could cause the entire world to unite in a new world government and a new world religion and to submit suddenly to the leadership of the Antichrist as world dictator?

To catapult the world into international political, religious, and ethnic peace and unity would take some inconceivable event of cosmic proportions. And that is exactly what the Rapture will be, as we shall see—God's catalyst to usher in Daniel's seventieth week and the final act in the drama of human history.

Consequently, the Rapture must occur before the tribulation period spoken of by Christ and detailed in Revelation. Many arguments are raised against such a view. For example, one of the verses quoted at the beginning of this chapter declares that the raising of the dead and transformation of the living will be "at the last trump." Therefore the Rapture can't take place at the beginning of the seven-year period, for the last trump isn't sounded until near the end (Revelation 11:15). So the argument goes.

First Corinthians 15:52 doesn't identify this "last trump," so we must ask, "The last trump of what?" It could be the last trump of the feast of trumpets (Leviticus 23:24) immediately preceding the Day of Atonement. Such is the belief of many students of prophecy. Or it could be some other "last trump." We aren't told that detail.

At Christ's descent from heaven there could be a series of trumpet blasts, one after the other in rapid and musical succession, as one might expect in announcing such an event. Then one final blast, the last trump, and the dead suddenly arise. The explanation may be as simple as that.

Certainly Paul doesn't identify the "last trump" as the one in Revelation 11:15. Indeed, it can't be, for as we shall see, a pre-tribulation Rapture is the key to the puzzle.

Chapter 14

An Incredible Growing Delusion

And as it was in the days of Noah, so shall it be also in the days of [the coming of] the Son of man. They did eat, they drank, they married wives, they were given in marriage, until the day that Noah entered into the ark, and the flood came, and destroyed them all. Likewise also as it was in the days of Lot; they did eat, they drank, they bought, they sold, they planted, they builded; but the same day that Lot went out of Sodom it rained fire and brimstone from heaven, and destroyed them all. Even thus shall it be in the day when the Son of man is revealed (Luke 17:26-30).

And take heed to yourselves, lest...that day come upon you unawares. For as a snare shall it come on all them that dwell on the face of the whole earth. Watch·ye therefore, and pray always (Luke 21:34-36).

Here we have additional evidence that argues powerfully for a pretribulation Rapture. The coming of Christ will be at a time similar to the days of Noah and Lot. These were times of great wickedness, and in that respect our generation is similar. However, that is not the point being made, for nothing is said about the evil of those days. The emphasis, instead, is upon the fact that life was normal (eating, drinking, buying, selling, planting, building) and the fact that the last thing expected was judgment. So it will be when Christ returns. Jesus Himself said so.

Once again we see that the Rapture and the Second Coming must be two separate events occurring at different times. Surely these verses from Luke do not describe either the economic situation or mood on earth at the time of the Second Coming. Consequently, another event must be the topic.

The Second Coming occurs in Revelation 19. The previous chapters have described the progressive devastation of earth that has at this time reached almost unimaginable catastrophic proportions. Life is not normal at all. Even eating and drinking is a problem, for famine has been rampant (Revelation 6:5,6), a third of the trees and all green grass has been burned up, a third of the ocean has turned to blood, and a third of earth's waters has become bitter and poisonous (Revelation 8:7-11).

Nor is buying, selling, planting, building, or any other part of life normal. More than a billion people have died from plagues and war. There have been cataclysmic upheavals of nature which have left earth pulverized and her inhabitants in desperate straits. Certainly the conditions on earth at the time of the Second Coming are exactly the opposite of those to which Christ refers. In the days of Noah and Lot, judgment from God was unknown, the last thing those about to suffer it would have expected.

Nor is the mood on earth just before the Second Coming at all like the happy-go-lucky, judgment-will-never-come attitude that prevailed just before the flood and just prior to Sodom's destruction. The inhabitants of the earth near the end of Daniel's seventieth week have long since realized that God's judgment is being poured out upon them. As early as Revelation 6:15,16, we read that everyone on the earth is attempting to hide from God and is crying out to the rocks and mountains to fall upon them to protect them from God's judgment.

Christ Could Only Have in Mind a Pre-Trib Rapture

When Christ says, "As it was in the days of Noah and Lot," it is absolutely certain that He is not describing conditions that will prevail at the time of the Second Coming. Therefore, these must be the conditions that will prevail just prior to the Rapture at a different time—and, obviously, before the devastation of the tribulation period. A pre-tribulation Rapture is, therefore, imperative.

"Ah, but the symbolism is wrong," objects someone. Christ's statement is put differently in Matthew 24:39. There it says, "And knew not until the flood came and took them [i.e., the wicked] all away." From this it is argued that it wasn't Noah and his family (a picture of believers) who were taken away, but the unbelievers. Thus there won't be a Rapture at all, but the wicked will be taken away to judgment and the righteous will remain upon the earth. So goes the common argument.

Actually, both Noah and those who rejected his preaching were taken away. Noah and his family were taken away by the ark, borne up on the water (a picture, though not a perfect one, of the Rapture), and the wicked were taken away to death by the waters of judgment.

When it comes to Lot, however, the symbolism is crystal clear. He and his family were definitely taken out of Sodom by the angels (a type of the Rapture), and, after their departure to safety, God's judgment fell (a type of the Great Tribulation). The pre-tribulation Rapture could not be depicted more accurately.

Rejection of the Rapture

As clear as the Scriptures are, the truth of the Rapture was largely lost for centuries because of the apostasy and domination of Roman Catholicism. Nor was it recovered at the Reformation. None of the Reformation creeds makes the essential distinction between the Rapture and the Second Coming. They refer only to a coming or return in a general sense. Nor was the Rapture found in the works of some of the most widely read Christian writers. C.S. Lewis, for example, failed even to mention the Rapture when he wrote his famous essay, "The World's Last Night," in which he dealt with the final events in world history.

A surprising number of today's evangelicals are rejecting the Rapture in favor of remaining here to take over the world. There is an entire movement known as Manifest Sons that rejects the Rapture. It is up to Christians, according to this teaching, to "manifest" themselves as "sons of God" by attaining to sinless perfection and immortality. This, they say, will not happen at the return of Christ, but must be accomplished to bring Him back. Overcomers who manifest themselves as sons of God in this way are then, in that power, to take over the world. When the Church has established the kingdom, Christ will return to earth, not to take anyone to heaven but to rule over the kingdom the overcomers present to Him.

This clearly unbiblical teaching originated in a Pentecostal revival in Canada around 1948. An alleged prophetic utterance gave the divine interpretation of Romans 8:19. If the listeners had simply read the context, verses 14-25, instead of blindly accepting a "prophecy," they would have seen how utterly false this idea was. The "manifestation of the sons of God" comes at "the adoption, to wit the redemption of our body" (v. 23—i.e., the resurrection of the dead and transformation of the living at the Rapture) and with the believer's glorification with Christ in heaven (v. 17).

Though immediately condemned as heresy by the Assemblies of God, and confined to a fanatical fringe for years, this teaching is lately gaining increasing acceptance among Pentecostals and charismatics. In complete disregard for Christ's promise to take us to heaven and for other Scriptures we have already cited, one of the leaders in the movement, writes:

> You can study books about going to heaven in a so-called "rapture" if that turns you on. We want to study the Bible to learn to live and to love and to bring heaven to earth.

Scripture Twisting Par Excellence

Just imagine: *We* are going to bring heaven to earth. What blind pride. Some of the statements by these men are so contrary to Scripture that one finds it difficult to believe that those who make them have even read the Bible. Indeed, they study it and still come to these conclusions. The pastor of a 12,000-member church near Atlanta and author of several books, though denying that he's part of this movement, teaches the same unbiblical doctrines. Note the complete twisting of Scripture in the following:

> We who are alive and remain are left here for one
> ultimate purpose: to conquer the last enemy, which
> is death. God has left us here to take dominion over
> death.

The rejection of clear biblical teaching could not be more deliberate. This popular author begins the statement with a partial quote from the Bible: "We who are alive and remain." He then substitutes his own words for the rest of the verse, directly contradicting what God has said. The Bible declares: "We who are alive and remain shall be caught up together with them [the resurrected ones] to meet the Lord in the air and so shall we ever be with the Lord." His comment that "we who are alive and remain" are *left here* is the direct opposite of being *caught up,* which the Bible wonderfully promises.

And *we* are going to conquer death? What folly! The teaching of Scripture is very clear. Christ is the One who has already conquered death. There is nothing we must or can do to "take dominion over death." Christ imparts the power of His resurrection to us in the forgiveness of sins and the gift of eternal life. Our bodies, however, remain subject to death until He returns to raise the dead and to transform the living and to catch them all together up to heaven.

Here is the sequence of events presented in 1 Thessalonians 4:13-17:1) the Lord descends from heaven to take His Church out of this world; 2) He shouts and the trumpet sounds and (at the "last trump" per 1 Corinthians 15) the dead are raised incorruptible and caught up to meet Him; 3) the bodies of the living in Christ are also transformed into immortality and caught up to meet Christ "in the air"; 4) our Lord takes the saints of all ages to heaven.

Paul elaborates further in 1 Corinthians 15:51-57, telling us that this incredible event will take place "in the twinkling of an eye, at the last trump: for the trumpet shall sound, and the dead shall be raised incorruptible, and we [the living] shall be changed...then shall be brought to pass the saying that is written, Death is swallowed up in victory."

The Word of God could not be clearer that the final victory over death takes place when Christ returns, raises the dead, and transforms the living. Only then is death "swallowed up in victory." It doesn't happen through our positive confession that we have victory over death, or by believing God for immortality. It is a work of Christ which He does when He returns to catch us up to heaven.

A Church That Does It All Before Christ Returns

Yet this same pastor, whose influence is growing through his books and Christian radio and television and conference speaking, declares: "The Church of Jesus Christ has not yet conquered death but this last enemy will be totally conquered before Jesus's return."

Before Jesus' return? That statement directly contradicts the verses we just quoted! More Scripture perversion follows: "The Church shall be changed in a moment, in the twinkling of an eye, and it will then become the great, glorified Church of Jesus Christ on the earth."

On the contrary, that happens when we are caught up to meet Christ in the air, and He takes us to heaven.

This man will insist that he believes in the Rapture when he is in the presence of those who do, and he will give the false impression that he means what they mean by that term. In fact, however, his "Rapture" has nothing to do with taking the Church to heaven. It is an allegorical term signifying a transformation of the Church into a higher spiritual state with dominion over all disease and death so that she can take over the world. He goes on to say, "I believe that when Christ returns, the Church will have taken such dominion over the earth that rulership will have already been established."

If the Church has taken over the world, Christ, at His coming, would have no need to destroy the Antichrist. That teaching would astonish Paul, who specifically declared under the Holy Spirit's inspiration: "Whom the Lord shall...destroy with the brightness of his coming" (2 Thessalonians 2:8). Nor does the Lord need to rescue Israel at Armageddon. The

Church is in control and has conquered, if not converted, Antichrist and all those he had deluded. We can do away with Ezekiel 38–39, Zechariah 12–14, Revelation 19, and numerous other Scriptures which these new prophets supersede with their modern revelations. To remove any doubt about what these men believe, this pastor's brother and assistant elaborates:

> For centuries God has waited for His Kingdom to be established [by us] on earth....God waits to signal His Son's return to earth. But this cannot and will not take place until the Body of Christ, the Church, is mature....We [mistakenly in the past] found it convenient to focus our attention on national Israel and ascribe to them the role of "God's timepiece." The scriptures clearly show that we, the Church, have become Israel. God's timepiece is not an identifiable ethnic group. God's timepiece is His Church, spiritual Israel!...But don't expect the "rapture" to rescue you....If you want to bring Christ back to earth, you can do it...WE CAN DO IT!...We hold the key to His return."

So *we* must establish the kingdom and by doing so *we* can bring Christ back to earth. Nor does Christ catch us up to meet Him in the air and take us to heaven. He comes down to earth to reign over the kingdom we have established for Him, thereby making it possible for Him to return. The Rapture is a delusion, an "escape theory" for those who aren't willing to get involved in changing the world. So this growing movement among professing evangelicals claims.

A Delusion with Serious Consequences

The consequences are rather severe for those who embrace this deception. The Scripture plainly declares that Christ is going to catch us up to meet Him in the air and take us to heaven. Therefore all those who meet a "Christ" with their feet planted on this earth—a "Christ" who hasn't come to take them to heaven but to reign over the kingdom they've established for him—have been working for Antichrist!

The teaching that the Church must take over the world so that Christ can return to rule is helping to prepare both the world and a false but professing church to embrace the Antichrist when he comes. His counterfeit kingdom will be established before Christ's millennial reign. Indeed, as we have seen, it is specifically to destroy Antichrist's kingdom that the Second Coming takes place.

It is often argued that belief in a pre-trib Rapture leaves one unprepared to face Antichrist and susceptible to deception. The facts are just the opposite. It is those who deny the Rapture who have set themselves up for the most horrible deception. Antichrist will pretend to be the very "Christ" whom they expect to come to earth to reign. He will congratulate them on the good work they've done in preparing the world for his rule. Hundreds of millions of those who call themselves Christians will be completely deceived.

In actual fact, a belief in the Rapture is the surest way to be kept from deception. Wherever a "Christ" comes from when he arrives on the scene, if he doesn't resurrect all dead Christians and catch them and the living up into heaven, then he is a fraud. That is something the Antichrist, for all his bag of tricks and lying signs and wonders, will not be able to perform. If one doesn't believe in the Rapture (in being caught up into heaven), it might then be conceivable that the Antichrist could put on such a psychic show of satanic power that many would think he was Christ. Paul warned of this "lawless one"—

> ...whose coming is after [by the power of] Satan with all power and signs and lying wonders, and with all deceivableness of unrighteousness in them that perish; because they received not the love of the truth, that they might be saved. And for this cause God shall send them strong delusion, that they should believe a lie: That they all might be damned who believed not the truth, but had pleasure in unrighteousness (2 Thessalonians 2:9-12).

A Strong Delusion from God

Antichrist will do exactly what the Bible foretells. For example, as a means of stabilizing world economies, he'll set up a worldwide system for buying and selling which will employ the number 666 in some way. We needn't speculate about the part that number will play. Those who don't obey him will not be allowed to buy or sell. He will set up his image in the temple—an image that all will be forced to worship on threat of death. How could one witness such events, all prophesied in Scripture and attributed to the Antichrist, and imagine that Christ was doing them?

Paul warns that God Himself will send a strong delusion to those who, prior to the Rapture, refused to receive the love of the truth. Those who reject the clear teaching of Scripture concerning the Rapture and opt instead to take over the world have already demonstrated their rejection of God's truth. They will be completely convinced that Antichrist is Christ and will follow him enthusiastically. He will fulfill all the expectations they had concerning Christ's return.

Won't the disappearance of scores of millions of Christians prove to the hundreds of millions of professing Christians who are left behind that the Rapture has indeed taken place? No. There will be explanations to prove that what occurred was not the Rapture. For example, part of the Manifest Sons teaching is that those who refuse to accept their doctrine and do not become overcomers will be instantly removed to judgment. This is their interpretation of "then shall be two in the field; the one shall be taken, and the other left. Two women shall be grinding at the mill; the one shall be taken, and the other left" (Matthew 24:40,41).

That those who embrace the Manifest Sons teaching have been left behind will not trouble them at all. Indeed, it will prove that they are the faithful ones. It is the missing, so they will believe, who have been taken away to judgment and who are thus to be mourned. What a setup for Antichrist!

Chapter 15

Pre-Trib—Key to the Puzzle

Immediately after the tribulation of those days shall the sun be darkened, and the moon shall not give her light....And then shall appear the sign of the Son of man in heaven....And he shall send his angels with a great sound of a trumpet, and they shall gather together his elect from the four winds, from one end of heaven to the other (Matthew 24:29-31).

And it was given unto him [by God] to make war with the saints, and to overcome them: and power was given him [by Satan] over all kindreds, and tongues, and nations. And all that dwell upon the earth shall worship him, whose names are not written in the book of life of the Lamb slain from the foundation of the world....And he [the second beast, Antichrist's false prophet] had power to...cause that as many as would not worship the image of the beast should be killed....And that no man might buy or sell, save he that had the mark, or the name of the beast...in their right hand, or in their foreheads (Revelation 13:7-17).

The verses from Matthew 24 above present the strongest Scripture for a post-tribulation Rapture. According to the advocates of this view, there simply is no argument against what seems to be stated in the plainest terms: "Immediately after the tribulation of those days...shall gather together his elect from the four winds."

The proper interpretation hinges upon the basic argument we have supported with biblical and historical evidence and with logic in so many ways in the previous chapters: There are two comings: 1) the Rapture, which must take place at the beginning of Daniel's seventieth week; and 2) the Second Coming, which clearly takes place at the end thereof in the midst of Armageddon. Yes, there is a coming of Christ "immediately after the tribulation of those days." It is not the Rapture, however, but the Second Coming. The evidence and arguments we have given overwhelmingly support this conclusion. So does the language of the verses we just cited.

There are several factors to take into consideration. The first is that the coming described in these verses takes place after the tribulation and is accompanied by unmistakable signs in the sky that are visible to and recognized by all mankind. Yet the Rapture takes place at a time when conditions are like those in the days of Noah—no tribulation has occurred and the last thing expected is God's judgment. There are no accompanying signs for the Rapture. The whole idea is surprise, which is why Christ warns us to watch and wait lest that day overtake us unawares.

Christ's Language Makes It Clear

Several times we've gone over Christ's "I will come again and receive you unto myself" (John 14:3). This was the wonderful promise He made at the last supper. It is an intimate pledge to His own to catch them up to His Father's house to be with Him forever. What Christ describes in the Matthew 24 passage above sounds altogether different from the Rapture.

Take the previous verse (27): "For as the lightning cometh out of the east, and shineth even unto the west; so shall also the coming of the Son of man be." Obviously the world is deliberately being notified of what is about to occur. The despised and rejected One is coming for vengeance. Christ is about to confront Antichrist face-to-face. Let the world tremble!

Surely the event being described is not the intimate catching away of His bride to His Father's house! One could argue that a miraculous sign in the sky at the time of the Rapture would add terror to the sudden mass disappearance of millions from earth. But Christ is not describing a "sign" that will add significance to a mysterious catching away of millions from earth. He is obviously describing His visible return to the scene of His rejection to execute judgment. He goes on to say, "And they shall see the Son of man coming in the clouds of heaven with power and great glory." It can only be at Armageddon, to the Mount of Olives, as John explained it in more detail later:

> Behold, he cometh with clouds; and every eye shall see him, and they also which pierced him: and all kindreds of the earth shall wail because of him. And I saw heaven opened, and behold a white horse; and he that sat upon him was called Faithful and True....His eyes were as a flame of fire, and on his head were many crowns....And the armies which were in heaven followed him upon white horses, clothed in fine linen, white and clean. And out of his mouth goeth a sharp sword, that with it he should smite the nations: and he shall rule them with a rod of iron: and he treadeth the winepress of the fierceness and wrath of Almighty God....And I saw the beast, and the kings of the earth, and their armies, gathered together to make war against him that sat on the horse (Revelation 1:7; 19:11-20).

Christ came once as the Lamb of God. Like a lamb dumb before its shearers, He was silent before His accusers, for He took our place and we had no answer to make to God's accusation against us. He was meek and submitted to man's hatred and abuse and allowed them to nail Him to a cross. Now He comes as the Lion of the tribe of Judah, in majesty and power, the Lord of glory, Creator of the universe, to execute judgment upon the ungodly. That is why the Second Coming will be like lightning flashing across the sky, visible to every eye.

The language isn't describing the Rapture of saints to heaven, but the visible descent of Christ to earth "with all the saints" accompanying Him. His mission at this time is not to catch up a bride to heaven, but to confront Antichrist upon earth, destroy his evil kingdom, and to set up His own reign of righteousness. This is not the catching up of His saints to the Judgment Seat of Christ in heaven, but the awesome execution of judgment upon the ungodly on this earth.

What About the Elect?

The previous arguments may sound logical, is the rejoinder of post-tribulation advocates, but this passage clearly says that He catches up His elect. That must refer to the Church, so this can only be the Rapture. There is the sound of a trumpet, too, just as in 1 Thessalonians 4 and 1 Corinthians 15. It couldn't be clearer: The Rapture takes place in conjunction with the Second Coming at the end of the Great Tribulation.

We have already shown why these two events cannot occur at the same time. Moreover, this passage, from its very language, confirms that fact. Look at Matthew 24:31 again, and note some contrasts between it and the Rapture passages. In 1 Thessalonians 4 we have "the voice of the archangel and the trump of God"; here we have "a great sound of a trumpet" but no archangel. At the Rapture it is Christ Himself who catches us up to meet Him in the air. Here it is "his angels" who "gather together his elect."

Nor is there anything about being caught up to meet Him in the air. The term "gather together" is altogether different. The gathering together is "from the four winds" or from the four corners of the earth under heaven—obviously to a single location on this earth, not to a rendezvous in the sky.

It is His elect who are being gathered together. Who would they be? That term is used for the Church, but also for Israel: "For Jacob my servant's sake, and Israel mine elect" (Isaiah 45:4). If it were the Church in view here, they would be caught up to meet Christ in the air. Instead, they are being gathered back to their own land for the Messiah's millennial reign exactly as the Hebrew prophets foretold:

> And I will bring forth a seed out of Jacob, and out
> of Judah an inheritor of my mountains: and mine
> elect shall inherit it, and my servants shall dwell
> there. I will rejoice in Jerusalem, and joy in my

people....And mine elect shall long enjoy the work of their hands...for they are the seed of the blessed of the Lord, and their offspring with them....The wolf and the lamb shall feed together...saith the Lord (Isaiah 65:9-25).

We can only conclude that "elect" here means the seed of Abraham, Isaac, and Jacob. They are being gathered by the angels from every part of earth and taken to Israel where Christ has arrived to destroy Antichrist, rescue His people, and set up His kingdom. All surviving Jews who have not yet returned to Israel will be gathered there from every part of the earth to meet their Messiah and participate in His millennial reign.

This is the promised regathering back to Israel to participate in Christ's millennial kingdom of all Jews who have been scattered in judgment to every nation on earth. The language of Scripture is explicit: "Then shall they know that I am the Lord their God, which cause them to be led into captivity among the heathen: but I have gathered them unto their own land, and have left none of them any more there" (Ezekiel 39:28).

The Rapture is an altogether different event. It has preceded by seven years what is being described in the above verses. In fact, as we shall see, had the Rapture not occurred the Antichrist could not have come to power. The final events described in Revelation require the Rapture both to set the stage and act as a catalyst to cause otherwise impossible alignments to take place. Moreover, without the Rapture "all the saints" (Zechariah 14:5) would not be in heaven ready to accompany Christ back to earth.

Let's Face the Reality of a Pre-Tribulation Rapture

Whether one believes in the Rapture or not, let us suppose for a moment that it actually happened. Here is an event so far beyond anything in history that it staggers the imagination. With no warning—in fact, when prospects are rosy and the world is congratulating itself that "peace and safety" seem assured (1 Thessalonians 5:3)—scores of millions of people from every nation and race and locality instantly vanish from the face of the earth.

Estimates place the number of Christians in China at upwards of 80 million, in Africa at 100 million, in the United States at 50 million. These figures may be high, especially in the USA. However, out of an estimated 1.8 billion professing Christians in today's world it would not seem unreasonable to suggest that 250 million truly know the Lord and would leave in the Rapture. That's almost the entire population of the United States! One cannot even imagine the impact of such a mass disappearance.

Hundreds of millions of people around the world have witnessed the impossible: A relative, friend, neighbor, acquaintance or total stranger have suddenly vanished. People have disappeared from escalators in shopping malls, instantly vanished from elevators in high-rise apartments or office buildings, and from airplanes in flight. In some cases the entire cockpit crew has vanished and the plane has crashed. Drivers of automobiles on all kinds of roads and highways have vanished. In sections of some freeways the tangle of wreckage may take weeks to clear for lack of operators of cranes and tow trucks, who have also mysteriously disappeared.

In the United States, unlike most other countries, there are familiar faces missing from top levels of government—from the White House staff, Cabinet, Congress, Senate, Pentagon. The military has been decimated: admirals; generals; colonels; fighter, bomber, and helicopter pilots; those holding key top-secret positions involving cryptography and nuclear arms have vanished by the thousands. Business and industry are similarly stripped of key personnel, from the factory to executive offices.

The United Nations Security Council (except for a few of its members who may have vanished as well) is meeting in emergency session almost around the clock. Haggard officials in every city of any size face the same unimaginable chaos. It will take months to unravel the tangle of insurance claims for missing persons, to sort out the credit card and banking confusion of accounts for whom no parties exist either to collect from or to pay.

Effect of a Pre-Tribulation Rapture on the World

All of the chaos described above is eclipsed, however, by the horrifying fact that hundreds of millions of infants suddenly vanished as well. If we believe that babies who die are covered by Christ's atonement and taken to heaven, then it would seem likely that at the Rapture all who are too young to be account-able would also be taken. There is scarcely a family anywhere in the world, of any nation or religion, that is untouched. Here is the most heartrending and terrifying aspect of this incom-prehensible disaster. The fact that missing babies and young children far outnumber adults who vanished gives the event its most ominous tone.

Where did they, the adults and children, all go? Who took them? Is some intergalactic power snatching slaves? Could the missing have been beamed aboard advanced spacecraft and taken off to populate another planet in some bizarre experi-ment? The inhabitants of earth would feel themselves at the mercy of a power that obviously had no mercy and against which there was no defense. At any moment millions more might vanish. Who might be snatched next?

Beyond the perplexity, mystery, and chaos is the unspeak-able terror that grips the world. Here at last would be something large enough and horrible enough to unite every warring faction on earth. The common terror shared by all of earth's inhabitants would unify them in a way that nothing else could. The sudden sense of oneness and mutual dependence experienced by the few survivors of a plane crash on an isolated mountain peak would pale in comparison to the unity created among the sur-vivors of this inconceivable and eerie catastrophe.

Conflicts between Muslims and Hindus in India, between Arabs and Jews in Israel, between Catholics and Protestants in Ireland, between ethnic groups in Yugoslavia or in the former Soviet Union would suddenly have become meaningless. Everything that had seemed so important the moment before— love or hate, war or peace, profit or loss, employment or unem-ployment, grades in school or salary at work, or whatever it might have been—would have lost all significance. There would be only one reality. The appalling fear gripping every individual would override even the grief of missing loved ones. Stark, raving terror and panic would reign.

Here we have the one event of such magnitude that it could remove all other considerations and unite the world completely as nothing else possibly could. There are those who suggest, for example, that World War III would have that effect and that out of the ashes of a nuclear holocaust would come the necessary unity. That is a doubtful scenario at best. No war yet has had such an effect, nor would it likely be the case for any war in the future. Wars leave deep wounds and fresh hatreds that can only increase division, not bring unity.

Any scenario for uniting the world must deal with 1.3 billion Muslims whose allegiance to Allah commits them to ultimate Islamic supremacy as the major article of their faith. No Middle East peace treaty, no pledges, no threats, no deals can ever change their underlying fanatical commitment to exterminate Israel and all Jews. Arabs are not even united among themselves but would be at each other's throats had they not a common enemy. The only thing that gives the Arab world any semblance of unity is their common passion to see Israel annihilated. Try to think of anything other than the Rapture that could instantly unite Islamic Arabs with the rest of the world. There is nothing else.

The Rapture alone would break down every barrier and unite the entire world. Even the most fanatical of Muslims would suddenly share a common terror with all survivors of this worldwide calamity—a terror so great that even the passion to annihilate Jews would be at least temporarily forgotten.

A Pre-Tribulation Rapture: Perfect Opportunity for Antichrist

Suppose, too, that suddenly in the midst of the terror and chaos a man arises who has an ingenious but sensible explanation for what took place. Moreover, he alone can guarantee that all those who submit to Him as world ruler will be safe from any further threat of disappearance from earth. He is not without unusual credentials that would generate confidence in his abilities and knowledge. Most convincing of all are the apparent miracles he is able to perform. While all is done by the power of Satan, he passes it off as mind or psychic power with the promise that all mankind can develop similar abilities under his guidance.

There are many possible scenarios from this point on. Let us consider only one. Suppose there are massive UFO sightings immediately following the Rapture. Huge spacecraft are seen everywhere, even in broad daylight, so that there can be no doubt as to their existence and power. Earth's military forces are helpless. This man, in a bold attempt at negotiation, consents to being taken aboard a huge spacecraft—or so everyone is led to believe—that hovers over the United Nations headquarters in New York. Of all earth's inhabitants he is singled out by these beings who, though they deny taking anyone from earth, declare that they know which intergalactic power did so and that they can prevent any recurrence in the future. The only man they will work with on earth is this one individual—and through him they guarantee protection if certain rules are followed.

Let such a man arise with an explanation that the world believes and with the apparent power to guarantee safety for everyone on earth, and the world is in his hands. He may even claim to be in negotiation with some intergalactic council for the ultimate return of those who have vanished. Still emotionally unhinged by the mass disappearance (hundreds of thousands have gone insane), those left behind would only be too happy to have Big Brother put his mark on their hand or forehead and know that he was watching out for them, promising that there would be no other such disaster.

There are other possibilities, but little point in presenting them. Whatever explanation may be given for the mass disappearance, and whatever accompanying circumstances may assist, one thing is quite clear: The Rapture is the one catalyst that could suddenly bring into being the New World Order with its world government and world religion so essential to Antichrist's world rule. The Rapture is the key to any scenario for uniting the world under Antichrist and giving him the absolute power that the Bible indicates he will have.

How This Scenario Fits Other Scriptures

We have given many biblical reasons for a pre-tribulation Rapture. We've shown that Daniel's seventieth week can't even start to run its course until the church is removed. We have noted that the saints must have previously been taken to heaven in order to come from there with Christ at the Second Coming. Now we have added a logical reason: Antichrist could not ascend to power without the Rapture terrifying the entire world into uniting under him. The Bible gives at least two reasons which support this view.

First of all is the timing of Antichrist's ascension to power. There are those who suggest that it cannot occur until the middle of the seven-year period. They can't imagine how he could gain control any earlier. Antichrist, however, makes a covenant of peace with the many for that entire week, as we've seen, so he must be in power at the beginning. He breaks that covenant "in the midst of the week," so he can hardly just come to power at that time, since it is a covenant which he has made three-and-a-half years earlier.

The conclusions we've arrived at present a cohesive picture. The seventieth week can't begin nor can Antichrist be revealed until the Church is removed in the Rapture. Yet he must be in full power immediately thereafter in order to make the covenant at the beginning of the seventieth week as Daniel declared. Logically, then, it is the Rapture itself which both allows Antichrist to be revealed and terrifies the world into an otherwise impossible unity and catapults him suddenly into control of the world.

Second, Paul tells the Thessalonians: "You know what withholdeth that he [Antichrist] might be revealed in his time. For...he who now hinders will hinder until he be taken out of the way. And then shall that Wicked be revealed" (2 Thessalonians 2:6-8). A Person is preventing the Antichrist from being revealed. Quite clearly He is no ordinary person, for He who prevented Antichrist's revelation in Paul's day 1900 years ago is still doing so today. He is not only timeless but omnipotent, for Satan cannot act until this One is out of the way.

Paul can only be referring to the Holy Spirit. But He cannot be removed from earth because He is omnipresent. Furthermore, there will be many converted through the gospel of the kingdom during the Great Tribulation, and for that to be possible the Holy Spirit must be present to convince and convict them. Then what is the meaning of "until he be taken out of the way"? How could that apply to the Holy Spirit?

The Church is described as "a habitation of God through the Spirit" (Ephesians 2:22). The bodies of all Christians are the "temples of the Holy Spirit" (1 Corinthians 6:19). God the Holy Spirit is present in this world in a unique way that was not true before the Church was formed nor will be so after the Church is removed in the Rapture. When the Church is taken to heaven, that special presence of the Holy Spirit will also be removed, though He will be here as God omnipresent as He eternally is throughout the entire universe.

More Reasons Why the Church Must Be Removed

The true Church would not tolerate the Antichrist for a moment. She would expose his identity, prove it from Scripture, and oppose him. She would actively warn others and stand solidly in the way of Antichrist and his diabolical machinations. Satan's plans through Antichrist cannot go forward until the Church has been removed.

Furthermore, if the Church were present during the Great Tribulation, she would be wiped out by the Antichrist. But that would not be allowed by God. He who protects the Church, who said "the gates of hell shall not prevail against" her, is the same One who gives Antichrist the power to "make war with the saints and overcome [kill] them...[and that] as many as would not worship the image of the beast [Antichrist] should be killed" (Revelation 13:7,15).

The only way both to protect the Church and allow Antichrist to kill all saints is to remove the Church. The saints who are killed by Antichrist are those who have become believers in Christ during the Great Tribulation. They pay for their faith with their blood:

> And I saw under the altar the souls of them that were
> slain for the word of God, and for the testimony
> which they held: And they cried, How long, O
> Lord...dost thou not...avenge our blood on them
> that dwell on earth?...And it was said unto them, that
> they should rest...until their fellowservants also and
> their brethren, that should be killed as they were,
> should be fulfilled. These are they which came out
> of great tribulation, and have washed their robes and
> made them white in the blood of the Lamb (Revela-
> tion 6:9-11; 7:14).

A post-tribulation "Rapture" would be a classic non-event.
There would be few if any believers in Christ to take to heaven.
They would all have been killed, for such is the fate of those
who refuse to take the mark of the beast (Antichrist) and worship his image. Submission to Antichrist is the only way to stay
alive during that horrible period. For those, however, who take
the mark of the beast and worship his image there is an even
worse fate:

> If any man worship the beast and his image, and
> receive his mark in his forehead, or in his hand, The
> same shall drink of the wine of the wrath of God,
> which is poured out without mixture....And they
> have no rest day nor night, who worship the beast
> and his image, and whosoever receiveth the mark of
> his name (Revelation 14:9-11).

Finally, a post-tribulation Rapture removes an essential
factor involved in the Rapture: imminency. The Bible, as we
shall see, teaches that Christ could have come at any time in
history. Nor is there anything that prevents Him from coming
at this moment.

CHAPTER 16

A Post-Trib Scenario

> For yourselves know perfectly that the day of the Lord
> so cometh as a thief in the night. For when they shall
> say, Peace and safety; then sudden destruction
> cometh upon them, as travail upon a woman with
> child; and they shall not escape. But ye, brethren, are
> not in darkness, that that day should overtake you as
> a thief. Ye are all children of light, and the children of
> the day....Therefore let us not sleep, as do others; but
> let us watch and be sober (1 Thessalonians 5:2-4).

One frequently hears the argument: "There is no record that the early Church believed in the imminent return of Christ. The idea of a pre-tribulation Rapture wasn't dreamed up until the 1830s." No matter how "early" it may have existed, any church is the wrong place to look for truth. Paul lamented, "All they which are in Asia be turned away from me" (2 Timothy 1:15). The Church of Paul's own day had already gone astray in many ways. Most of his epistles had to be written to correct error that was already in the earliest Church.

Don't be deceived by those who cite some "early Church father" and suggest that we must accept his interpretation of Scripture as authentic because he "knew Peter" or "was a contemporary with the apostle John." Those who lived in the days of Peter and John had already embraced serious heresies. Paul had to warn the Ephesian elders, "After my departing shall grievous wolves enter in among you, not sparing the flock. Also of your own selves shall men arise, speaking perverse things, to draw away disciples after them" (Acts 20:29,30). If the elders at Ephesus whom Paul had trained could go astray, then no so-called "early Church father" may be safely looked to as authoritative.

The Word of God is the only sure source of truth. Never mind what some "early Church" did or didn't believe. The New Testament will tell us what the first Christians believed, where they went astray, and what we ought to believe and practice today. Nor can there be any doubt, when one reads the New Testament, that the Church of Paul's day believed in and fervently awaited the imminent return of Christ to Rapture her to heaven. There is no earlier Church to provide an example than that one!

A Troubling Rumor

As we shall see, the early Church believed in and actively watched and waited for Christ's imminent return. Consequently, they must have believed in a pre-tribulation Rapture, though that term is not used. Christ's imminent return is a major theme running throughout the New Testament. It was a "blessed hope" (Titus 2:13) that all were anticipating at any moment. This fact is clear once again from what Paul wrote in his second epistle to the Thessalonians:

> Now we beseech you, brethren, by the coming of our Lord Jesus Christ [Second Coming], and by our gathering together unto him [Rapture], That ye be not soon shaken in mind, or be troubled, neither by spirit, nor by word, nor by letter as from us, as that the day of Christ is at hand (2 Thessalonians 2:1,2).

What was this "day of Christ" to which Paul referred, and why should the believers at Thessalonica be concerned if it had come? The answer to that question has a direct bearing upon our topic. In trying to calm their concern, Paul appeals both to the Rapture and to the Second Coming. Therefore both must have an important relationship to "the day of Christ."

Paul had mentioned that day in his first epistle to the Thessalonian saints in the verses quoted at the beginning of this chapter. He had emphasized that it would come like a thief when the world would not expect it. The Christians, however, would not be caught by surprise if they were watching and waiting for Christ's return. The thought that this day of the Lord had already come had shaken the believers in Thessalonica. Apparently they had been caught unaware. Their concern, however, went beyond that possibility.

Paul had no doubt discussed the "day of Christ" with them so they knew it was going to be a time of great destruction from God upon this earth. In fact, it would include the Great Tribulation, as Paul reminded them in the opening verses of this his second epistle to the Thessalonians. After commending them for patiently, and with faith in God, enduring "persecutions and tribulations" at the hands of the ungodly, Paul writes:

> Seeing it is a righteous thing with God to recompense tribulation to them that trouble you; and to you who are troubled rest with us, when the Lord Jesus shall be revealed from heaven with his mighty angels, in flaming fire taking vengeance on them that know not God and that obey not the gospel of our Lord Jesus Christ: Who shall be punished with everlasting destruction from the presence of the Lord...when he shall come to be glorified in his saints, and to be admired in all them that believe in that day (2 Thessalonians 1:6-10).

The reference is obviously to Christ's Second Coming in power and glory at Armageddon to wreak vengeance upon the godless. "In that day," doubtless refers to the day of Christ, thus identifying it as the time of His revelation to the world as the Avenger of God's persecuted people.

Post-Tribbers Would Not Be Troubled

Other than being caught by surprise, which they shouldn't have been, why would the Thessalonian believers be upset to be told that the day of Christ had arrived? There was no reason to be "shaken in mind" if they believed in a post-tribulation Rapture. There was, however, sound reason for being shaken if they believed in a pre-trib Rapture. Clearly, then, the latter was their view.

If the Thessalonians knew they had to go through the Great Tribulation in order to arrive at the Rapture, which they looked forward to with eager anticipation, then it would not have troubled them to know that the day of Christ had come. Their reaction rather would have been, "Praise God! The time has come for us to face Antichrist and prove our love and faithfulness to our Lord. If we are martyred, we have a special crown. If not, and we endure to the end, then we will be caught up to meet Christ on His descent to the Mount of Olives." After all, the coming of the day of the Lord and the revelation of the Antichrist with the accompanying tribulation was certainly what they had anticipated if they believed in a post-trib Rapture. Not exactly a "blessed hope," but surely nothing to be "shaken in mind" or "troubled" about.

If, on the other hand, the Thessalonians were expecting Christ before the tribulation period and it had arrived without their leaving in the Rapture, they had something, indeed, to be "shaken in mind" about! Had they been rejected by Christ? Why hadn't they been taken? And why was Paul still there and all of the other Christians? No one had been caught up to heaven.

If the day of Christ had arrived without Christ taking His own out of the world, then perhaps they had been misinformed not only on this subject but on many others as well. That possibility was enough to shake them.

The point is, the Thessalonians would have had no reason to be "shaken in mind" if they believed in a mid-trib or post-trib Rapture. The fact that they were badly shaken at the thought that they were in the tribulation only shows they had been taught that Christ would rapture them prior to that horrible time.

Paul, however, did not use the term "Great Tribulation" or even "tribulation." Here he refers to "the day of Christ." Elsewhere he calls it "the day of the Lord Jesus." Both terms are the New Testament equivalent of "the day of the Lord," an expression used many times in the Old Testament.

The Day of the Lord/Christ

That the day of the Lord is not a literal 24-hour day is clear from reading only a few of the references to it. Far too much happens to occur in one day. In fact, as we noted concerning the coming of Christ, so it is with the day of the Lord. Seemingly contradictory statements are made about it that must be reconciled with each other—and which require a far longer period to be worked out than a literal day.

Frequently "the day of the Lord" is referred to as a day of woe, evil, vengeance from God, of indescribable destruction: "the day of his [God's] wrath" (Psalm 110:5); "a destruction from the Almighty" (Joel 1:15); "great and very terrible, who can abide it?" (Joel 2:11); "woe...darkness and not light" (Amos 5:18); "the day of the Lord's anger" (Zephaniah 2:2,3); "that shall burn as an oven; and all the proud, yea, and all that do wickedly, shall be stubble...saith the Lord of hosts" (Malachi 4:1). Such descriptions leave no doubt that the day of the Lord includes the Great Tribulation period.

The Day of the Lord pertains especially to Israel and involves the Messiah coming to her rescue at Armageddon and executing judgment upon those who have mistreated her. That fact is also clear from reading the context of the few verses just referred to as well as from the large number of other passages dealing with this subject.

It is interesting to note how Christ handled the Scripture (Isaiah 61:1,2) that He read in the synagogue of Nazareth on that important day when He declared His mission in coming to earth:

> And he came to Nazareth, where he had been brought up: and, as his custom was, he went into the synagogue on the sabbath day, and stood up for to read. And there was delivered unto him the book of the prophet Esaias. And...he found the place where it was written, The Spirit of the Lord is upon me, because he hath anointed me to preach the gospel to the poor; he hath sent me to heal the broken-hearted, to preach deliverance to the captives, and

recovering of sight to the blind, to set at liberty them that are bruised, To preach the acceptable year of the Lord. And he closed the book....And he began to say unto them, This day is this scripture fulfilled in your ears (Luke 4:16-21).

He was, of course, declaring to those in His hometown who knew Him only as the carpenter that He was the fulfillment of the passage He had just read, i.e., the Messiah. They were enraged at such blasphemy and tried to kill Him. Most interesting is the fact that He stopped reading in mid-sentence. The next phrase, which He avoided, says, "and the day of vengeance of our God."

Again the Necessity for Two Comings

Here we have another example of an Old Testament Scripture with a double meaning that required the Messiah to come twice. Jesus read that part which pertained to His first advent and refrained from reading that which pertained to His Second Coming. "The day of vengeance" is another description of "the day of the Lord." We can now see its intimate relationship to the Messiah and His Second Coming. Jude, as already noted, reminds us of Enoch's prophecy that the Lord (Yahweh) will come "with ten thousands [i.e., an innumerable company] of his saints, to execute judgment upon all."

So the day of the Lord, this day of vengeance and judgment from the Almighty, includes the Second Coming. Therefore, in the New Testament it is called the day of Christ, for it is the day when He will be "revealed from heaven in flaming fire taking vengeance upon them that know not God." The Messiah is the One who will proclaim that day and execute that vengeance; therefore, it is rightly called the day of Christ.

In stopping His reading where He did, Christ was indicating that the day of vengeance was being deferred. Had Daniel's seventieth week followed immediately the consummation of the sixty-ninth, the day of the Lord would have begun right after His crucifixion, but it did not. It has been delayed for reasons we have already discussed.

This day of the Lord, however, includes more than the Great Tribulation ("the time of Jacob's trouble"—Jeremiah 30:7) and Armageddon. It is also a day of great blessing for Israel under the Messiah's millennial reign as Zechariah 14 (and other Scriptures) makes clear:

> Behold the day of the Lord cometh....I will gather all nations against Jerusalem to battle; and the city shall be taken....Then shall the Lord go forth, and fight against those nations....And his feet shall stand in that day [the day of the Lord] upon the mount of Olives...and the mount of Olives shall cleave in the midst thereof toward the east and toward the west, and there shall be a very great valley....And it shall be in that day [the day of the Lord] that living waters shall go out from Jerusalem [through the newly formed valley]....And the Lord [Christ] shall be king over all the earth [ruling on the throne of his father David in Jerusalem]: in that day [the day of the Lord] shall there be one Lord, and his name one [i.e., no false religions allowed]....And it shall come to pass, that every one that is left of all the nations which came against Jerusalem shall even go up from year to year to worship the King, the Lord of hosts [Jesus Christ], and to keep the feast of tabernacles (Zechariah 14:1-4,8,9,16).

There is yet more to the day of the Lord. It also includes the destruction after the millennium of the entire universe by fire and the ushering in of a new universe. Peter confirms Paul's statement about this day arriving as a thief (1 Thessalonians 5:2), then goes on to explain further what John later recon-firmed in Revelation:

> But the day of the Lord will come as a thief in the night; in which the heavens shall pass away with a great noise, and the elements shall melt with fervent heat, the earth also and the works that are therein shall be burned up....Nevertheless we, according to

his promise, look for a new heavens and a new earth,
wherein dwelleth righteousness (2 Peter 3:10,13).

And I saw a new heaven and a new earth: for the
first heaven and the first earth were passed away;
and there was no more sea. And I John saw the holy
city, new Jerusalem, coming down from God out of
heaven, prepared as a bride adorned for her hus-
band (Revelation 21:1,2).

While agreeing that the day of the Lord begins with the
Rapture, the chief proponent of a "pre-wrath Rapture" places
it at the end of Revelation 6 just prior to the opening of the seventh seal by Christ. Such a timing is impossible. Six of the seven
seals of judgment having already been opened, the world is in
chaos, suffering from famine, wars, and unprecedented
upheavals of nature.

The opening of the second seal "took peace from the earth"
(v. 4). Yet the day of the Lord comes when the world is exulting
in having achieved "peace and safety." The whole world rec-
ognizes that "the great day of his [Him that sitteth upon the
throne and the Lamb] wrath is come" (vv. 16,17) and cries out
to the rocks and mountains to hide them from God's wrath. Yet
the day of the Lord or the day of Christ comes as a thief, when
the last thing the world's inhabitants expect is God's judgment.

We can only conclude that the day of the Lord begins
before any signs or warnings or disasters occur. Such are also
the conditions at the Rapture. We know that the Rapture marks
the beginning of Daniel's seventieth week, which we can now
see coincides with the start of the day of the Lord. This scenario
agrees with Christ's warning that He would come as a thief
(Matthew 24:43; Luke 12:39) when even believers would be
caught by surprise (Matthew 24:44; Luke 12:40) and at a time
similar to the days of Noah: of eating, drinking, building, marrying, business as usual. Such conditions certainly no longer
prevail upon the earth at the end of Revelation 6, much less in
the midst of Armageddon.

But What About "The First Resurrection"?

A major post-tribulation argument is that the Bible teaches a post-tribulation resurrection, so that has to be when the Rapture takes place. For example, Revelation 20:4-5 declares that the "first resurrection" takes place after the battle of Armageddon, so the Rapture must occur then. Moreover, Christ said, "No man can come to me except the Father which hath sent me draw him: and I will raise him up *at the last day*." The expression "last day" could hardly be referring to the beginning of the Great Tribulation!

First of all, it must be noted that Revelation 20:4-5 is only a partial resurrection. It does not refer to the resurrection of *all* believers, but only to those martyred by Antichrist during the Great Tribulation: "them that were beheaded for the witness of Jesus, and for the word of God, and which had not worshipped the beast, neither his image, neither had received his mark."

One must ask, what about Abraham, David, Peter, Paul, Spurgeon, Moody, and Christians who have died more recently, none of whom were slain by Antichrist? When are they resurrected? It is stated very clearly that they are resurrected at the Rapture: "The dead in Christ [all of them] shall rise first: then we which are alive and remain shall be caught up together...to meet the Lord in the air" (1 Thessalonians 4:16,17).

Therefore, the Rapture, which coincides with a general resurrection of all those who have died trusting in Christ, is another event and must occur at another time. Before or after Armageddon? Obviously it occurs before, because the resurrected saints are already in heaven and accompany Christ from there to Armageddon. Revelation 19:7-9 describes "the marriage supper of the Lamb" involving, of course, His bride, the Church (Ephesians 5:23-32). She is clothed in fine linen, white and clean (v. 8). Next, Christ descends with "the armies which were in heaven...[also] clothed in fine linen, white and clean" (v. 14) to confront and destroy Antichrist at Armageddon. The Church clearly comprises at least a large part of that army.

As we have already noted, Enoch prophesied that Christ would return to this earth "with ten thousands [i.e., an innumerable company] of his saints, to execute judgment" upon

Antichrist and his followers (Jude 14,15). Zechariah 14:4-5 states that when Christ comes to earth to rescue Israel and "His feet stand in that day upon the mount of Olives...all the saints" come with Him. These are not disembodied spirits waiting to be resurrected! The saints who are present at the marriage supper of the Lamb and who accompany Christ from heaven to reign on earth must be in their glorified bodies—and they must have been taken to heaven previously in order to descend from there with Him at Armageddon.

That this resurrection after Armageddon specifically involves only "the souls of them" who were martyred by Antichrist is, in fact, another argument for a pre-trib Rapture. It indicates that all other saints have previously been resurrected. Then why wait until this late time for these martyrs to be raised? We are told why.

Some of these same souls are seen earlier:

> I saw under the altar the souls of them that were slain for the word of God...and it was said unto them, that they should rest...until their fellowservants also...that should be killed as they were, should be fulfilled (Revelation 6:9-11).

Since all Great Tribulation martyrs are resurrected together—and Antichrist kills believers to the very end—their resurrection must await the end of Armageddon.

If the resurrection of believers who lived and died prior to the tribulation took place seven years previously, why is the resurrection in Revelation 20 of those slain by Antichrist called "the first resurrection"? It must be in order to show that these martyrs are part of that company, the Church, which has already been resurrected. It specifically says that they "reign with him [Christ] a thousand years" (Revelation 20:6) as do the saints of all ages.

What about Christ raising all believers "at the last day"? As we have just seen, this "last day" cannot be the 24-hour period in which these martyrs are raised, for there are many more days that follow during the millennium. The "last day" is a reference to what is also called "the day of the Lord [God]" (Isaiah 2:12; Jeremiah 46:10; Ezekiel 30:3; Joel 1:15, etc.) or "the day of Christ" (1 Corinthians 1:8; Philippians 1:10; 2 Thessalonians 2:2), which we have just discussed. As we have seen, it begins with the Rapture and includes Daniel's seventieth week, the millennium, the destruction of this old universe and the creation of a new one.

A Post-Tribulation Scenario

Those who believe in a post-tribulation Rapture must place the beginning of the day of the Lord at Armageddon. It can hardly be placed any later, such as the beginning of the millennium, because of the great destruction and judgment upon Israel and all the nations which it unquestionably involves. At the end of the tribulation, however, the conditions are the exact opposite of those that Christ warned would prevail at the time of the Rapture and the beginning of the day of the Lord.

Let us assume a post-tribulation Rapture in order to see that it doesn't fit our Lord's exhortations and warnings. We look in upon a few beleaguered Christians who have gathered together in secret at the risk of their lives. It is the end of the Great Tribulation. They are certain of that fact, because every event Christ foretold in His Olivet discourse and all the events John laid out with such precision in Revelation have happened exactly as prophesied. They have agonizingly witnessed it all.

The Antichrist established his New World Order, recovered from his deadly head wound, continues to perform great signs and wonders, and the world worships his image in Jerusalem's rebuilt temple. All who would not worship him as God have been killed, except for a very few new believers in Jesus who have escaped and are being hunted down by the world police whose informers are everywhere. The natural disasters have followed their course just as foretold. Worldwide television has covered the two witnesses preaching repentance in the streets of Jerusalem. Their execution by Antichrist, resurrection, and ascent into heaven have also been witnessed by the world. There can be no doubt that the seven years of Daniel's seventieth week have gone according to schedule and the calendar is about to run out.

Having gathered together the armies of the world, Antichrist has invaded Israel, and a nuclear exchange has begun. Refusing to go down to defeat like a lamb to the slaughter, Israel opted to use her ultimate weapon as she had warned. Nevertheless, the forces arrayed against her are overwhelming and she is doomed. It is a replay of Hitler's "final solution to the Jewish problem," only this time on a massive scale and engineered by the Antichrist himself.

Our small group of Christians is meeting in a cave deep in a forest somewhere. Having refused to take the mark of the beast, unable to buy or sell, they are destitute, starving. Marked for death for refusing to worship the Antichrist's image, they have managed somehow to escape and barely survive. As they have followed the events of the past seven years, they have noted in the margins of their worn and precious Bibles each time a prophecy was being fulfilled. In that process, they have arrived at Revelation 19 and now mark in the margin that Armageddon is in full execution.

One of their number rises and asks uncertainly, "Do you think it is now time for the Lord to come?" He is hooted down. "Of course not," the others snort. "Look at conditions around you. If there was ever a time when He wouldn't come, this is it. Now let's get some sleep." Such a post-trib scenario is unbelievable.

A Scenario Beyond Belief

The scene above is so far from the "at such an hour as ye think not the Son of man cometh" which Christ described as to be beyond belief. Is there eating and drinking, buying and selling, marrying and feasting, business as usual, and no expectation of God's judgment just as it was in Noah's day? Are those conditions prevailing at the end of the Great Tribulation in the midst of Armageddon? One would have to be mad to imagine such a setting for a post-trib Rapture. The world is on the brink of total destruction! Christ warned that unless He intervened no flesh would be left alive (Matthew 24:22).

A complacent Church is sleeping soundly, the wise along with the foolish? Antichrist has had power to kill all Christians for many months—and he and the other world leaders sharing in his New World Order have even turned against the false church and destroyed her (Revelation 17:16,17)! How could Christ come as a thief now, when every sign has been fulfilled so that everyone knows He is "right at the door" (Matthew 24:33)? Even Antichrist and his armies know Christ is coming and have "gathered together to make war against him" (Revelation 19:19).

A post-tribulation coming of Christ? Indeed, there will be, but it will be the Second Coming in power and glory to rescue Israel and destroy Antichrist and his kingdom and armies. The post-trib coming will most assuredly not be the occasion of the Rapture of His bride. She has been in heaven, the marriage has taken place, and now she accompanies Him back to earth to share His triumph.

Don't confuse the Rapture with the Second Coming! When the latter takes place all the signs will have been given and the whole world will know that Christ is about to descend bodily to the earth with heaven's armies. When it comes to the Rapture, however, our Lord is talking surprise and imminency. No signs. No warning. He could come at any moment! One cannot read the New Testament with any understanding at all and come to any other conclusion.

It requires no complicated theological reasoning from obscure verses to realize that a post-trib Rapture couldn't possibly fit Christ's description of a peaceful, prosperous, thriving world and a complacent, sleeping Church. It is as simple and as plain as the meaning of the commonest of words: "Watch! Be ready! At such an hour as ye think not the Son of man cometh!" And that could be at any moment.

CHAPTER 17

Imminency

How ye turned to God from idols to serve the living and true God; and to wait for his Son from heaven, whom he raised from the dead, even Jesus, which delivered us from the wrath to come (1 Thessalonians 1:9,10).

And unto them that look for him shall he appear the second time (Hebrews 9:28).

Let your loins be girded about, and your lights burning; and ye yourselves like unto men that wait for their lord…that when he cometh and knocketh, they may open unto him immediately. Be ye therefore ready also: for the Son of man cometh at an hour when ye think not (Luke 12:35-40).

Reading the first epistle to the Thessalonians, one can see that Paul was thrilled with the transformation in the lives and with the spiritual growth of those who had come to know Christ in Thessalonica. That ancient Greek city occupied a strategic position at the crossroads of trade routes converging on the Balkan peninsula. Travelers passed through Thessalonica going in all directions, and reports were spreading far and wide about the faith of these former pagans who had "turned to God from idols to serve the living and true God."

Something else was also being reported about them. The information had reached Paul's ears and pleased him greatly. The Christians at Thessalonica, though fairly new in the faith, not only had begun to worship the true God, but they were "wait[ing] for his Son from heaven...even Jesus." Paul had obviously taught them this truth and it is equally clear that he considered it to be of great importance.

Waiting for Christ's Return

Paul certainly had not advised them that Christ wasn't coming for at least 1900 years and therefore they shouldn't give much thought to His return. Nor had he told them that Christ wouldn't come until the Antichrist first appeared or until the end of the Great Tribulation. He must have taught them that Christ could come at any moment, or they wouldn't have been *waiting* for Him.

Paul commends the Thessalonian believers for "waiting" for Christ's coming. He reaffirms that such should be the attitude of every follower of Christ—as much the mark of a true Christian as was turning to God from idols. To encourage this anticipation and to reinforce what he had previously taught them, Paul presents in chapter four of this epistle (likely the first one he ever wrote) the clearest description of the Rapture that we have anywhere.

"To wait for his Son from heaven" has an expectant ring. It is much more specific than the general belief in His return expressed in the creeds. It goes beyond accepting the doctrine that Christ will return one day in the distant future. The Thessalonian believers were waiting for Him to return right then. Obviously, Paul had taught them that Christ could come at any moment, or to "wait for Him" would make no sense. One doesn't go to the airport in July to "wait" for Aunt Jane if she has written to say she is coming in November.

"Waiting for Christ" would not have been the attitude of the Thessalonian believers had they been taught by Paul that any signs or events would precede His coming. A person who doesn't believe Christ can come until after the first six seals are opened, or until Antichrist appears, or until the end of the Great Tribulation or millennium would not be "waiting" for Christ.

Belief in a post-*anything* Rapture would eliminate the expectant "waiting" for which Paul commends the Thessalonians. The language of Scripture—waiting, watching, looking for Christ—cries, "Imminency! Christ could come at any moment!"

Imminency and Expectancy in the New Testament

Clearly the Christians Paul commends at Thessalonica did not believe in a post-tribulation Rapture. They would not have been watching and waiting for Christ's return had they been taught that at least seven years lay between them and that longed-for event. Paul's language demonstrates conclusively that the early Christians expected the Rapture as the next event on the prophetic timetable. They did not believe they would be on earth enduring the trials and tribulations of Daniel's seventieth week. No point in watching and waiting for Christ now if He would not come until Israel was surrounded by the world's armies and Armageddon was underway—whenever that might be.

If Antichrist must come first, or if some event must happen before the Rapture, then one would not be watching and waiting for Christ but for that earlier event. If Antichrist must come first, then it would be senseless to watch for Christ until Antichrist had been revealed. Christians would be watching not for Christ, but for Antichrist or for Armageddon or whoever or whatever must precede Christ's coming.

Significantly, there is no record in the New Testament of *anyone* ever watching and waiting for Antichrist. Nor is there any record of *anyone* ever being instructed to do so. Christ exhorted us, His own, to watch for His return—not for Antichrist or some necessary prior event.

Paul ends the Thessalonian epistle with a further reference to Christ's return: "I pray God your whole spirit and soul and body be preserved blameless unto the coming of our Lord Jesus Christ" (5:23). That soon-coming event was much on his heart and is a constant theme in his epistles. Surely such language would be folly if Christ wasn't coming until the end of the millennium! No one was going to live that long.

From even a cursory reading of the New Testament there can be no doubt that it was considered normal in the early Church to expect Christ at any moment. Paul greeted the

Christians at Corinth as those who were "waiting for the coming of our Lord Jesus Christ" (1 Corinthians 1:7)—again language that requires imminency. He urged Timothy to "keep this commandment without spot, unrebukable, until the appearing of our Lord Jesus Christ" (1 Timothy 6:14). While not demanding imminency, the language includes that as a possibility and certainly implies that the Rapture could occur within Timothy's lifetime. Once again we see the expectancy of the Rapture that Paul himself maintained and encouraged in others.

Indications of such expectancy are found elsewhere throughout Paul's epistles. For example, he begins his epistle to "all the saints in Christ Jesus which are at Philippi" with an expression of his confidence that the One who had "begun a good work" in them would "perform it until the day of Jesus Christ [i.e. the day of His coming]" (1:6). This statement reflects Paul's expectation that these believers could be alive when Christ returned. Paul didn't say, "perform it until you die," which he should have if Christ could not come for hundreds or thousands of years.

That the saints at Philippi (along with Paul, for he includes himself) were definitely expecting Christ's return at any time is again clear from a verse which we have already quoted: "For our conversation [citizenship] is in heaven; from whence also we look for the Saviour, the Lord Jesus Christ" (3:20). The only conclusion one can draw from such language ("we *look* for the Saviour") is that Paul was encouraging the believers at Philippi to expect the resurrection of the dead, transformation of the living, and the Rapture of all together into heaven at any moment. Otherwise it would be foolish to be looking for Christ when He couldn't come until something else occurred first.

The "Blessed Hope"

If, in fact, we must face Antichrist and the Great Tribulation before the Rapture can occur, then Paul is badly misleading us here and in his other epistles. There is never a word of warning about the horrible trials of the Great Tribulation, no encouragement to be strong even though it will mean death for not taking the mark of the beast. Here is a vital topic which should at least have been addressed, if not for his contemporaries, then for us today. Any reference, however, to going through the Great Tribulation, how to identify the Antichrist, encouragement to faithfulness in the face of such unusual deception, and warnings not to take his mark is conspicuous by its absence in all of Paul's epistles and in those of the other apostles as well.

Paul called the prospect of the imminent Rapture "the blessed hope" (Titus 2:13). It would hardly be a blessed hope to know that to experience it one must first endure the Great Tribulation with its devastation of planet Earth by war, famine, and natural disasters. Hardly a blessed hope if it couldn't occur until after most if not all Christians had been hunted down and slain for refusing to take Antichrist's mark and worship him as God! Hardly a blessed hope to know that God would give Antichrist the power to kill all Christians (Revelation 13:7) at least three-and-a-half years before the Rapture! Hardly a blessed hope to know that by the time the Rapture occurred in the midst of Armageddon very few if any believers would be left alive for Christ to catch up to meet Him on His way down to rescue Israel! Better to call the Rapture a cruel hoax than a blessed hope if that were the case!

Let us logically consider the meaning of language. A "hope" is something which might possibly occur in time to be of some benefit in an existing situation. For example, a person who finds himself dying in the wreckage of a car might hope to be rescued in time for his life to be saved. Suppose, however, one has been told by a prophet, "You will be among 100 survivors of a plane crash, but the wreckage will lie under 50 feet of salt water slowly seeping inside. No help will arrive to rescue anyone until 98 people have died of injuries and dehydration. At that point an underwater rescue team will manage to save one of those still alive." Would that be a blessed hope?

One could not begin to hope for rescue while there were still 75 people alive, 50, 25, 10. Nor could any Christian who found himself in the Great Tribulation have any hope of being Raptured until the earth was virtually destroyed and Armageddon was in process. To offer to the Church such a Rapture and to call it a "blessed hope" would be the ultimate deception. It could hardly be what Christ had in mind when He said, "I will come again and receive you unto myself, that where I am, there ye may be also."

If language has any meaning, then one could not possibly call a post-tribulation Rapture "the blessed hope." To do so would be a mockery. Moreover, Paul said that Christians should be *looking* for that blessed hope" (Titus 2:13)! If the Rapture won't occur until the end of the Great Tribulation, then there is no point in looking for it until then. The fact that Paul tells Christians to be *looking* for that blessed hope right now proves conclusively that no sign or event must precede it.

The Rapture could only be a *blessed* hope if one knew that Christ could come at any moment, right now, tomorrow, or the next day. Only a pre-tribulation Rapture could be a blessed hope. To be a blessed hope one must know that the Rapture will come in time to rescue one from the most horrible devastation and suffering the world will ever see. Such is a blessed hope indeed, and one to wait and watch for at the present time!

Waiting, Watching—Normal Christian Attitude

As with the Thessalonians, the fact that the Philippians were *looking* for Christ certainly indicated that they had been taught that He could come within their lifetime. But it indicated more than that. One doesn't *look* for Uncle George if he has written to say that he may come within the next 20 years. That's too uncertain and possibly distant to actually start *looking* for him. The Church we read of in the New Testament was waiting, looking, watching, obviously expecting Christ at any moment. How unlike the Church today!

In referring to the Lord's return, the epistle to the Hebrews uses similar terminology—"unto them that *look* for him." Its author, inspired of the Holy Spirit, seems to consider such watchfulness to be the normal attitude of every true Christian. Consider this Scripture again:

And as it is appointed unto men once to die [no reincarnation], but after this the judgment [no second chance]: So Christ was once offered to bear the sins of many; and unto them that look for him shall he appear the second time without sin unto salvation (9:27,28).

"Unto them that *look* for him shall he appear." Does that mean that if one doesn't happen to be looking into the sky, or at least thinking of Christ's return when He comes to catch away His bride, he'll be left behind? Surely not. Our going to heaven at the Rapture does not depend upon whether we even believe in that blessed hope much less are *looking* for Christ at that particular moment. Our ticket to heaven is the finished redemptive work of Christ on the cross. If one's faith is in the Lord Jesus Christ as his personal Savior, he will be taken to heaven at the Rapture even if he has never heard of such an event.

If all Christians are included, then why does it say, "Unto them that look for him"? Simply because it is expected of all Christians to be looking for Christ. Reference is not to an elite group of Christians, those who continually look for Christ, as the only ones who will be Raptured. The Bible does not teach a "partial Rapture" of the worthy (however that is defined), leaving the unworthy behind.

To the author of the epistle to the Hebrews (which was more than likely Paul), looking for Christ was clearly considered the normal attitude for every Christian. He didn't even exhort his readers to maintain that expectancy. Rather it is taken for granted. So "unto them that look for him shall he appear" is just another way of saying, "unto all Christians shall he appear." Isn't that redundant? No. He's speaking of the Rapture, and at that time Christ appears only to His bride as He catches her up to heaven.

A "Secret" Rapture?

It is increasingly popular, even among evangelicals in these last days, to mock the idea of a "secret" Rapture. Yet this is the teaching of Scripture and it makes good sense. The world will not see what transpires, for at least two reasons. First of all, the Rapture is an intimate meeting between Christ and His bride and has nothing to do with those who have rejected Him, so why should they be allowed to witness it? They were invited to participate but refused (Luke 14:16-24). Secondly, if all the world witnessed this event, the mystery would be removed and the false explanation that helps Antichrist seize power would not be possible.

It is not God's will for the world to understand the truth about what has happened. From the moment of the Rapture, all those who refused the love of the truth are under a strong delusion from God to believe the lies of Antichrist and Satan. The last thing they would believe, or that God wants them to believe, is that the Rapture has occurred.

Books and newsletters have been written to show that a belief in the secret pre-tribulation Rapture was popularized by Plymouth Brethren founder, J.N. Darby. He presumably picked it up from a false "revelation" related to a Scottish Pentecostal revival and received by a young woman, Margaret MacDonald, in early 1830. A great deal of time and effort and relentless research has gone into establishing this thesis. Much time and effort has been expended in rebuttals as well. Such proofs and disproofs are beside the point.

What Margaret MacDonald did or did not mean by her rather convoluted and vague "revelation"—and what part it played in Darby's thinking—may well be of historical interest for those who have the time to pursue such matters. It has, however, nothing whatsoever to do with the controversy between pre- and post-tribulation Rapture beliefs. That controversy can only be settled by what the Bible does or doesn't say. That is the only issue.

The First Teacher of Imminency

The expectation held by the New Testament Church of Christ's imminent return was not attributable only to the teaching of the apostles. It came first of all from the words of

Christ Himself. He taught repeatedly that His coming was imminent.

One could not use stronger language than we quoted at the beginning of this chapter: "Let your loins be girded about, and your lights burning; and ye yourselves like unto men that wait for their lord....Blessed are those servants, whom the lord when he cometh shall find watching." Here Christ urges upon His followers two things: 1) to maintain a high state of *readiness* for His return; and 2) to continue to *watch* for His return. That He is teaching the imminence of and thus a pre-tribulation Rapture cannot be denied.

It is incredible that anyone could read the words of our Lord Himself and conclude that He could not return until the Antichrist had first appeared, or until the middle or end of the tribulation period, much less the end of the millennium! In Matthew 24, we have the same exhortations: "*Watch* therefore: for ye know not what hour your Lord doth come" (v. 42); and "Therefore be ye also *ready:* for in such an hour as ye think not the Son of man cometh" (v. 44).

Would any Christian who had survived the Great Tribulation and saw Armageddon in process possibly be surprised by the Lord's coming, much less say to himself, "I don't think Christ will return now"? Though Christ does come in the midst of Armageddon, surely there must also be another coming at another time that fits the description He gives! Scripture demands, as we have documented, two comings or two stages in Christ's return: the Rapture and the Second Coming. Which one is being referred to is indicated, if not by the description of the event itself, then by the description of the conditions in the world and Church which prevail at the time.

A Complacent, Sleeping Church

In Matthew 25, Christ warns that the Church will likely be asleep when He comes to catch His bride away. Yes, five virgins are wise and five foolish. Apparently because the five foolish do not have oil in their lamps (a symbol of the Holy Spirit) they are not genuine Christians. Be that as it may, the following declaration from the Lord is more than sobering:

"While the bridegroom tarried, they *all* slumbered and slept" (Matthew 25:5).

The wise slept along with the foolish! "The bridegroom tarried" and somehow it just didn't seem as though he'd be coming in the next few hours, so they took that opportunity to get some sleep—and that's when he came! Now we see why the Lord coupled His exhortation to *watch* and to be *ready* with the warning that He would come at a time when we wouldn't expect Him—when somehow it just wouldn't seem that He'd be coming then. That description just doesn't fit the end of the Great Tribulation!

Again we have imminency. He could come at any time: Watch, be ready! We also have as clear a presentation as one could ask for of the fact that He won't come at the end of Daniel's seventieth week in the midst of Armageddon. No one would be complacently sleeping then or doubting that it was the right time for Him to come!

A Practical Question About Timing Remains

What about Paul's statement that the dead are raised at the "last trump"? The question comes up again and again. We have commented earlier that the idea of the "last trump" in 1 Corinthians 15 being the seventh trumpet in Revelation 11 is not confirmed in Scripture. Nor does it fit the criteria of a time of complacency, peace, business as usual, and no expectancy whatsoever of God's judgment and Christ's return.

There are many possible last trumps and Paul doesn't give us any criteria for identifying the one to which he refers. Moreover, the timing of the seventh trumpet in Revelation 11 precedes Armageddon by at least several months, so if the Rapture took place then it would be a separate event from the Second Coming as well. But why then?

There must be a better reason for the timing of the Rapture than to coincide with a trumpet blast! But that theory also destroys imminency if the Rapture must wait upon the sounding of this trumpet. Therefore such a belief must be rejected as unbiblical.

There is a growing following for the idea that the "last trump" Paul had in mind is the last trumpet to sound on the Feast of Trumpets. We can now see the fatal flaw in that theory as well. If Christ didn't come at the Feast of Trumpets in a particular year, then we would know we had another year before He could come—but that would destroy imminency and therefore must be rejected. He might very well come at that time, but we cannot state it as a certainty.

Having made the case for imminency, we know that Christ could return to catch His bride away at any moment. But we still have not answered our question, "*When* will Jesus come?" One practical problem remains that must be settled first.

Even though there are no preconditions and no signs for the Rapture, there are many for the Second Coming. We know that seven years, the seventieth week of Daniel, separates the Rapture and Second Coming. Is there time for all that is prophesied to take place within that seven-year period without any preparation beforehand? If not, then we've lost the case for imminency after all.

CHAPTER 18

Timing Factors

For then shall be great tribulation, such as was not since the beginning of the world to this time, no, nor ever shall be. And except those days be shortened, there should no flesh [on earth] be saved [i.e., this is a worldwide phenomenon] (Matthew 24:21,22).

For as a snare shall it come on all them that dwell on the face of the whole earth (Luke 21:35).

Because thou hast kept the word of my patience, I also will keep thee from the hour of temptation, which shall come upon all the world, to try them that dwell upon the earth (Revelation 3:10).

L et us state our present concern once again. We have arrived at the conclusion that Christ and His apostles taught and the church we read of in the New Testament believed and watched for, a pre-tribulation and imminent Rapture. If we are correct, nothing at any time in history could have stood between the church and the Rapture. There were no signs and no conditions that needed to be fulfilled in the past nor are there any today. Such is definitely the impression one obtains from reading the New Testament.

Have we not, however, given some conditions? For example, that Christ would come at a time when the Church would not expect Him. That statement, of course, could be as much a description of the Church's spiritual lethargy as of conditions in the world. Certainly it was not long before the Church lost its sense of expectancy, so the parable of the sleeping wise and foolish virgins applied throughout history as it does today. How many of those who call themselves Christians around the world are presently really watching, waiting, and looking for Christ's return? A very small percentage!

So this criteria, which has always been met, did not point to a particular time in history during which Christ must come, and thus it did not affect imminency. Instead, as we have seen, it identified the time when the Rapture *could not* occur—i.e., the end of the Great Tribulation. At that time booming business, complacency, no thought of judgment as it was in Noah's day, and surprise are out of the question. Even Antichrist will know that Christ is coming. Thus these criteria, rather than working against pre-trib imminency, actually preserve it by eliminating a post-trib Rapture.

"As It Was in the Days of Noah"

Yes, but what about those criteria: "As it was in the days of Noah"—eating, drinking, buying, building, with no expectation of judgment? Remember, Christ is speaking of conditions worldwide. While there have always been times of famine, war, pestilence, and upheavals of nature in parts of the world, never have these disastrous conditions prevailed worldwide. They will during the Great Tribulation after the Rapture, but not until then. Similar conditions to those prior to the flood have always prevailed in many if not most parts of the world. That fact is supported by the comments of those who remain skeptical of coming judgment even today:

> Knowing this first, that there shall come in the last days scoffers, walking after their own lusts. And saying, Where is the promise of his coming? for since the fathers fell asleep, all things continue as they were from the beginning of creation (2 Peter 3:3,4).

These scoffers insist that world conditions are and always have been as they were in the days of Noah. Yes, many of the Christians who were being hunted, imprisoned, and killed under communist regimes in Russia, China, Laos, Cambodia, and in Muslim and Catholic countries have at times thought they were already in the Great Tribulation. They had, however, no biblical basis for such fears. The Great Tribulation will be far worse and it will be experienced not only in a few countries but by the entire world all at once as the verses at the beginning of this chapter assure us.

Therefore, this criteria, too, rather than pointing to a special time when the Rapture *must* occur, defines the time when it *could not*—i.e., during and especially at the end of the Great Tribulation, when conditions are anything but like those in the days of Noah.

Unusual Signs Unknown to Previous Generations

In an earlier chapter we mentioned that in addition to the well-known signs of the nearness of His return cited by Christ (wars, pestilence, famine, earthquakes, etc.) there are some other signs unlike anything known to previous generations. Ours is the first generation for which these prophecies, seemingly impossible before, even make sense. Does that mean, then, that we have lost imminency after all? Let us look at some of these peculiar signs.

In the verses quoted at the beginning of this chapter, Christ declared that the Great Tribulation would involve dangers to life unlike anything ever known. So horrendous, in fact, would the weapons be, that "except those days be shortened, there should no flesh be saved." That statement seemed outrageous for more than 1900 years. There were no weapons capable of wiping out all life on this planet. None, that is, until our generation came along. Not only the nuclear arsenals which are now common knowledge fall into that category, but other secret weapons equally deadly have been developed. A major deterrent to the use of these star wars weapons has been the fear that a disaster of cosmic proportions could be unleashed which would make any kind of life on this planet impossible.

How amazingly accurate was Christ's prophecy made more than 1900 years ago! Once again we have confirmation of Christ's deity and of the fact that the Bible is God's Word. Confirmation, too, that these are the last days of which He spoke.

In our day, for the first time in history, the fulfillment of Christ's frightening prophecy—a prophecy that seemed impossible for so many centuries—is simply a matter of using existing weapons. This terrifying development in destructive capabilities means that Christ's prophecy could become reality at any time.

This fact, however, confronts us with an important question. If weapons that have only been developed in our generation had to be in existence at Armageddon, did this not prevent Christ from coming in the past? The answer, of course, hinges upon whether or not previous generations might have been able to develop such weapons during the seven years between the Rapture and Armageddon.

Would it have been possible for a previous generation to go from knights in armor, for example, to nuclear arms in such a short period of time? That particular leap in technology may not have been necessary. There may be other weapons more ingenious and far more horrible which could have been developed and used more simply and quickly. No one can dogmatically rule out such a possibility. Human genius is unpredictable.

"That No One Might Buy or Sell [Without]...the Mark"

Revelation 13 declares that Antichrist will control all banking and commerce in the entire world. Once again that concept seemed unbelievable in the past. Then along came our generation and developed the computers and communications satellites with which to fulfill this prophecy. We are rapidly heading toward a cashless society for reasons of efficiency and crime control. Holdups, kidnapping, extortion, drug dealing, and money laundering as well as counterfeiting and cheating on income tax could all be eliminated by doing away with cash and requiring that all transactions be electronic. For these reasons such a system is inevitable.

The one smart card, however, could be stolen, lost, or forgotten. A tiny computer chip painlessly and quickly implanted just under the skin in hand or forehead will likely become the means of fulfilling this prophecy. We already have the technology and equipment for implementing such worldwide control at any time. Certainly Antichrist's mark involving 666 and the purpose for imposing it upon the world will not seem to be evil but something overwhelmingly beneficial which our generation has conceived and produced.

Again we must ask whether such sophisticated electronics could have been developed, for example, by a feudal society. Moreover, this system for controlling all buying and selling would have to be in place long before Armageddon, so there would only be the first few years of Daniel's seventieth week in which to complete the task. Could it have been accomplished by previous generations?

Once again, while admitting that such a feat would not seem likely under ordinary circumstances, one cannot say it would have been impossible. There may well be some other more ingenious method of accomplishing more simply the same end which could have been developed quickly had the Rapture occurred at any previous time in history.

It is certainly possible that some former generation, with incredible genius, *could* have developed within seven years or less the weapons and technologies necessary to fulfill all prophecies concerning Daniel's seventieth week. That simple possibility preserves imminency. The Rapture could have come at any time and these developments followed immediately and swiftly, perhaps with techniques even more ingenious than our generation has used.

The Rapture did not occur in the past. Today we are confronted with a solemn reality. Unlike previous generations, ours is the first one which *already possesses* everything necessary to fulfill all remaining prophecies. Moreover, the fact that this unusual and necessary capability has suddenly developed within a generation adds to the sense of expectancy. Why now? Surely for a reason!

While the Rapture could have come at any time, its occurrence in the past would have necessitated some rapid developments. These essential preparations have suddenly occurred in our generation. Today the props are all in place on the stage ready for the final act. Thus it is not only *possible* for the Rapture to occur at any moment, as it always has been, but now it is highly probable—certainly more probable than at any time in history!

What About the Temple?

A major factor, of course, is the necessity for Israel to be back in her land, where last days prophecies place her, immediately after the Rapture. This is required by the fact that Antichrist makes a covenant involving Israel at the very beginning of Daniel's seventieth week. Would that not mean, then, that the Rapture could not occur until Israel had once again become a nation? If so, we have lost imminency.

In fact, it would not be necessary for Israel to be back in her land before the Rapture. Suppose Antichrist had risen to power with Jews still scattered around the world without a homeland. Part of the covenant He makes with "the many" would have been to create that homeland and the nation of Israel immediately—which is no longer necessary, for Israel is already in her land.

Prophecy also indicates that the Jewish temple must be rebuilt in Jerusalem. Not *if* but *when* this will occur remains the only question. As we noted in an earlier chapter, Antichrist will seat himself in the temple of God and declare that he is God (2 Thessalonians 2:4), so it must be in existence at that time. He will also "cause the sacrifice and the oblation to cease" (Daniel 9:27), which again tells us that during Daniel's seventieth week (the seven-year tribulation period) the temple must be in existence and functioning with sacrifices being offered.

More than likely, as part of a Middle East peace treaty immediately following the Rapture, Antichrist will allow the Jews to rebuild their temple. According to Daniel, Antichrist will "confirm [this covenant] for one week" (obviously Daniel's seventieth week). Then, in the midst of that week, he will go back on his word. It may be at this time that he unveils his image in the temple and requires that it be worshiped in conjunction with his claim that he is God. These events start the world on the road to Armageddon.

Today the barriers standing in the way of the temple being rebuilt seem insurmountable. Islam's third holiest shrine, the

Dome of the Rock, occupies the place where the temple once stood. Try to move that! It was allegedly to this rock, Al-Aqsa, over which this shrine has been built, that Muhammad journeyed from Mecca and from which he ascended to heaven on his magical horse. That claim, however, was the invention of Yasser Arafat's uncle, Haj Amin el-Husseini, during the 1920s when he was Grand Mufti of Jerusalem. Haj Amin worked with the Nazis for the extermination of the Jews. In order to arouse Arabs against any Jewish presence in Jerusalem, he invented the idea that the Dome of the Rock had been constructed over Al-Aqsa.

The Dome of the Rock

That the rock over which this shrine was built was not considered at the time to be the fabled Al-Aqsa is clear. Sura 17:1, the only verse in the Koran to mention Al-Aqsa, is conspicuously absent among the many Koranic scriptures inscribed in Arabic inside the Dome. The idea that this was Al-Aqsa was not even dreamed of in those days.

In fact, the rock under the Dome, being the highest point of Mount Moriah, was very likely, as tradition holds, the place where Abraham offered Isaac (Genesis 22). David later purchased it from Ornan the Jebusite and built an altar there (1 Chronicles 21) and it was upon this site that Solomon built the first temple (2 Chronicles 3:1).

The Dome of the Rock was constructed in A.D. 691 by Abd-al-Malik to replace the Ka'aba in Mecca, which had been destroyed. He hoped to garner revenues from pilgrims coming to Jerusalem just as the Meccans made huge profits from pilgrims to the Ka'aba. The latter was restored, however, and Abd-al-Malik succeeded in capturing Mecca and with it the Ka'aba in 692. Jerusalem, not mentioned even once in the Qur'an, was meaningless to Muslims; and with the Ka'aba restored, the idea of pilgrimages to the Dome of the Rock never took hold. The myth that this is Al-Aqsa was invented in the 1920s by Haj Amin al-Husseini, Grant Mufti of Jerusalem and Arafat's uncle—and is maintained today to prevent the Jews from rebuilding the temple.

It is believed by some Jewish archaeological experts that the Holy of Holies in the original temple was directly over this rock. Other experts believe it was adjacent. Whatever the precise location when it is finally established, the Dome of the Rock would have to be moved in order for the Jewish temple to be rebuilt. Impossible? No. Suppose Antichrist should reveal the location of what Islamic leaders would agree was the true Al-Aqsa. The Dome of the Rock, in that case, could very well be moved to that site. The Jews have the technology and are prepared to move it piece by piece wherever necessary. There are other possibilities which we need not explore.

In any event, given the catalytic force of the sudden mass disappearance of hundreds of millions at the Rapture, Antichrist could bring about the relocation of the Arabs' third holiest shrine. That would open the door for the peaceful reconstruction of the Jewish temple at its authentic site on the temple mount.

Many Orthodox Jews believe that only the Messiah can point out the proper location of the temple and oversee its rebuilding. The accomplishment of that feat would seem to validate Antichrist's claim to be the Messiah. If he brought peace to the world, had the Dome of the Rock moved, pointed out the precise site for the temple, granted permission, and very likely even financed much of the construction, most Israelis would be convinced that he was the Messiah.

How it happens is a mere detail. The fact is that the temple will be rebuilt and swiftly, most likely immediately after the Rapture. According to Jewish experts involved in plans for the reconstruction, it could be accomplished in a matter not of years but of months. So again we have no hindrance to imminency. At any time in history Christ could have Raptured his Church, the nation of Israel could have been born immediately, and the temple built very quickly thereafter.

Here again, however, our generation is the first one in history to see Israel already established in her land and preparations for rebuilding the temple finalized. That this essential ramification occurred within the same generation that has seen the development of the technology necessary to fulfill all other prophecies can hardly be a coincidence. Once more, though the *possibility* remains the same, the *probability* that Christ will return momentarily has increased greatly.

Ready to Be Rebuilt

Some Jews today are not in favor of rebuilding the temple. They feel no religious need and are concerned that its construction would only further alienate Israel from the world community. Nevertheless, for most Jews, only with the rebuilding of the temple will Israel finally be functioning in her land and able to fulfill her divine calling. While this sense of destiny may have more to do with a commitment to tradition than with genuine faith in God, it runs deep and strong in Jewish consciousness. Its connection to the temple is most amazing.

One need only recall the intense emotion among Jews worldwide when the temple mount was recovered. Israeli paratroopers took the holy site on the fourth day of the Six-Day War in June 1967. These hardened soldiers wept uncontrollably and found themselves unable to leave the mount, as though some mystical force held them there. However, because of diplomatic pressure, Israeli Defense Minister Moshe Dayan gave the administration of the mount back to the Arabs, who control it to this day. In fact, by Jewish law no Jews are allowed to enter the mount because of the sacredness of the site and the uncertainties surrounding the exact location of the Holy of Holies.

In the meantime, plans have been meticulously laid to erect a third Jewish temple. It will replace Solomon's, built about 950 B.C. and destroyed by Nebuchadnezzar in 586 B.C., and Zerubbabel's temple originally completed in 515 B.C. Remodeled and enlarged by Herod beginning in 20 B.C., the second temple was destroyed by the Roman legions in A.D. 70 and has lain in ruins for more than 1900 years. Today, however, there is an awakening among Jews that the time has come for the long-anticipated recovery of their spiritual center.

The extent of preparations both for construction of the temple and for reinstitution of animal sacrifices which one discovers by a visit to Jerusalem is astounding. The cornerstone has been quarried, temple garments have been manufactured, the instruments to be used in connection with the sacrifices have been fashioned, and the priests are being trained. Even the ancient harps necessary for the singing that accompanies worship are now being handmade in Jerusalem. Everything is in readiness.

An Incredible Phenomenon

Here we are in the first decade of the twenty-first century. Ours is an age of space travel, computers, nuclear weapons, and highly advanced technology. It seems incredible, therefore, that today's modern Jews, who are among the best-educated and most scientifically minded people on earth, should have a passion to see the temple rebuilt—and even insist upon the precise location which it occupied in the past. Why? Few Israelies are religious. Most are sophisticates, agnostics, humanists, atheists, New Agers. The masses seldom if ever attend sabbath religious services. What could move these people to desire with such passion the reinstitution of the ancient temple worship?

Why this return to the past? The temple ceremonies date back to Moses and the fantastic (for most Jews) claim that he received the instructions for these rituals directly from God. These are ancient, archaic, strange practices involving incense and anointing oil whose formulas date back thousands of years. At the heart of the temple ceremonies are rituals which involve thousands of animal sacrifices. What will the animal rights activists say to that!

These highly symbolic ceremonies all looked forward to the sacrifice of the Jewish Messiah who, as the Lamb of God, would bear away the sins of the world. What other meaning could they have, especially to a people so irreligious? The rituals they are reviving will be performed by a priesthood that wears archaic garments whose design was given to Moses on Mount Sinai about 3500 years ago. The priests and their garments must be purified in ceremonies which require the ashes of a red heifer. It all seems so empty if the true meaning is missed—yet Israel is aflame with the passion to see the temple rebuilt!

On the one hand it seems incredible that intelligent modern people would involve themselves in such an ancient and formal religion in the twenty-first century. Tradition seems inadequate to explain this phenomenon. For those who believe the Bible, however, it is not surprising, for it must happen in order to fulfill prophecy.

So the temple will be rebuilt. How long would it take? Herod was 46 years in building the last temple (John 2:20). We are told by Israeli temple designers and builders that this latest temple, with the modern technology and construction methods of today, could be built in a few months. Here again we have an essential criteria that can be satisfied within the seven-year period and does not hinder imminency. Christ could have come at any time in history and the temple could have been rebuilt and functioning in the early part of Daniel's seventieth week in fulfillment of prophecy.

What About Ezekiel 38 and 39—World War III?

Many students of prophecy believe that the next event on the calendar is World War III, and that only thereafter can the Rapture take place. It is commonly taught that this conflict is foretold in Ezekiel 38 and 39. Based upon these two chapters, and long before the Soviet Union became a world power, students of prophecy declared that Russia would lead a coalition, which would include the Arab nations, in a devastating attack upon Israel and be defeated by God.

The collapse of the Soviet Union, rather than weakening this scenario, seems to have strengthened it. Significantly, Russia remains the largest entity to come out of this breakup of the Communist empire. The new independent Russia retains the nuclear warheads and the military manpower to fulfill Ezekiel's prophecy. Furthermore, several of the now-independent former Soviet republics are largely Muslim. Their independence has made it possible for a closer alliance between them and Iran, Iraq, Syria, and other radical Islamic regimes that are determined to annihilate Israel. The collapse of communism seems to have moved the players on the stage much closer to this great battle.

Some Christian leaders are convinced that only out of this global conflict and the miraculous defeat of Russia can the Roman Empire (which they conceive of as ten nations in Western Europe) be revived with Antichrist at its head and take its place as the dominant world power. Once again, if this interpretation is correct and this great war must precede the Rapture, then we have lost imminency. Let us examine these two chapters in Ezekiel briefly to see whether this is the case.

We lack the space, nor is it necessary, to go into detail concerning this conflict. As one reads these two chapters one is impressed with the finality of the language used in some of the verses. The following are a sample:

> It shall be in the latter [last] days, and I will bring thee against my land [Israel], that the heathen may know me (Ezekiel 38:16).

> Surely in that day there shall be a great shaking in the land of Israel; So that the fishes of the sea, and the fowls of the heaven, and the beasts of the field...and all the men that are upon the face of the earth, shall shake at my presence, and the mountains shall be thrown down (38:19,20).

> And I will be known in the eyes of many nations, and they shall know that I am the Lord (38:23).

> So will I make my holy name known in the midst of my people Israel; and I will not let them pollute my holy name any more: and the heathen shall know that I am the Lord, the Holy One in Israel (39:7).

> Speak unto every feathered fowl...assemble yourselves...ye shall eat the flesh of the mighty, and drink the blood of the princes of the earth (39:17,18).

> And I will set my glory among the heathen....So the house of Israel shall know that I am the Lord their God from that day and forward (39:21,22).

> Neither will I hide my face any more from them [Israel]: for I have poured out my spirit upon the house of Israel, saith the Lord God (39:29).

The language in these two chapters makes it very clear that this battle is Armageddon and not some earlier conflict prior to the Rapture. Note the magnitude of the shaking of the earth and the fact that the destruction is directly attributed to the presence of the Lord. It sounds like the description of Armageddon in Zechariah and Revelation when Christ Himself comes with the armies of heaven. The call to the fowls (39:17,18) is too similar for coincidence to the same invitation at Armageddon "to all the fowls that fly [to] eat the flesh of kings...captains...and of mighty men" found in Revelation 19:17,18.

The principle objection to this being Armageddon is the fact that the weapons of the defeated armies will be burned as fuel for seven years. It sounds like a neat fit if this should come at the beginning of the Tribulation—otherwise the burning and the purifying and burying of corpses goes on into the millennial reign of Christ. Why not? Fuel will be used during the millennium. Nor will the earth be suddenly and miraculously cleaned up by God. People will have much work to do. So this objection cannot be sustained, particularly in view of the language used concerning the heathen and Israel knowing God as a result of this conflict.

The repeated declaration that all the heathen will know that God has done this deed, that He has rescued Israel, and that they are His people is conclusive. The phrase "from that day forth" or similar words are used several times. Israel ever after knows God and that she belongs to Him. Moreover, Israel will never again pollute His holy name and can never again be forsaken of God.

Such language could not be used of anything except Armageddon, for God would have to violate this pledge to allow the destruction of Israel by Antichrist. Thus such a transformation in Israel and pledge from God could not come before Armageddon but only as a result thereof. At Armageddon, as described in Zechariah 12–14, we find the people of Israel, for the first time, realizing who Christ is and returning to God. Yet that is described as happening as a result of the conflict in Ezekiel 38 and 39. These chapters must therefore be a description of Armageddon and could not be referring to some earlier battle.

Imminency Remains

In summary, then, there are certain unusual prophecies which pertain to the last seven-year period known as Daniel's seventieth week or the tribulation. If any of these elements could not be developed within a seven-year period immediately following the Rapture of the Church, then we would have lost imminency. Something would have had to occur prior to the Rapture.

In fact, all of these unusual signs of the Second Coming could have developed within the seven-year period no matter at what point in history the Rapture might have taken place. The great battle described in Ezekiel 38 and 39, too, is clearly Armageddon and not some earlier conflict which must precede the Rapture.

Most interesting is the fact that now, for the first time in history, the means for fulfilling all of these unusual prophecies are already fully in place. Furthermore, this unique capability has come about rather suddenly within the same generation that has seen Israel back in her land. That these developments have rapidly converged on our generation could hardly be coincidence.

Everything necessary for the fulfillment of last days prophecies is now in place. Why should it be held in readiness far ahead of time? All of the signs indicate that the Rapture and the commencement of Daniel's seventieth week will very soon, and without further warning, be upon us.

CHAPTER 19

Israel, the Messiah, and the Church

And there appeared a great wonder in heaven; a woman clothed with the sun, and the moon under her feet, and upon her head a crown of twelve stars...and behold a great red dragon, having seven heads and ten horns....And the dragon stood before the woman which was ready to be delivered, for to devour her child as soon as it was born. And she brought forth a man child, who was to rule all nations with a rod of iron: and her child was caught up unto God....And the woman fled into the wilderness....The dragon persecuted the woman...and went to make war with the remnant of her seed, which keep the commandments of God, and have the testimony of Jesus Christ (Revelation 12:1-6,13-17).

Although the book of Revelation is almost entirely about the future, there is, in the passage above, a brief recapitulation of history. The woman can only be Israel. The man-child, of course, is the Messiah. The red dragon is none other than Satan himself. Indeed, later in this same chapter he is described as "the great dragon...that old serpent, called the Devil, and Satan, which deceiveth the whole world." The picture is of Satan's past and future determination to destroy first of all the Messiah, and having failed that, to destroy Israel and all Christians as well.

Satan waited long and apprehensively for the virgin birth of the promised One. Here was the Messiah who would be his antagonist in the battle for control of the universe. As we have already seen, that inconceivable cosmic warfare began with Lucifer's rebellion against God eons ago. The Messiah's coming was first promised by God to Adam and Eve immediately after their sin and just prior to their expulsion from the Garden of Eden. Interestingly enough, it was to Satan, who had communicated to Eve through a serpent, that God spoke on this occasion:

> And I will put enmity between thee [the serpent] and the woman, and between thy seed and her seed; it [the seed of the woman, i.e., Messiah] shall bruise [literally crush] thy head, and thou shalt bruise his heel (Genesis 3:15).

Our introductory verses from Revelation 12 depict Satan down through history, waiting, watching for the birth of the Messiah, poised to destroy Him. One such satanically inspired attempt was made upon the child Jesus by King Herod when, after learning of His birth, he sent his soldiers to kill all the male infants in Bethlehem and the surrounding countryside (Matthew 2:16-18). That slaughter of the innocents fulfilled yet another prophecy by Jeremiah (31:15). There is no mystery about these prophecies if we allow the Bible to speak for and to interpret itself.

Self-Serving "Translations"

Here we must issue a word of caution. Unfortunately, some cults have tampered with the biblical text in order to promote their own peculiar doctrines. Obviously, any teachings that require an alteration of God's Word for their support are not authentic. The Jehovah's Witnesses are an example. They deny so much biblical doctrine, including the deity of Christ and salvation by grace through faith, that they have found it necessary to produce their own *New World Translation*. It is not, however, a translation from the Hebrew and Greek manuscripts, but a self-serving perversion, as a comparison with numerous other more widely accepted translations will quickly reveal.

Their proprietary "Bible" was specifically designed to support their peculiar heresies.

The Catholic Douay Bible is another case in point. In its attempt to glorify Mary, it has long rendered this passage from Genesis as follows: "I will put enmities between thee and the woman, and thy seed and her seed: she shall crush thy head, and thou shalt lie in wait for her heel." So Mary, not the Messiah, is presented as the one who will destroy Satan. The marginal note says, "In art Mary is frequently pictured with her foot on the head of a serpent."

Demonic Apparitions of "Mary"

Indeed, in one of numerous demonic impersonations embraced by Roman Catholics, "Mary" appeared to Catherine Labouré in November 1830, in Paris as the "woman clothed with the sun, and the moon under her feet, and upon her head a crown of twelve stars" (Revelation 12:1). This apparition substituted Mary for Israel. Moreover, this counterfeit "Mary" appeared standing with her foot upon a serpent's head which she was crushing beneath her heel. The vision gave seemingly miraculous support to Rome's dishonest rendering of Genesis 3:15. While some modern Catholic translations have in recent times corrected this verse, the teaching that Mary is the one who crushes the serpent's head remains solidly entrenched in Roman Catholicism.

Catherine Labouré's vision has been preserved in a medal minted in 1832, to be worn around the neck for protection by the Roman Catholic faithful. The medal depicts "Mary" as Catherine saw her, crushing the serpent's head. Obviously the apparition, now known as "Our Lady of the Miraculous Medal," was not the true Mary of the Bible, for it perverted the Scripture and gave to Mary a power and a work that belong to Christ alone.

Whether Catherine hallucinated, made up the whole story, or was deceived by a demon impersonating Mary is irrelevant. The fact is that this heretical picture of Mary is honored as the truth by the Roman Catholic Church to this day. This favorite medal, to which many miracles have been credited, has been worn by scores of millions of Catholics around the world. It continues to rank in popularity and official Church recognition next to the rosary and the scapular of "Our Lady of Mount Carmel."

Of course, the Bible gives no such honor to Mary, nor did the real Mary claim it. There are no prophecies in the Old Testament about the coming of the woman, but there are scores of prophecies concerning the coming of the "seed of the woman," i.e., the virgin-born Messiah, as we have already seen. He has come once and defeated Satan by dying for our sins upon the cross. He must come again. This time He will confront Antichrist face-to-face and destroy this Satan-empowered impersonation of evil and his worldwide kingdom (2 Thessalonians 2:8).

Antichrist and the Dragon

In Revelation 13, John makes it clear that the dragon (Satan), is the real power and the Antichrist is his puppet. He puts it like this:

> All the world wondered after the beast [Antichrist].
> And they [the whole world] worshipped the dragon
> which gave power unto the beast: and they wor-
> shipped the beast....All that dwell upon the earth
> shall worship him (Revelation 13:3,4,8).

This time of "great tribulation," as it is called, will be the most horrible period the earth has ever experienced or ever will thereafter (Matthew 24:21). The scourge of Nazism and communism and the unspeakable terror and devastation that numerous evil dictatorships with their death camps have brought to the earth will pale by comparison.

The description of the dragon with seven heads and ten horns, presented at the beginning of this chapter, is most instructive. In Daniel 7:7, we also meet a beast with ten horns. We are told that it represents the fourth world empire, which was Rome. Verse 24 declares that the ten horns "are ten kings that shall arise." These are the same ten kings encountered in Daniel 2, represented by the ten toes on the image. Since they did not reign over the ancient Roman Empire, they must be involved with it in its revived form. It is specifically "in the days of those kings" that Christ will return to earth to destroy Antichrist and the revived Roman Empire and to establish His millennial kingdom on David's throne.

In Revelation, chapters 13 and 17, we meet this beast again, there described more fully as having seven heads as well as the ten horns. That beast, as we shall see, represents both the Antichrist and the revived Roman Empire, over which he will rule. His power, we are told in Daniel 8:24, is not his own. It comes from Satan according to Revelation 13:2. This fact is reinforced by the similarity in the description of the dragon (Satan) and the beast, both of whom have seven heads and ten horns. This striking similarity tells us that the Antichrist and his kingdom will be controlled and empowered by Satan.

Israel's Strategic Role

Getting back to Revelation 12, the dragon, having failed to destroy the man-child, hates and persecutes the rest of her seed—i.e., Christians and Jews. We have noted that there has been, down through history, an unmistakably diabolical element in the persecution of Jews around the world. There can be no doubt that Satan has attempted to inspire their enemies to destroy them so that the Messiah could not come into the world.

That the Jews, because of their physical relationship to the Messiah, would have to be preserved unto the "last days" and brought back to their land is at the very heart of most prophecies in the Bible. Unfortunately, in spite of their preservation to this day, the prophets with one voice warned that the worst time for Jews around the world lies ahead. It will be even worse than the holocaust in Nazi Germany—the time of "Jacob's trouble" (Jeremiah 30:7) to which we have already referred. Only one-third of all Jews on earth will survive.

Revelation 12 presents a picture of God's preservation of that remnant of Israel for "a time, times and half a time" (three-and-a-half years) during the last half of Daniel's seventieth week, called the Great Tribulation. Daniel 7:25 speaks of this "time and times and the dividing of time" as the period during which the Antichrist destroys all who will not worship him. Satan will actually be in control, for he is the one who gives this beast of a man—yes, the Antichrist is shown as a beast—his power.

Suppose Satan had succeeded in exterminating the Jews. Couldn't God have started over with another people? No, that would be impossible. The forces of darkness would have remained in control of this earth. God is called the "God of Israel" 203 times in the Bible. His integrity is tied to the survival of Israel.

Moreover, God had committed Himself to bring the Messiah into the world through the descendants of Abraham, Isaac, and Jacob, through the tribe of Judah and specifically from the line of King David. Numerous prophets declared it. If those prophecies were not fulfilled, God would be a liar. He would have lost control of history and of His universe. Satan would have won by default. This fact is the only explanation for anti-Semitism throughout history!

It takes little insight to recognize that Satan is still determined to destroy Israel. Why? What good would it do now after Christ has come and has defeated Satan on the cross? Here we discover one of many reasons why one cannot, as is becoming increasingly popular, declare that God is finished with Israel and that the Church has taken her place.

The Necessity of Israel's Survival

Christ is coming back, is He not? That was His clear promise and it is the subject of this book. But if God is finished with Israel, what would be the purpose of Christ's return to the earth? He has promised to take the Church out of this world to heaven, so what further interest would Christ have in this earth if Israel no longer had any part in prophecy?

Of course, Christ is coming to confront and destroy the Antichrist. But why? He comes to destroy Antichrist's kingdom and to set up His own millennial reign. Where will His throne be? New York? Washington, D.C.? London? Paris? Berlin? Moscow? Indeed not. It will be in Jerusalem, where He will reign on the throne of His father David over the people of Israel.

The Jewish people scattered all over the earth must have survived as an identifiable ethnic unit and must be together in the promised land when the Messiah returns. It can't be otherwise. The prophets have declared it unequivocally and repeatedly.

The survival of the Jews as a national and ethnic group brought back into their land in the "last days" is absolutely essential to Christ's Second Coming. And so it will be. The Jews have been preserved as God promised. Hitler failed in his "final solution to the Jewish problem." The Muslims have failed repeatedly and will continue to fail to wipe out Israel.

The attempts will continue, for if Satan can succeed in destroying the Jews, he will have achieved at least a stalemate with God. The Bible's major prophecies, which all pertain to Israel back in her land when Messiah returns, could not be fulfilled. God would be proved a liar, discredited in His own universe. Thus, the fulfillment of the prophecies concerning Israel is crucial for God in His battle with Satan.

Replacing Israel

In spite of the clarity of the prophecies we have mentioned, there is a growing movement even among evangelicals today to deny that Israel any longer has any part in prophecy. Yes, it is admitted, the Jews may come to Christ for salvation and become part of the Church just as Gentiles may—but as a nation they have no place any longer in God's program. They have been rejected and cut off because they crucified their Messiah.

So goes this diabolical theory. By that reasoning, there is no significance whatsoever to the fact that the nation of Israel exists once again in her own land and that Jews are gathering there in unprecedented numbers from around the world. We have been robbed of a major verifiable evidence for the existence of God and that the Bible is His Word.

The further consequences are equally devastating. Thousands of verses must be ripped out of God's Word, leaving it mutilated beyond recognition. "Spiritualizing" the prophecies concerning Israel in an attempt to make them apply to the church is no better, for it strips Scripture of its literal application and thus of its strength.

Nearly every prophecy concerning the Second Coming is directly tied to Israel as a nation and to the land she must inhabit when her Messiah returns. The angels said that Jesus would come back to the Mount of Olives. When and why? Certainly not at the Rapture. He doesn't come there to catch away His bride, which is composed of the redeemed from every nation scattered all over the earth.

Neither the Mount of Olives nor the land of Israel has any special significance for the Church. Christ would have no reason to return to Israel unless His people were there and unless He intended to occupy the throne of David and rule over them from Jerusalem. That He would do so was stated repeatedly by the prophets as a solemn promise from God. Those prophecies must and will be fulfilled at the Second Coming—and are unrelated to the Rapture.

The Importance of the Land of Israel

Those who insist that the Church has replaced Israel often argue that there are no references in the New Testament to Israel restored to her land, and therefore such promises from the Old Testament are no longer of any effect. That statement simply isn't true. When he told Mary that she would give birth to the Messiah, the angel Gabriel declared explicitly that this One would reign "upon the throne of his father David." Here is a New Testament reference to Israel restored to her land and a reaffirmation of the promise to David concerning the messianic kingdom.

Other New Testament references to Israel's future in her land concern Armageddon (Revelation 16:16; 19:17-21) and Christ's rescue of Israel. Moreover, Christ, who is acknowledged as "the King of Israel" by His disciples (John 1:49; 12:13), promised the 12 that they would reign with Him over "the twelve tribes of Israel" (Matthew 19:28; Revelation 20:4, etc.)—obviously in the land of Israel.

The message of the angels at Christ's ascension, to which we have referred, was another New Testament reference to the land. They declared that it would be to the Mount of Olives just outside Jerusalem that He would return. That statement was a reaffirmation of Zechariah 14:4, which is all about the land of Israel. Furthermore, promises such as Jeremiah 31:35-37, which we have earlier quoted, hardly need to be reaffirmed!

Why does Jesus come back to the land of Israel? Surely it is not because the Church inhabits that land! He comes to rescue Israel at Armageddon. For that to be the case, God's ancient people must have been reestablished there. How, then, dare anyone say that Israel's national presence in her land today means nothing!

An Unbelieving Israel Must Be in the Land

Yes, Israel is back in her land in unbelief, but that is exactly what the Bible said would be the case. Israel as a whole will not believe in her Messiah until she sees Him come in power and glory to rescue her. At that time those who have rejected Christ will look upon Him whom they pierced and believe (Zechariah 12:10). That event will also fulfill two New Testament prophecies, one by Christ, the other by Paul: "But he that shall endure unto the end, the same shall be saved" (Matthew 24:13) and "all Israel shall be saved" (Romans 11:26).

There are those, both Jews and evangelicals, who argue against the presence of Israel in her land from a slightly different point of view. While admitting that the Jews will be returned by God to their land someday, they insist that this return to Israel cannot take place until after the Messiah has come. It takes little reflection to realize how utterly unscriptural such a view is.

The Messiah doesn't come to a land that is empty of inhabitants, or that is crowded with some other people who must be put out to let the Jews in. He comes back to a land that is occupied by His own people who rejected and still don't know Him. They are surrounded by the armies of the world determined to exterminate them.

Christ comes both to rescue His people at Armageddon and to reveal Himself to them. Where is Armageddon? It is in Israel. Why is this battle going to be fought? Because the Jews occupy that land. It is to His people, back in their land, that Christ comes! If they are not there, the Second Coming has no meaning and cannot even occur!

Israel's Central Role in the Kingdom

During the exciting 40 days that Christ spent with His disciples after His resurrection, He conversed with them "of the things pertaining to the kingdom of God" (Acts 1:3). He undoubtedly corrected their previous misunderstandings. One question remained, however, and the disciples asked it: "Lord, wilt thou at this time restore the kingdom to Israel?"

The wording of that question revealed the disciples' basic understanding of the teaching they had just received from Christ concerning the millennial kingdom: 1) that the kingdom would indeed be restored to Israel; 2) that the kingdom had not yet been established; and 3) that Christ, not the Church, was the only One who could restore it. Had any of these assumptions which are implied by their question been false, Christ surely would have corrected them. That He did not, leaves these three points intact.

Certainly He didn't say, as some teach today: "Don't you realize that since they crucified Me God has excommunicated the Jews? Israel no longer has any special place in God's plans. She has nothing to do with the kingdom. It all pertains to the Church now!" Instead, He simply replied: "It is not for you to know the times and seasons, which the Father hath put in his own power" (Acts 1:6).

Serious Consequences

We have noted some of the consequences of asserting that while God chose Israel and gave her special promises in the past, He rejected her when she crucified her Messiah. The most obvious logical deduction from this belief—and it is a growing teaching even among evangelicals—is that Israel, in spite of scores of prophecies to the contrary, has no more right to the land she now possesses than do the Arabs. That teaching makes God a liar.

Nor, according to this reasoning, is the land where God put His name (1 Kings 11:36) and which He said He would never forget (Leviticus 26:42), in spite of Israel's sins, any longer of any significance in God's plans. The Church, according to this doctrine, is now spiritual Israel, and all the promises God gave to Israel belong to her. The land, however, is an obvious exception.

The Church, being composed of scores if not hundreds of millions of people living around the world, has no need of the land of Israel. Indeed, the entire Church couldn't possibly all live in that tiny area. Therefore, the land no longer has any significance. This teaching is a direct denial of scores of prophecies promising the land to Israel forever.

Blessings and Curses

Of course, those who identify the Church with Israel are only interested in claiming her blessings, while leaving Israel with the curses God pronounced upon her. Such an approach encounters two major problems: 1) Most of the blessings God gave Israel, by their very nature, could never apply to the Church; and 2) the curses and the blessings go together, so that the Church cannot claim the one without accepting the other also.

Israel's greatest blessings, in fact, come in the restoration of that which she lost because of the curses of God that resulted from her disobedience. That fact alone makes it clear that Israel and the Church are two distinct entities.

No one tries to apply God's curses upon Israel (to be removed from her land and scattered throughout the world) to the Church, for they so obviously don't apply. Then the blessings that result from the undoing of those curses could not apply either. Yet almost every blessing that lies ahead for Israel is of that nature, and thus could not possibly be claimed by the Church.

Two Distinct Destinies

It is clear from even a cursory study of the prophecies pertaining to the Church and Israel that distinct destinies lie ahead for each. For example, the destiny of the people of Israel is to be brought back into their own land from every place where God has scattered them. The Church never had a land of its own, was never removed from it, and certainly can't be brought back to it. Her destiny is in heaven.

Both Israel and the Church play significant roles in the last days and specific prophecies pertain to each. Failure to distinguish between the two results in a serious distortion of biblical prophecy, especially that which pertains to the Rapture and the Second Coming of Christ.

The distinctives which separate Israel and the Church make inapplicable to the latter, for all time, the promises that God gave to Israel as recorded in numerous places in the Bible. The very nature of God's promises to Israel requires that they pertain to a specific ethnic group of people who lived in a particular location on the earth, were scattered from it, and returned thereto in the last days. In contrast, the Church, which was not in existence when these promises were made and isn't even mentioned in the Old Testament, far from being a single, ethnically identifiable people, is comprised of multitudes from "every kindred, and tongue, and people, and nation" (Revelation 5:9).

It cannot be stated too strongly that if we are to understand the Rapture and the Second Coming, then we must distinguish Israel from the Church. Otherwise we will confuse the distinct roles which each is to play. If we substitute the Church for Israel, then we will be hopelessly confused on prophecy and will not be able to discern the times in which we live, which are described in Scripture as "the last days."

CHAPTER 20

"This Generation"

> So likewise ye, when ye shall see all these things,
> know that [my coming] is near, even at the doors.
> Verily I say unto you, This generation shall not pass,
> till all these things be fulfilled (Matthew 24:33,34).

Christ here seems to be giving criteria by which His coming could possibly be dated, at least approximately. There is a generation which will not pass away until everything He has prophesied for the last days has been fulfilled. We know that all must be fulfilled also at the end of Daniel's seventieth week, so this should help us to discover when that will occur. Obviously what Christ has to say here is of great importance in our attempt to discern how close we are to His return.

There are, as always, some problems. To whom is Christ speaking—to Israel or to the Church? Is He referring to the Rapture or to the Second Coming? Who or what does He mean by "this generation"? Furthermore, as we have noted in an earlier chapter, the above statement seems, at least upon its face, to contradict verses 42 and 44: "For ye know not what hour your Lord doth come....For in such an hour as ye think not, the Son of man cometh."

A time was coming when all the signs of which He spoke would have been fulfilled before the eyes of a particular generation. On that basis they would realize that Christ's coming was right at the door. Yet at the same time He declares that no one will know when He will return. In fact, even those who are watching for Him are likely not to think that He is coming when He really is. Of course we know that both of these seemingly contradictory statements from our Lord are true and that there is no contradiction.

We have already pointed out that there is only one rational and Scriptural way to reconcile these two statements. Christ can only be referring to two different events: the Rapture and the Second Coming. There are no signs for the Rapture, which will take almost everyone by surprise. The signs are all for the Second Coming—which is why those who heed His Word would know exactly when He is right at the door about to enter the world scene once again. This time He comes not as a lamb to be led to the slaughter, but in power and glory and to take vengeance upon the enemies of God.

Two Opposing Views

Which generation will know exactly when the Second Coming is about to occur? Before whose eyes will all these signs be visibly fulfilled in such a way that they cannot mistake them? Since we know that these things must take place during the seventieth week of Daniel, the generation alive at that time is the one to whom Christ refers. But which generation is that?

As for the latter question, there are two major opposing views. They are held by preterists on the one hand and by futurists on the other. Preterists believe that all of the prophecies of the Olivet discourse and of the book of Revelation through midway into chapter 20 have already been fulfilled (most of them around the time of A.D. 70). Consequently, they consider "this generation" to refer to the generation of those who were alive at the time Christ spoke these words in A.D. 32. If we consider the length of a generation to be 40 years, then it would seem that the date of A.D. 70, when the temple and Jerusalem were destroyed, would support this view.

The futurists, while accepting as fulfilled those prophecies which can definitely be identified in that manner (such as the destruction of Jerusalem in A.D. 70), believe that most of these Scriptures just mentioned are yet to be fulfilled in a future period of time known as the "last days." They therefore believe that by "this generation" Christ referred to a future generation yet to live on earth.

Some futurists simply say that Christ was indicating that when these signs began to occur they would all take place within the lifespan of one generation. It seems unlikely, however, that Christ would be indicating that view. Daniel had already told us that everything would have to be fulfilled within a shorter period of time—the seven years of his seventieth week. Christ would certainly not extend that seven-year period to a generation, for to do so would contradict Daniel.

A Disappointing Interpretation

Other futurists hold the view that "this generation" refers to the generation alive when Israel returns to her land. Therefore, all the prophecies will have been fulfilled within a generation from 1948, when Israel became a nation again. Unfortunately, some futurists, calculating that 40 years represented a generation, predicted that all the signs would have come to pass including the end of the Great Tribulation, Armageddon, and the Second Coming in 1988. Those who believed in a pre-tribulation Rapture subtracted seven years from that date and arrived at 1981 as the year of the Rapture.

Of course, the Rapture didn't occur according to that schedule. Even the post-tribbers were disappointed, because the tribulation didn't arrive nor was the Antichrist revealed. The only option left for those who held this view was to suggest that a generation could be much longer than 40 years. One verse that is given to justify a much longer period as the length of a generation is Genesis 15:16. God tells Abraham that his descendants will come into the promised land of Canaan "in the fourth generation." Since Exodus 12:40 declares that the children of Israel spent 430 years in Egypt, "one generation," by that reckoning, would be more than 100 years.

While we still have nearly 50 years to wait to see whether the latter view is correct, it takes no time at all to demolish the preterist position. It is irrefutable that all of the signs and events of which Christ spoke in Matthew 24 had not occurred by A.D. 70. One wonders how anyone could hold to this position. Yet many do. Let us mention just a few of the reasons why the preterist view is a serious misperception.

A Past Fulfillment of All Can't Possibly Be True

In verse 21, Christ declared that a "great tribulation" was coming, "such as was not since the beginning of the world to this time, no, nor ever shall be." It is that last phrase, "nor ever shall be," which destroys the preterist view. The destruction of Jerusalem and slaughter of Jews at A.D. 70 may indeed have been the greatest tribulation until that time, but there have been some since that have been far worse. One need only mention the Nazi Holocaust to prove the point.

Verses 29-31 tell us that "immediately after the tribulation of those days shall the sun be darkened, and the moon shall not give her light, and the stars shall fall from heaven...and then shall appear the sign of the Son of man in heaven...and all the earth...shall see the Son of man coming in the clouds of heaven with power and great glory. And he shall send his angels...and they shall gather together his elect from the four winds, from one end of heaven to the other."

These events are very spectacular and would certainly be observed by the whole world, yet they are all conspicuous by their absence from recorded history. Obviously none of them had happened by A.D. 70, nor have they occurred to this day. That fact is not surprising inasmuch as the Great Tribulation which they are to follow has not taken place.

One scarcely need mention the plagues and devastation foretold in Revelation that will strike over the entire earth—none of which had occurred by A.D. 70—to provide further evidence that by "this generation" Christ did not mean the one living at the time He spoke these words. The Antichrist hadn't appeared (Nero, as we've seen, certainly didn't qualify), the Roman Empire hadn't been revived (it hadn't even been destroyed by A.D. 70)—and on and on we could go. These prophecies and many more are yet future and will run their course, as we have seen, in that seven-year period of great tribulation that coincides with Daniel's seventieth week and awaits the Rapture of the Church before it can begin to be fulfilled.

Is there any alternative at all to waiting another 40-plus years to see whether everything has been wrapped up by 2048? Yes, there is another interpretation of what Jesus meant by "this generation"—a view which the writer always held and perhaps others have held it as well. This view is clearly supported by Zechariah 12.

"This Generation"—An Oft-Used Phrase

The Olivet discourse was not the only time Jesus made reference to "generation." In fact, on numerous occasions He was rather specific in His description of a particular generation, the one I believe He had in mind in the prophecy in question. Twice He used the term "this generation," first of all in Matthew 11:16. There He seemed to refer to those alive at the time, for He made specific mention of their rejection of, and complaints they had voiced about, both John the Baptist and Himself. All other references to "generation" have a different quality about them.

The second reference to "this generation" would seem to be an unreasonable statement if He meant only those living at the time:

> That upon you may come all the righteous blood shed upon the earth, from the blood of righteous Abel unto the blood of Zacharias son of Barachias, whom ye slew between the temple and the altar. Verily I say unto you, All these things shall come upon this generation (Matthew 23:35,36).

The Zacharias to whom Christ refers was no doubt the priest named Zechariah who was stoned in the temple court when, in the days of King Joash, he called upon the people of Judah to repent (Zechariah 24:20,21).

That the full punishment for all the righteous blood shed upon earth, from Abel's death in at least 4000 B.C. to a priest's death by stoning about 1000 A.D., would all come upon one generation of Jews which was not alive at either time hardly makes sense. Thus we confront the probability, indeed, the necessity, that Christ had a larger meaning for "this generation."

Two verses earlier (23:33), we get a hint from these words of Jesus: "Ye serpents, ye generation of vipers, how can ye escape the damnation of hell?" Peter explained the only escape in his sermon at Pentecost; and his use of the same word hints further at a larger meaning: "And with many other words did he testify and exhort, saying, Save yourselves from this untoward generation" (Acts 2:40).

Characteristics, Not Time Period

An "untoward [perverse] generation" or a "generation of vipers" identifies a group of people not by the time in which they lived but by their characteristics. Certainly anyone living at any time who exhibited the same evil tendencies would also be part of that "generation of vipers." In fact, Christ used the same expression earlier and similar expressions often. Here are some of them, all from Matthew:

> 12:34—generation of vipers
> 12:39—evil and adulterous generation
> 16:4—wicked and adulterous generation
> 17:17—faithless and perverse generation

Jesus repeatedly linked the words *evil, wicked, adulterous, perverse,* and *faithless* with His use of the word *generation.* Certainly the generation to which He spoke was characterized by these adjectives of rebuke. However, Jesus also linked His hearers in their sin and unbelief to previous generations of Jews, whom He called the "fathers." In fact, Jesus does exactly that in the process of calling His hearers a "generation of vipers":

> Woe unto you, scribes and Pharisees, hypocrites! because ye build the tombs of the prophets, and garnish the sepulchres of the righteous. And say, If we had been in the days of our fathers, we would not have been partakers with them in the blood of the prophets. Wherefore ye be witnesses unto yourselves, that ye are the children of them which killed the prophets. Fill ye up then the measure of your

fathers. Ye serpents, ye generation of vipers, how can ye escape the damnation of hell? (Matthew 23:29-33).

It is quite clear that Christ indicts His hearers with the sins of their fathers. Why? Because they are related not only physically but by their evil hearts. If His hearers are a generation of vipers, then so must have been their "fathers" who lived before them and with whose sins He indicts them.

In his bold and convicting speech to those who were about to stone him, Stephen indicates that all the generations of Israel in the past have been idolaters and rebels against God and murderers of His prophets. One must read his entire brilliant discourse to savor the power of his argument, but we can't quote it all here. At the end he indicts those to whom he speaks with being the children of their fathers—i.e., resisting God and killing the prophets as the entire perverse and unbelieving generation of Israel has done since the beginning:

> Ye stiffnecked and uncircumcised in heart and ears, ye do always resist the Holy Ghost: as your fathers did, so do ye. Which of the prophets have not your fathers persecuted? and they have slain them which shewed before of the coming of the Just One; of whom ye have been now the betrayers and murderers: who received the law by the disposition of angels, and have not kept it (Acts 7:51-53).

It is clear from what both Jesus and Stephen said and from the record of Scripture that Israel has always been a perverse and evil generation of vipers. They have persistently rebelled against God and rejected and even killed the prophets He sent to them. The attitude of the Jews in His time toward Jesus was nothing new, nothing that had not been prophesied, nothing that was not to be expected—and it would continue.

What Jesus was saying, then, was that this same attitude among the Jews (not every individual but as a people) would persist until all was fulfilled. The generational sins of Israel would manifest themselves perpetually until the very end (though many individuals would repent and believe in their Messiah and thereby become part of the Church). The chosen people, generally, would remain resistant to God in their blindness and perversion until the very moment when Christ would appear in the midst of Armageddon to rescue them. Indeed, this is exactly what Zechariah prophesied as we have already noted:

> For I will gather all nations against Jerusalem to battle; and the city shall be taken....Then shall the Lord go forth, and fight against those nations....And his feet shall stand in that day upon the mount of Olives....And I will pour upon the house of David, and upon the inhabitants of Jerusalem, the spirit of grace and of supplications: and they shall look upon me whom they have pierced, and they shall mourn for him, as one mourneth for his only son, and shall be in bitterness for him, as one that is in bitterness for his firstborn. In that day there shall be a great mourning in Jerusalem....In that day there shall be a fountain opened to the house of David and to the inhabitants of Jerusalem, for sin and for uncleanness. And one shall say unto him, What are these wounds in thine hands? Then he shall answer, Those with which I was wounded in the house of my friends (Zechariah 12:10–14:4).

A Generation That Won't Pass Until All Is Fulfilled

One hears the complaint increasingly voiced among Christians these days: "Those unbelieving Jews don't deserve to be in that land! They are a bunch of atheists, agnostics, Christ-rejectors. It's merely a coincidence that they happen to be there. God's blessing can't possibly be upon them!"

Ah, yes, they don't deserve to be in that land any more than we deserve the forgiveness of our sins that has come by God's grace through the redemptive work of Christ. Nor are they there because they are worthy, but because of the promise which God made to Abraham, Isaac, and Jacob to bring their descendants back to their land in the last days.

Today's Jews are simply following in the footsteps of their fathers, proving that they are part of that same stubborn and unbelieving generation to which Christ referred. Their ancestors throughout history continually disobeyed God, yet He brought them into the promised land and patiently endured their perverseness for hundreds of years before finally casting them out. So what is new? And how else could the Messiah return to Jerusalem and find His people there being attacked by the armies of the world and have them repent when He rescues them? They *must* have returned there in unbelief. That "generation" could not have passed away.

Jesus said that "this generation" of perverseness and unbelief would not pass away until all was fulfilled. Exactly as He foretold, Israel remains a generation of unbelievers. Paul wrote, however, that all Israel would be saved. When will that take place? Not until "all these things be fulfilled," as Jesus said. When will that be? At Armageddon when Christ comes to rescue Israel.

Armageddon is the last event of the seventieth week. By this time all of the signs Christ gave have been witnessed on earth. Israel is surrounded by the armies of the world intent upon annihilating her. At that point, all signs having been fulfilled. Anyone who has studied the Bible would know that the Second Coming was about to occur. Even Antichrist knows Christ is coming and goes out to do battle with Him. We've already covered the Scriptures that assure us of this fact.

When they see the Lord Jesus Christ, whom they have rejected, coming to rescue them, all of Israel who have survived will at last know the truth and believe in Him. Only then will that generation of unbelieving rebels have passed away, but not until then.

While this chapter hasn't brought us any closer to knowing when the Second Coming will occur, it has dealt with a key element in understanding prophecy which we can't ignore. It is necessary to know what Christ meant by "this generation," lest we come to false conclusions concerning the timing of the Rapture.

CHAPTER 21

What About the Kingdom?

And this gospel of the kingdom shall be preached in all the world for a witness unto all nations; and then shall the end come (Matthew 24:14).

Now this I say, brethren, that flesh and blood cannot inherit the kingdom of God (1 Corinthians 15:50).

Verily, verily, I say unto thee, Except a man be born again, he cannot see the kingdom of God (John 3:3).

Fear not, little flock; for it is your Father's good pleasure to give you the kingdom (Luke 12:32).

Wherefore we receiving a kingdom which cannot be moved, let us have grace (Hebrews 12:28).

Many evangelicals believe that Matthew is declaring in the first verse cited above that the gospel must be preached to every tribe and tongue—and even, as some suggest, to every person on earth—before the Rapture can take place. If so, then Christ has set a precondition for His return that denies imminency. Surely He would not have said, "Let your loins be girded about, your lights burning; and ye yourselves like unto men that wait for their lord" (Luke 12:35,36) if He could not return until the gospel had been preached to every person on earth! Nor would Paul have encouraged the early Church to look, watch, and wait for the Lord's return. Therefore, such an interpretation cannot be accepted.

In fact, Christ is not setting a condition for the Rapture. That "blessed hope" should rather be called "the beginning" than "the end," for it ushers in the Day of the Lord and Daniel's seventieth week. It is "the end" which cannot come until the gospel of the kingdom has been declared to all nations. One must ask, "The end of what?" And what is meant by "witness unto all nations"?

Restoring God's Sovereign Rule

Since some preliminary end is not specified, Christ must mean the final end of Satan's and mankind's rebellion and the ushering in of God's new universe. That "the end" coincides with the final establishment of the kingdom of God in its eternal fullness is confirmed by Paul:

> Then cometh the end, when he [Christ] shall have delivered up the kingdom to God, even the Father; when he shall have put down all rule and all authority and power (1 Corinthians 15:24).

By "the end," Paul obviously means the consummation in final victory of God's battle with Satan and a full recovery, through Christ, of God's rightful rule over His universe. Christ destroyed Satan on the cross (Hebrews 2:14,15) and conquered death through His resurrection. He must yet rule over earth from David's throne, bringing the benefits of His victory to God's chosen people in fulfillment of prophetic promises. Ultimately, He must put down the final rebellion instigated by Satan at the end of the millennium. Thereafter, God will rule supreme over His eternal kingdom in a new universe into which sin and rebellion can never enter.

It is widely taught and thought that the "kingdom" in Scripture is the millennium. This is only partially true. The millennial reign of Christ is a temporary and earthly manifestation of the eternal kingdom. That the millennium, however, is not the ultimate kingdom is clear. The millennium is of limited duration and ends in a war, whereas the kingdom embodies endless peace. Obviously, the millennium does not measure up to the following descriptions of the kingdom:

Thy kingdom is an everlasting kingdom (Psalm 145:
13; Daniel 4:3; 2 Peter 1:11).

Of the increase of his government and peace there
shall be no end, upon the throne of David and upon
his kingdom, to order it and to establish...for ever
(Isaiah 9:7).

Flesh and blood cannot inherit the kingdom of God
(1 Corinthians 15:50).

Except a man be born again, he cannot see...[much
less] enter into the kingdom of God (John 3:3,5).

If God's true kingdom is eternal, then the "gospel of the
kingdom" prepares those who receive it, not for the millennium, but for eternity. Then what is the millennium?

What Is the Millennium?

In contrast to the above, the millennium is not eternal, its
peace is terminated by a war, and many flesh-and-blood people
who have not been born again inhabit the earth during that time.
They are the ones who will rebel against Christ when Satan is
loosed after 1000 years of imprisonment in the "bottomless pit"
(Revelation 20:2,7).

Christ's thousand-year reign upon David's throne is the
fulfillment of God's promises to Abraham, Isaac, Israel, and
David—but it is more than that. It is the final proof of the incorrigible nature of man's sinful heart. Christ is present in Jerusalem,
ruling the world, and the saints of all ages in resurrected bodies
administer the kingdom righteously under His direction. All evil
is prohibited and punished immediately. Even Satan is locked
away so that he cannot in any way influence mankind.

The earth becomes an Edenic paradise again, and it lasts for
1000 years. At the end of that time, Satan is released and is
given access to earth once more. Incredibly, he immediately
deceives multitudes of those who have known the benevolent
rule of Christ, have experienced only peace and plenty, and

who have until then been kept from demonic temptation. They follow Satan!

There has been no child abuse for 1000 years, no "dysfunctional families," no poverty or deprivation. None of the reasons given today for wrong behavior are present, yet evil lurks in the human heart and springs forth when it has the opportunity. This final rebellion of mankind against God will constitute the ultimate proof that the theories of the sociologists and psychologists, which blame evil upon environment and circumstances, are false.

Of course, the folly of such theories had already been fully demonstrated in the Garden of Eden. At the end of the millennium, however, it will no longer have been only Adam and Eve, but millions of their descendants who, in a perfect environment, nevertheless turn against God and give their allegiance to Satan. Morever, these millennial rebels will have had the full proof of sin's destructiveness and God's love and redemption—for the crucified and resurrected Christ has been reigning and living among them. The futile attack upon Jerusalem to tear Christ from His throne is the final attempt by Satan to take control of God's universe.

Clearly, these rebels, though they experienced Christ's millennial reign of perfect peace and righteousness, were never part of His kingdom. They had never believed the "gospel of the kingdom." What is that gospel?

There is only one true gospel. It offers eternal life as a free gift of God's grace through faith in the Lord Jesus Christ. Truly believing that He died for one's sins brings a new birth into God's family. That transformation brings one into loving submission to God's sovereign will throughout all eternity—a new life that will never end.

What did Christ mean that the gospel of the kingdom must be preached in all the world for a witness to all nations before the end could come? Surely, that gospel will be proclaimed in the fullness of its truth and power by Christ Himself during the millennium, and by us, the redeemed, reigning with Him in our resurrected, glorified bodies. But it will also be proclaimed in a most unusual and powerful way during the tribulation.

A Powerful Proclamation to the World

Christ is certainly not saying that this gospel must be preached to *every person*. Millions have already died without hearing it. Rather, it must be proclaimed in "all the world *for a witness to all nations*." That phrase sounds as though the day is coming when not only individuals but all the nations of the world will be powerfully confronted by the gospel and the consequences of rejecting it. John seems to have been shown such a time in his vision:

> And I will give power unto my two witnesses, and they shall prophesy a thousand two hundred and threescore days [1260 days, three-and-a-half years] clothed in sackcloth....And if any man will hurt them, fire proceedeth out of their mouth, and devoureth their enemies....These have power to shut heaven, that it rain not in the days of their prophecy: and have power over waters to turn them to blood, and to smite the earth with all plagues, as often as they will (Revelation 11:3-6).

What a dynamic and compelling message from God these two amazing evangelists will bring to "all nations"! No one can write them off as crazies, for they display incredible supernatural powers and defy the Antichrist and his underlings to stop them. No doubt they will be seen daily on international television in every corner of the earth as they warn mankind of God's coming judgment. The world police and even the military will be powerless to silence them. Anyone who attempts to stop them from preaching is instantly destroyed. Even Antichrist's satanic powers are no match for these two fearless and God-empowered preachers of truth.

There can be no doubt that these two witnesses will have the attention of the entire world! Their message will be a declaration to all the nations on this earth to repent and to acknowledge that Jesus Christ is the world's rightful ruler. The three-and-a-half years of their compelling preaching would seem to coincide with the first half of Daniel's seventieth week.

Many will believe the gospel they proclaim and will thereafter refuse to worship the Antichrist or to take his mark—and will be martyred for their faith.

At the end of 1260 days, Antichrist will at last be allowed by God to slay these two witnesses. Their dead bodies will lie in the street in Jerusalem for three-and-a-half days—one day for each year of their incredible testimony. Then, in the sight of a stunned and watching world, they will be resurrected and caught up to heaven.

At this same time ("in the midst of the [seventieth] week"—Daniel 9:27) Antichrist breaks his covenant with Israel, causing the temple sacrifice and worship to cease. He then sets his image in the temple and demands to be worshiped as God. From that time, his evil empire begins to unravel under the outpouring of God's wrath as the world moves ever closer to all-out war against Israel.

The Great Tribulation

Thus commences the last half of Daniel's seventieth week, known as the Great Tribulation. Antichrist's betrayal of Israel marks the beginning of a period of worldwide persecution of Jews which is far more intense than anything they have experienced in the past. Jeremiah calls it "the time of Jacob's trouble" (30:7). Israel will not take this lying down. The growing conflict will engage all nations and culminate at last in Armageddon.

Most likely at this same time Antichrist is given authority by God "to make war with the saints and to overcome them" (Revelation 13:7). If the Church has been Raptured, who are these "saints"? They can only be those who had not rejected the gospel before the Rapture but who, during the tribulation period, hear it and believe in Christ. Those who have previously heard and rejected the gospel—"received not the love of the truth that they might be saved" (2 Thessalonians 2:10)—will be given a "strong delusion that they should believe [Antichrist's] lie" (v. 11). Apparently, no one in this category will any longer have the opportunity to believe the truth.

Instead, God will help them to believe the very lie they have wanted to believe in rejecting the gospel.

Inasmuch as those who believe the gospel during the tribulation and become followers of Christ will be killed, a post-trib Rapture would be a classic nonevent. There would be few if any believers to catch up to heaven, all of them having been slain by Antichrist for refusing to worship him and to receive his mark (Revelation 13:15). Multitudes will believe the gospel and be true to Christ during Daniel's seventieth week and will pay for that faith with their lives:

> I saw under the altar the souls of them that were slain for the word of God, and for the testimony which they held: And they cried with a loud voice, saying, How long, O Lord, holy and true, dost thou not judge and avenge our blood on them that dwell on the earth? And white robes were given unto every one of them; and it was said unto them, that they should rest yet for a little season, until their fellowservants also and their brethren, that should be killed as they were, should be fulfilled. After this I beheld, and, lo, a great multitude, which no man could number, of all nations, and kindreds, and people, and tongues, stood before the throne, and before the Lamb....These are they which came out of great tribulation, and have washed their robes, and made them white in the blood of the Lamb...and they loved not their lives unto death (Revelation 6:9-11; 7:9-14; 12:11).

The "Gospel of the Kingdom"

What is this "gospel of the kingdom" which the two witnesses and the 144,000 Jewish evangelists (Revelation 7:3-8) will proclaim and which leads to the martyrdom of those who believe it? Many evangelicals distinguish between the gospel of Christ which we now preach, and the gospel of the kingdom which Christ and His disciples announced at the beginning and which will be proclaimed during the tribulation period. They suggest that those who believe this "gospel of the kingdom" are not part of the Church, but will be allowed to continue on earth into the millennial reign of Jesus Christ.

Allegedly, this gospel pertains only to the millennial kingdom and was offered by Christ exclusively to the Jews. In other words, the gospel of the kingdom presumably called upon Israel to recognize her Messiah and to submit herself willingly to Him as the One whose right it was to rule over her from David's ancient throne. When Israel rejected and crucified Christ, the gospel of the kingdom ceased, the Church was born and began to proclaim the gospel of the grace of God. Such a "dispensational" view, however, cannot be sustained from Scripture.

Mark 13 is the passage parallel to Matthew 24. It gives the same statement by Christ about the gospel being preached throughout all the world prior to the end, but leaves out the phrase, "of the kingdom." Mark simply says, "And the gospel must first be published among all nations" (13:10). Which gospel? There is only one. It is called "the everlasting gospel" (Revelation 14:6).

"The gospel of the kingdom" was the only gospel which Christ preached: "And Jesus went about all Galilee... preaching the *gospel of the kingdom*" (Matthew 4:23). It must therefore have been the gospel of which Christ spoke when He told His disciples to "go into all the world and preach the gospel" (Mark 16:15). There is no indication that He meant any other gospel than the one He had been preaching and which He must have trained them to preach as well. Clearly, it was the only gospel the disciples knew, even after the resurrection (Acts 8:12). It was also the gospel Paul preached:

> And now, behold, I know that ye all, among whom I have gone preaching the kingdom of God, shall see my face no more [Paul to the Ephesian elders] (Acts 20:25).

> And Paul dwelt two whole years in his own hired house [during his imprisonment in Rome], and

> received all that came in unto him, preaching the
> kingdom of God (Acts 28:30,31).

"The gospel of the kingdom" is an expression that occurs
only five times in the Bible (Matthew 4:23; 9:35; 24:14; Mark
1:14,15). Nowhere in the New Testament is there any hint that
it differed from the gospel we preach today. Nor is there any
indication of a time when a transition was made from a gospel
which brought hearers into the kingdom to a gospel which
brought hearers into the Church.

The question arises, however, how, prior to the death and
resurrection of Christ, the disciples could preach a gospel
which included those truths when they did not as yet understand them. The fact is that every promise of salvation in the
Old Testament, either to Israel or to the Gentiles, depended
for its realization upon the coming Messiah and His redemptive
death upon the cross. That He would be rejected and die for
our sins in fulfillment of the Old Testament sacrifices was foretold by the prophets, as we have seen. Although the disciples
did not understand these truths, nevertheless they pointed their
hearers to the One whom they believed to be the Messiah.

That the "everlasting gospel" has not changed from the
beginning is clear from the fact that Paul could take the Old
Testament and preach from it the same gospel we preach
today. The Bereans checked Paul's preaching against the Old
Testament and found it biblical (Acts 17:11). Paul preached
what he called "the gospel of God, which he promised afore
by his prophets in the holy scriptures, concerning his Son Jesus
Christ our Lord" (Romans 1:1-3). It was preached according to
the progressive revelation available at the time. Today, we
enjoy the full revelation of its meaning.

If we do not preach this gospel in its fullness—the very same
gospel which Paul preached—we are cursed (Galatians 1:8,9). Is
it the "gospel of the kingdom"? Indeed it is, for only those who
believe it can be made new creatures in Christ Jesus and inhabit
the new universe God will one day make. That perfect, eternal
state in which the redeemed of all ages will ultimately dwell in
loving submission to God is the promised kingdom.

True "Apostolic Succession"

If the gospel of the kingdom was what Paul and the apostles preached both to Jews and Gentiles, then it must be the very gospel which we are to preach today. If ours is a different gospel from that preached by Christ and His disciples, how were we to learn about this new gospel and when were we commissioned to preach it? There is no answer to such questions in Scripture.

Just as Christ discipled the 12, so they were told to make disciples. These new disciples were to be instructed to observe everything which Christ had taught and commanded the original 12 to observe. Christ's disciples were commanded by our Lord to pass on to their converts everything He had taught them during those years when they had been under His discipline and instruction day and night: "Teaching them to observe [obey] *all things* whatsoever I have commanded you" (Matthew 28:20).

How could the disciples' converts obey everything Christ had commanded the original 12 unless they received the same authority and power to do so? If words mean anything, then all powers and responsibilities which Christ conferred upon His original disciples were to be passed by them to their converts. These new disciples, in turn, were to make more disciples, who would likewise be taught to obey all that Christ had commanded the original 12. Here was true "apostolic succession"!

Apostolic succession does not bestow (as the Roman Catholic Church falsely claims) privileges, responsibilities, and powers upon a select class of clergy, priests, bishops, and popes. No, these blessings accrue equally to every person who becomes a disciple of Christ. This chain of command from Christ through His disciples to their converts and on to their converts' converts has come down to every Christian today. By God's grace, we have been given the same obligation and privilege of preaching in all the world the same gospel of the kingdom which the original apostles preached, for we are the disciples of those who were made disciples by them. Every true Christian is a successor to the apostles!

Confusion concerning the kingdom has relegated many of Christ's teachings, such as the Sermon on the Mount, to Israel and the millennium, causing Christians today to miss much of value for their own lives. Some evangelicals go so far as to say that the four Gospels are only for Israel and the millennium, while the epistles are for the Church. Yet, it was in the Gospels that Christ founded His Church, and it is there that we find the foundational truths.

At the other extreme are the Reconstructionists, the Reformed or Covenant theologians, and the Kingdom Now Dominionists who take for the Church what belongs to Israel. These generally imagine that we are in the millennial kingdom right now and that the Church has the responsibility to establish this kingdom by progressively taking over the world in the name of Christ. Some even teach that Satan is locked up, though one would certainly not suspect it. Some of the leaders in these movements even suggest the use of physical *violence* to accomplish their misguided takeover of the world.

Are We Already in the Kingdom?

Speaking to a group of Pharisees who were questioning Him, Christ said, "The kingdom of God is within you" (Luke 17:21). Unfortunately, the King James rendering, though generally the best, needs improvement here. Surely, the kingdom of God was not within the *Pharisees*. Yes, the kingdom of God is established in the hearts of those who believe in Jesus, and He begins to reign as Lord in their lives. But Christ was speaking to unbelievers in whom He did not dwell. The Greek also means "in your midst" or "among you," which was no doubt what Christ meant. He, the King, was in their midst, but they were going to reject and even crucify Him.

While the kingdom is here now, it only exists invisibly in the hearts of believers where the King already reigns. There is as yet no outward, visible manifestation of the kingdom taking authority over the ungodly and even animals living at peace with one another and mankind as there will be when Christ personally rules upon earth. That He will do so is promised repeatedly by Old Testament prophets and is also declared in the New Testament. The angel Gabriel told Mary:

> And behold, thou shalt conceive in thy womb, and bring forth a son, and shalt call his name Jesus. And he shall be great, and shall be called the Son of the Highest: and the Lord God shall give unto him the throne of his father David: And he shall reign over the house of Jacob for ever; and of his kingdom there shall be no end (Luke 1:31-33).

God's promises to Abraham, Isaac, and Jacob concerning the future of Israel are repeated and reaffirmed both in the Old and New Testaments, and cannot be annulled. Yet Reformed or Covenant and Dominion theology replaces Israel with the Church. As a corollary, it denies the personal reign of Christ in a future millennium. Covenant theologians insist that God's visible, worldwide kingdom is in place now and that He is reigning over it from heaven through the Church. This rejection of a future kingdom for Israel and application to the Church of prophecies meant for Israel has created a popular and dangerous teaching among many of today's evangelicals—a teaching which could not be more in opposition to Scripture.

A Dangerous Delusion

The Bible declares that when Christ resurrects the dead saints He simultaneously catches up all living Christians together with them to meet Him in the air and to escort them to heaven. The language concerning the resurrection and the Rapture, which we have quoted already, could not be clearer:

> For the Lord himself shall descend from heaven with a shout...and the dead in Christ shall rise first: then we which are alive and remain shall be caught up together with them in the clouds, to meet the Lord in the air: and so shall we ever be with the Lord (1 Thessalonians 4:16,17).

Nevertheless, as we have already noted, it is being taught that at His return, rather than taking Christians to heaven, Christ joins them upon earth to rule over a kingdom which the Church has established for Him. While this is not Reformed theology, it is closely related thereto, and those of Reformed persuasion, especially Reconstructionists, often identify with the charismatics and Pentecostals who promote the "Kingdom Now" teaching.

The irreconcilable contradiction between such beliefs and the Bible could not be more obvious nor could the consequences be more serious. While we have earlier referred to these consequences, the warning bears repeating.

The real Jesus Christ will catch us up to meet Him in the air and take us to heaven. Then what of those who look forward to meeting their "Christ" with their feet planted upon earth—a Christ who has arrived to take over the "kingdom" they've established for Him? They have been working for Antichrist! His counterfeit kingdom will be established upon earth through a great peace-and-unity movement which will eliminate all political and religious differences worldwide. It is that new world order which Christ will destroy at His Second Coming (Daniel 2:44; 2 Thessalonians 2:8).

"Reformed" and "Dispensational" Views

The system of belief which includes a pre-trib Rapture and a distinction between Israel and the Church is broadly called "dispensationalism." This systematic way of interpreting the Bible has been attributed to J.N. Darby and C.I. Scofield, among others, and is widely taught among evangelicals and at such dispensationalist institutions as Dallas Theological Seminary. There are, however, several variations within dispensationalism—distinctions of which it is not necessary to take note.

The major opposition to dispensationalism among evangelicals comes from "Reformed" or "Covenant" theology. Again there are variations within these views which we don't have time to discuss, so we will be speaking broadly. Proponents of Reformed theology claim that its view of eschatology (post-millennial or amillennial) is the majority view today and that it

234 ço When Will Jesus Come?

held sway throughout history until the early 1800s, when Darby popularized dispensationalism. Indeed, post-millennialism or amillennialism (the small distinction between the two is unimportant to our discussion) did dominate the religious scene because they were Roman Catholic doctrines and anything else was punished as heresy.

It seems odd for those who claim a Reformation heritage to defend their views by saying that they were always held by the Roman Catholic Church! Indeed, when it comes to eschatology, Reformed theology is poorly named. It retained Roman Catholic views which had developed as a result of Rome's apostasy. Claiming to be the true Israel, the Roman Catholic Church became obsessed with taking over the world and lost the hope of the Rapture.

Following in Rome's footsteps, Luther and Calvin made their alignments with the secular powers of this world. Reformed theology retained the Catholic view that we are in the millennium now, that the Church is in the process of taking over the world and even that Satan has already been locked up. Imminency is rejected. Christ is allowed to return only at the end of the millennium.

Revelation 20 twice declares that the saints reign with Christ over the earth for 1000 years and that this reign follows a future battle of Armageddon. Nevertheless, such Scriptures are not taken literally by those of Reformed persuasion. Instead, the millennium is already present and will last not a literal 1000 years but for an indefinite period of time—perhaps many thousands of years.

While some Covenant theologians claim to believe that a rapture will occur at the end of their indefinite and very lengthy "millennium" (or non-millennium, as the case may be), it is certainly not what is described in 1 Thessalonians 4:13-18. Rather they propose simply a final judgment followed by the commencement of the eternal state. Nor does a rapture of any kind that far in the future have any motivating effect upon us today.

Armageddon, rather than being a future literal battle involving earth's armies in an attack upon Israel as the prophets testify, is seen as symbolic of the ongoing spiritual conflict between Christ and the forces of darkness. The fact that the resurrection clearly takes place before the millennium begins (Revelation 20) is again ignored. Whatever doesn't fit their theories is spiritualized to bring it into harmony with the Reformed, Covenant, or Dominion view.

Loosely Handling the Word of Truth

There is no recognition that Daniel's seventieth week has not yet run its course. Instead, it is vaguely assumed that all 70 weeks have come and gone without accounting specifically for the events which were to have occurred within that time frame. Daniel 2:44 is taken to mean that the kingdom will be established during the days of the ancient Roman Empire, thus supporting the teaching that it began when Christ was here the first time. That this verse specifically states that the kingdom will be established when ten kings (the ten toes) are reigning is ignored. Thus, there is no need for the Roman Empire to be revived at all, much less under ten heads.

Amazingly, the unscriptural view that the Church must gradually take over the world for Christ and in this manner establish the kingdom is growing in popularity. Yet the prophecies clearly indicate a cataclysmic inauguration of the kingdom by Christ's personal intervention. Surely the "stone cut out without hands" (a type of Christ, the Rock) which smashes Nebuchadnezzar's image and fills the whole earth indicates a sudden destruction of the kingdoms of earth and the establishment of God's kingdom by Christ's intervention. The same is true of the account in Revelation 19 where Christ comes to intervene at Armageddon, as well as the parallel account in Zechariah 12–14 and other passages. All of these are generally spiritualized or explained away in Reformed, Covenant, and Dominion eschatologies.

Christ's statement, "All authority is given me in heaven and earth" (Matthew 28:18), becomes the basis for the claim that Christians are therefore, in the strength of that authority, to take over the media, the schools, and the government until they reign over the world for Christ. Most Reformed theologians are Calvinists, so there is no room for human choice and thus no explanation for varying degrees of evil in the world. Everything depends upon how much "irresistible" and "common" grace God provides. As He apportions more and more, the world will gradually improve and the percentage of Christians will grow. Why God has not extended such grace in larger quantities and earlier is not explained.

The simple fact is that God has always been sovereign. Even so, His supreme authority did not prevent the rebellion of Satan in heaven, nor the disobedience of Adam and Eve on earth. They each made their independent choice just as people are doing today. Yet with God's authority the Church is expected to do what God Himself hasn't done—take over the world. Anyone who is not willing to exercise Christ's authority for that purpose is considered a defeatist.

Seemingly forgotten is the fact that Christ and His apostles were slain by the ungodly. The cross was Christ's great triumph. Those who are victorious over Antichrist die as martyrs at his hands: "And they overcame him by the blood of the Lamb, and by the word of their testimony; and they loved not their lives unto the death" (Revelation 12:11). Here is true victory, the way of the cross!

God's kingdom is made possible through the cross of Christ. Evil is not conquered by bluster and force, but by submission to God's will. And that means accepting His remedy for sin. Only then can paradise be restored fully and eternally.

Paradise Restored

When Adam and Eve were cast out of the garden for rebellion, the Tree of Life was guarded by the flaming sword of God's judgment. Mankind fled that sword, for its piercing would bring eternal death. The world has alternately cowered, complained that such judgment was too harsh, and even denied that it was real. But there was no way around that sword. Mankind must die and be reborn into God's family.

One day a perfectly sinless man who was, in fact, God and man in one Person, walked up to that sword and took its deadly blow in His heart for us. His blood quenched its flame and thus gave access to the Tree of Life. He is "the way, the truth and the life" to all who believe that He took God's just judgment for them.

Amazingly, the world rejected Him and plunged its own sword of hatred and pride through His heart. For to accept His sacrifice one had to admit one's sin, that God's penalty was just, and that restoration to fellowship with God could only come as a free gift of His grace through Christ's death in our place. Pride has prevented that admission for multitudes and robbed them of God's gracious forgiveness and the eternal life He gives.

Kings and priests, gurus of religion and humanism, ecologists, anthropologists, psychologists, sociologists, revolutionaries, and political leaders of all stripes have offered their solutions. There was, after all, so they promised, a way around that sword. Paradise could be restored if we would all get together, cooperate, love one another, share equally—and especially follow them. But their self-improvement programs miserably failed. Evil masqueraded as good and the world grew worse.

God is patient, but His judgment comes at last. Evil was so great in Noah's day that finally God cleansed the earth with a flood. The wickedness of Sodom and Gomorrah became such a stench that God destroyed them with fire. Today's Sodomites have become a favored class wielding great power. They educate our children in our schools, propagandize through the media, hold public offices, and even preach from our pulpits.

God is not mocked. His patience wears thin. Babies are murdered in the womb by the millions; marriage is ridiculed; sex, science, success, and pleasure are worshiped. Perversion of all kinds is flaunted in God's face. Judgment must fall upon a world that is at least as wicked and probably more so than the world of Noah and Lot. How close are we?

Paradise will be restored. A new universe will be created. But the cleansing of judgment must come first. That righteous retribution cannot be delayed much longer. Praise God, He has promised that the Rapture comes before God's wrath is poured out in vengeance upon this earth. We must be very close indeed to that most wonderful event—and, unfortunately, to the horror for unbelievers that will follow.

Chapter 22

How Close Are We?

> But and if that evil servant shall say in his heart, My Lord delayeth his coming....The Lord of that servant shall come in a day when he looketh not for him (Matthew 24:48-50).

> While the bridegroom tarried, they all slumbered and slept. And at midnight there was a cry made, Behold the bridegroom cometh; go ye out to meet him.... Watch therefore, for ye know neither the day nor the hour wherein the Son of man cometh (Matthew 25:5,6,13).

Let us summarize briefly the conclusions we have reached from carefully comparing Scripture with Scripture. In the preceding chapters we have noted a number of seeming contradictions in what Christ and the apostles said about His return: He comes at a time of peace and yet in the midst of war; He comes when no one would expect Him and yet He comes when all of the prophesied signs have been displayed to the world and even Antichrist knows He is about to descend to earth; He comes when judgment is the last thing anyone on earth would expect, yet He comes to a world very much aware that God's divine wrath and judgment are being poured out upon it.

We have found that the only possible way to reconcile these contrary statements is to recognize that they are referring to two separate events: the Rapture and the Second Coming. The differences may be simplified in this way: 1) At the Rapture, Christ comes for His saints at a time of peace and business as usual before the tribulation; whereas 2) at the Second Coming seven years later, He comes from heaven with all of His saints (they must have previously been taken there) to rescue Israel in the midst of Armageddon at the end of the Great Tribulation.

Two Solemn Warnings

There are two solemn and related warnings that Christ gave concerning His coming again. First of all, He repeatedly and earnestly declared that He was coming very soon and should be expected at any moment. That He hasn't come in almost 2000 years, far from discrediting that promise, makes it all the more urgent that we heed it in our day. By heaven's reckoning Christ has been gone a very short time; and His coming is nearer now than it ever was.

He told His disciples nearly 2000 years ago, "Let your loins be girded about, and your lights burning; and ye yourselves like unto men that wait for their lord" (Luke 12:35,36). If that was to be their attitude, how much more should we be anticipating His momentary coming in our day! Christ's words are clear and to the point. They cannot be reinterpreted to fit one's theories. In the plainest, unmistakable language He told us to expect Him at any moment. Dare we ignore His command?

Yet most Christians live as though Christ never made such statements. It is almost frightening to see and hear those who claim to believe in the Rapture deny it with their lives and lips. Christian businesspeople become absorbed in long-range programs stretching all the way to retirement. Pastors enthuse over their five-year and ten-year building programs and rehearse their meticulous plans for future church expansion. Housewives and students have their long-range dreams as well—all involving this present world.

We are not suggesting that plans should not be made, but only that recipes for one's future on this earth should always be contingencies *in case* the Rapture should not occur. One's expectation of Christ's return should be greater than one's expectation of remaining here upon earth. Sadly it seems to be the opposite. The qualifier, "If the Lord tarries and spares us," is scarcely heard as Christians talk and even boast of what they expect to be doing tomorrow, next week, next year, and on into the future.

The Second Warning

Secondly, He warned us about preoccupation with the things of this life. Christ knew the attraction that the pleasures and ambitions of this world, wicked though we realize it to be, can have for each of us. So He warned us that unless we kept the thought of His return fresh in our hearts at all times we would be caught by surprise at His coming.

He warned that He would come when the Church would be characterized by sleepy complacency and when many would even be entertaining wishful thoughts of a delay to His return. It would be at a time when He was least expected and even His own were in danger of being caught by surprise. Such warnings, which could not apply to Israel, clearly tell us that the Gospels, contrary to what some teach, are not only for Israel but for the Church as well.

Most dispensationalists insist, for example, that the Rapture is not in the Gospels. Specifically they say it isn't to be found in the Olivet discourse, which they claim is only for Israel. Obviously that can't be true. What coming will catch Israel by surprise? Surely not the Second Coming to rescue her at Armageddon, for all the signs have been displayed and even Antichrist knows Christ is about to descend from heaven to confront him.

Surely the complacency Christ warned about and the desire for the Messiah to delay His coming would not fit the Jewish situation when Christ comes to rescue Israel. It will be just the opposite. Far from sleepy and complacent, Israel will be in desperate straits under all-out attack by the armies of the world's most powerful nations.

Seeing the Vital Distinction Again

Undergoing destruction by overwhelmingly superior forces and about to suffer total defeat, Israel's only possible hope would be the immediate appearance of the Messiah to effect a miraculous rescue. It is, therefore, inconceivable that any Jew at that time would be hoping for a delay in Messiah's coming. On the contrary, Israel's inhabitants will be desperately crying out for Him to appear—not necessarily out of any real faith, but driven by the hopelessness and horror facing them.

Here we see again the clear distinction between Israel and the Church and between the Rapture and the Second Coming. Christ's warnings in Matthew 24 and elsewhere about complacency and surprise at His coming and even desiring it to be delayed could not apply at all to Israel in the midst of Armageddon. None of the statements by Christ quoted at the beginning of the chapter could possibly apply to Israel and the Second Coming.

Such language could only apply to the Church and the Rapture. We are forced to conclude that Christ did not have the Second Coming in mind when He warned that He would come like a thief when His followers would be complacently establishing themselves in the world and making long-term plans. "Watch, therefore...lest coming suddenly he find you sleeping" (Luke 13:35,36) is an exhortation that would certainly be unnecessary in the midst of Armageddon!

It is, however, a warning which Christians need to hear and heed. Moreover, there is an even more solemn forecast from our Lord. Complacency and finding one's hopes and joys in the world are bad enough. Yet Christ warned that He would come when the Church would not only be sleeping, but would be convinced that He was *not* coming: "Therefore be ye also ready: for in such an hour as ye think not the Son of man cometh" (Matthew 24:44).

It seems inconceivable that any Christian could ever think or say, "I don't think Christ is coming now." Jesus declares that He is coming at precisely such a time. How that warning should stir our hearts to watch and wait and to be ready for His return at any moment!

A Day Which Anyone Can Date

We discover another contrast between the Rapture and the Second Coming. Concerning the former, Christ declared unequivocally: "But of that day and hour knoweth no man, no, not the angels of heaven, but my Father only" (Matthew 24:36). How do we know He's referring to the Rapture and not the Second Coming? Very simply, because the day of the Second Coming can and will be known.

Daniel, who gave the precise date Jesus would enter Jerusalem and be hailed as the Messiah, provides similar data for calculating the exact day of Christ's return in triumph to the City of David. He tells us that Antichrist will break his covenant with Israel "in the midst of the week...[and] cause the sacrifice and oblation to cease" (9:27). One need, therefore, only count three-and-a-half years (1260 days) from that event to know the very day of the Second Coming at the end of Daniel's seventieth week of years.

The book of Revelation gives additional data confirming this timetable. The two witnesses are killed 1260 days into the last week of years—i.e., "in the midst [middle] of the week" (Revelation 11:3,7). Again, one need only count, from that event as well, 1260 days to arrive at the date of the Second Coming. As we have already seen, the woman of Revelation 12, obviously a symbol for Israel inasmuch as she gives birth to the Messiah "who was to rule all nations with a rod of iron" (v. 5), is persecuted by Satan for 1260 days (v. 6). She is protected by God for "a time [one year], times [two years], and half a time" [a total of three-and-a-half years].

Thus, Revelation tells us in more than one way that three-and-a-half years into the tribulation period ("in the midst of the week"—Daniel 9:27), when Antichrist breaks his covenant and stops the temple worship, he will begin to persecute Israel. At this point, the period known as the Great Tribulation begins. It will last for another three-and-a-half years or the last half of Daniel's seventieth week. Using this criteria also, one need only count 42 months from Antichrist's image being placed in the temple to arrive at the end of "the time of Jacob's trouble" (Jeremiah 30:7) and the Second Coming.

Of course, the date of the Second Coming cannot be known as yet. Everything hinges upon the Rapture (which cannot be dated) and is calculated from the moment of that event. Once the Church has gone, whose formation stopped God's time clock concerning Israel at the end of 69 weeks, and whose continued presence perpetuates that hiatus, Daniel's seventieth week will begin to run its course. Counting seven years from that time, the day of the Second Coming can be determined and even double-checked by following the fulfillment of the other prophesied events we've mentioned.

Why the Day of the Rapture Must Remain Unknown

It takes little thought to realize why God must keep the date of the Rapture as His secret. Suppose, for example, that the Bible indicated the date of the Rapture to be 2003. What a discouragement it would have been for believers during the 19 centuries leading up to this time! And what an encouragement to carnality and worldly living it would have been to know that the Lord couldn't come at any moment and catch one by surprise doing, perhaps, those things that no Christian should. Much would have been lost by giving the date of the Rapture—and nothing would have been gained.

If 2003 could have been calculated from Scripture as the time for the Rapture, the early Church would not have been waiting and looking for Christ, as indeed she was. The "blessed hope" could not have been a hope at all, even for us today, for one doesn't "hope" for something to happen if he knows exactly when it will occur. Of course, "hope" for the Christian has an element of confidence as well, for he is assured of its realization. But if the event couldn't take place for many years, then hope would be lost until that time arrived.

Hope purifies: "Everyone who has this hope in him purifies himself even as he is pure" (1 John 3:3). Yes, we know this event will occur eventually. However, the major impact of that hope in its purifying effect would have been lost to the Church through the centuries had a date been given for either the Rapture or the Second Coming. Nor would the Church today have that "blessed hope" (Titus 2:13) of being Raptured at any moment if Christ could not come until some future date or until after Antichrist's appearance, or after the tribulation or some other event or until some prior condition was met.

Of course Christ has always known exactly when He would rapture the Church. He knew that almost 2000 years would go by before His return. Why, then, would He urge His saints to watch for His coming when hundreds of millions would be watching in vain? Ah, no one watches in vain. The expectation of Christ's imminent return is the major motivation for godly living. Christ did not want to rob His own of that purifying expectancy.

How close are we? The Rapture could always have been—and still could be at this moment—only a heartbeat away. To wish to know the date of Christ's return, however, is to wish for that which He will not give and which would not be for our good. If we knew that He wouldn't come until a year from now, we would have lost the hope that He could come at any moment. Lost, too, would be that hope's motivating power which comes from knowing that we might not have another day and so must live and witness for Him as though each day were our last.

Such is the problem with the thesis, now gaining increasing acceptance, that the Rapture will occur when the last trump sounds at the Feast of Trumpets. Christ may indeed rapture His bride at that time. However, if that were clearly stated in Scripture, then each time that date passed with hope unfulfilled, one would know that His return would be delayed for another year. That knowledge, as Christ makes very plain, would not be in the best interests of the Church, but would most assuredly foster evil.

How Close Do You Want It to Be?

How close are we? Christ could come at any moment—before I finish writing this page, or before you finish reading it. Does that thought bring joy or regret—perhaps even fear? The honest answer to that vital question reveals one's spiritual condition and the measure of one's love for Him.

Whether or not we truly long for Christ's return and are ready for Him to come at any moment will obviously affect how we live. To awaken each morning with the joyful anticipation that this could be the day when Christ will catch away

His own from earth to heaven transforms our daily lives as nothing else could. The firm conviction that Christ could come at any moment—and the desire for Him to do so—is surely the secret to victorious and holy living.

Such is the message which Paul conveys in Colossians 3. One cannot find another chapter in the Bible that contains a more complete description of what the Christian life ought and ought not to be. And the key to victory which Paul presents is the hope of Christ's return.

Verse 5 begins by telling us to put to death the deeds of the flesh. The list goes on for several verses: "immorality, impurity, passion, evil desire, and greed...anger, wrath, malice, slander, and abusive speech and lying." Verses 12-25 list the Christlike virtues we are to embody as He lives through us: "a heart of compassion, kindness, humility, gentleness and patience; bearing with one another, and forgiving each other...as the Lord forgave you, so also should you...and put on love and let the peace of Christ rule in your hearts."

A key word in verses 5 and 12 was deliberately left out in the paragraph above. The word is *therefore*. It takes us back to the first four verses in the chapter. Here is what they say:

> If ye then are risen with Christ, seek those things which are above, where Christ sitteth on the right hand of God. Set your affection on things above, not on things on the earth. For ye are dead, and your life is hid with Christ in God. When Christ, who is your life, shall appear, then shall ye also appear with him in glory. Mortify *therefore* your members. Put on, *therefore,* as the elect of God.

Imminency: Its Purifying and Motivating Power

The life we live as Christians draws its incentive and strength from the realization that we are dead to sin, self, and this world, and draws equally from the hope of momentarily seeing Christ and of being eternally in His presence. All that we say and do is with the sure knowledge that our life is hid with

Christ in God and that when He shall appear we will appear with Him to God's glory. That hope inspires us to mortify the deeds of the body and to put on the virtues of Christ.

Contrary to what the critics say, the hope of Christ's imminent return doesn't lead to spiritual lethargy or an escapist mentality which shuns responsibility and trial. Rather it causes us to witness more earnestly and to live holier lives, knowing that very little time for doing so may remain.

Such was the impact this hope had upon the early Church, a motivating and purifying influence which has been largely lost and surely needs to be recovered. Paul himself indicates that the love of Christ's appearing was the driving force of his life:

> For I am now ready to be offered, and the time of my departure is at hand. I have fought a good fight, I have finished my course, I have kept the faith: Henceforth there is laid up for me a crown of righteousness, which the Lord, the righteous judge, shall give me at that day: and not to me only, but unto all them also that love his appearing (2 Timothy 4:6-8).

What has been the result of rejecting imminency? It could not help but foster a more worldly orientation. It surely has not increased the love Christians have for their Lord. Nor has the tragic loss of imminency fostered holy living or an increased sense of urgency in spreading the gospel. Instead, Christians have set their hope and affection on the status, security, pleasures, and possessions offered by this evil world.

Not expecting, until they die, to leave the earth they love so much, and hoping to delay the inevitability of death as long as possible, Christians have become as earthly minded as the worldlings around them. Building an estate, a bank account, trusting in insurance policies, and planning for retirement, have preoccupied a Church that no longer hopes for Christ's imminent return to take her to heaven. Believers have become much like the rich man to whom God said, "Thou fool, this night thy soul shall be required of thee: then whose shall those things be, which thou has provided?" (Luke 12:20).

Hoping for Heaven—But Not Yet

For most Christians heaven is a place they desire to reach eventually, but not until they have lived out their full days on earth. Their hopes, ambitions, and interests, contrary to what Christ taught and the early Church lived, are really bound up in the life they aspire to live in this world. Heaven is a distant and unreal destination they reluctantly expect to reach at the end of life, but it is not desired before then. To be suddenly Raptured to heaven would be, for most Christians, an unwelcome interruption of their earthly plans and ambitions.

Unfortunately, such an indictment applies even to many who intellectually believe in the pre-trib Rapture. Though mental assent is given to the doctrine, the truth of imminency has not gripped them. The awesome reality of suddenly at any moment being caught up to meet Christ in the air has not affected their lives. Instead, the Rapture is like a tale that has been told, something they believe in theoretically but which they have little if any expectation of experiencing in their lifetime.

Tragically, even those who claim to believe in the imminent return of Christ often do not live as Christ said they should, with "loins girded about and lights burning...as men who wait for their lord when he will return" (Luke 12:35,36). Only if His imminent return is our constant hope will we live as true followers of Christ—those who live as citizens of heaven and who are looking for their Lord to catch them up to His Father's house at any moment.

Was there ever a bride truly in love who didn't eagerly anticipate the wedding day when she and her fiancé could be united and begin to share their lives together? One longs to be with the one loved; and if that possibility is not a distant or vague hope but one which could be realized at any moment, then love is strengthened by it. To know, however, that one cannot see or be with the one loved for many years does not help the relationship.

The Choice: Heaven or This Earth

Let us be reminded that Christ always equated the thought of a delay in His coming with evil. Not only the first two verses quoted at the beginning of the chapter but others as well reiterate this same sober rebuke. What a convicting reprimand He gives to those who hope for a delay in His return! Nor could any stronger argument for imminency be given, for Christ's reprimand is always accompanied by the warning that He will return at a time when He is least expected:

> But and if that servant say in his heart, My lord delayeth his coming; and shall begin to beat the menservants and maidens, and to eat and drink, and to be drunken; the lord of that servant will come in a day when he looketh not for him (Luke 12:45,46).

There are some who desire the Rapture to be delayed, and many who think they have biblical reasons for believing that it cannot occur until after Antichrist appears, or the Great Tribulation has ended, or even until the end of the millennium. Yet Christ says that such thoughts are the first step in the wrong direction. It is always an "evil" servant who imagines his Lord won't come just yet and therefore he has time to live for self.

The very words John uses—"everyone who has this hope in him purifieth himself"—argue for imminency. If he is simply referring to some distantly future coming in which we could not possibly participate, such as a post-millennial coming, then there is no hope at all and thus no purifying effect. Nor would a post-tribulation Rapture, as we have already seen, qualify as a purifying "hope" for the reasons we have given.

It is argued that John was referring to the confidence shared by all Christians of meeting the Lord at one's death. In a sense that is true. John must, however, have had more than that in mind, for who hopes for death? He must be referring to something that has an even more powerful purifying impact than the thought of death. It can only be the hope of the imminent return of Christ to rapture His bride to His Father's house of many mansions.

John is not, of course, recommending a fanatical, other-worldly mindedness that foolishly ignores any common-sense provision for this life. We are to live as those who long to leave this earth and who expect to depart at any moment, yet who also make contingency plans in case the Rapture is delayed. One must prudently plan and provide for this life without resting one's hope or placing one's affection upon it.

The pre-trib Rapture goes to the heart of the battle between God and Satan for the souls of mankind. The choice we each face, surprisingly, is not heaven or hell. If that were the case, who would not choose heaven? The real choice we must and do make—daily, hourly—is between heaven and this earth. Only the possibility of an imminent Rapture confronts us with that choice.

Our attitudes and actions continually reflect our unconscious answer to the question: "Am I willing to leave this earth right now for heaven, or is there something that holds me here and thus something of earth which stands between my Lord and me at this moment?" When we honestly face that choice, we begin to understand why Paul exhorted, "Set your affection on things above, not on things on this earth."

The Real Question

The battle that is fought in man's heart began as a choice between two worlds—the world as God made it and the world which man, as a little god in partnership with Satan, intended to make. Adam bartered the world God made for another world which man, as the new presiding deity, would fashion to his own liking. In fact, we are in the process of destroying this world in spite of programs for ecological salvation and promises of a new world order.

One day God will "destroy them which destroy the earth" (Revelation 11:18) so that Christ can rule in righteousness. At the end of His millennial reign, following man's final rebellion, God will destroy this doomed universe and create a new one for "new creatures in Christ"—a perfect and eternal universe into which sin will never be able to enter.

Make no mistake, the actual choice we all face moment by moment is between man's new world and God's. Moreover, the real test is whether we truly long to make that exchange *now,* when life is vibrant, exciting, enjoyable. Of course, everyone wants to exchange sickness, death, hell for heaven—but do we, *right now,* want to exchange the best this world offers for God's presence? Such is the unique challenge of the imminent Rapture!

The Rapture is the focus of the closing verses in Scripture: "And the Spirit and the bride say, Come. And let him that heareth say, Come" (Revelation 22:17). In reply to this appeal, we read Christ's final words to His bride, "Surely I come quickly" (22:20).

Quickly? The question of why the long delay is not ours to ask. John's response is instant: "Even so, come, Lord Jesus." May this be our constant prayer as well.

Wait a minute! Such a prayer would be unbiblical and unreasonable if Christ can't come until after Antichrist appears or until the end of the great tribulation. Precisely. This final statement inspired by the Holy Spirit in Scripture is one more proof that Christ could come at any moment.

When will Jesus come? The real question is, rather, how close we desire the Rapture to be. Such is the heart-searching impact of imminency and of Christ's many warnings to watch and wait and to be ready for His return at any moment.

Is the Rapture something we really want right now, or do we wish for a delay? Yes, our hearts are torn because we long for unsaved friends and loved ones to receive Christ before it is forever too late. But nothing must stand in the way of our love for Him. May the hope of His imminent return become our passion and produce its purifying fruit in our lives—and, through us, impact many others before it is forever too late!

The author's free monthly
newsletter may
be received by request. Write to:

Dave Hunt
The Berean Call
P.O. Box 7019
Bend, OR 97708

Other Books by Dave Hunt

Death of a Guru
Descended from a long line of Brahman priests, Maharaj with bestselling author Dave Hunt, traces his difficult search for meaning, and his struggle to choose between Hinduism and Christ.

In Defense of the Faith
Drawing from the most-asked questions of his years in ministry, noted cult and prophecy expert Dave Hunt addresses the toughest questions that Christians and non-Christians ask.

Occult Invasion
Channeling, extraterrestrials, mystic religions, and psychology are infiltrating our schools, homes, and churches. Hunt gives signs to look for and practical steps for countering this invasion.

The Seduction of Christianity
One of the most talked about books in Christian circles. Examines dangerous extra–biblical practices, and helps people become aware of false doctrine

A Woman Rides the Beast
An eye–opening book about prophecy, Catholicism, and the last days. Has the view of the Church of Rome as the woman who rides the beast in Revelation 17 become outdated? Hunt carefully sifts through history and prophecy to provide an answer.